PLAYBUILDING AS QUALITATIVE RESEARCH

Developing Qualitative Inquiry
Series Editor: Janice Morse
University of Utah

Books in the new Developing Qualitative Inquiry series, written by leaders in qualitative inquiry, will address important topics in qualitative methods. Targeted to a broad multidisciplinary readership, the books are intended for mid-level/advanced researchers and advanced students. The series will advance the field of qualitative inquiry by describing new methods or by developing particular aspects of established methods.

Volumes in this series:

Autoethnography as Method, Heewon Chang

Interpretive Description, Sally Thorne

Developing Grounded Theory: The Second Generation, Janice M. Morse, Phyllis Noerager Stern, Juliet Corbin, Barbara Bowers, Kathy Charmaz, and Adele E. Clarke

Mixed Method Design: Principles and Procedures, Janice M. Morse and Linda Niehaus

Playbuilding as Qualitative Research: A Participatory Arts-Based Approach, Joe Norris

Poetry as Method: Reporting Research through Verse, Sandra L. Faulkner

PLAYBUILDING AS QUALITATIVE RESEARCH

A Participatory Arts-Based Approach

Joe Norris

Brock University

Walnut Creek, California

LEFT COAST PRESS, INC.
1630 North Main Street, #400
Walnut Creek, CA 94596
http://www.LCoastPress.com

ISBN 978-1-59874-476-7 hardcover
ISBN 978-1-59874-477-4 paperback

Library of Congress Cataloguing-in-Publication Data:

Norris, Joe.
  Playbuilding as qualitative research: a participatory arts-based approach / Joe Norris.
      p. cm.—(Developing qualitative inquiry)
Includes bibliographical references and index.
ISBN 978-1-59874-476-7 (alk. paper)—ISBN 978-1-59874-477-4 (pbk. : alk. paper)
1. Improvisation (Acting) 2. Playwriting—Study and teaching. I. Title.
PN2071.I5N67 2009
792.07'2—dc22

2009033491

Performance rights to the scripts contained within must be obtained from Mirror Theatre. Contact the author, who will assemble the Board to grant performance rights.

Printed in the United States of America

♾ ™ The paper used in this publication meets the minimum requirements of American National Standard for Information Sciences—Permanence of Paper for Printed Library Materials, ANSI/NISO Z39.48–1992.

09 10 11 12 13 5 4 3 2 1

Contents

Dedication

To my wife, Pauline, and my daughters, Carmen and Jessica, who best taught me how to live playfully and responsibly in community with others.

To my students and A/R/Tors, who have shared part of this journey of trying to understand and to improve the human condition.

To audiences, who have joined the casts of Mirror Theatre in our quest. Their insights on both the substance of our work and the theatrical forms used have taught us as much as we have taught them.

Preface

This book is written for researchers who wish to use the dramatic arts in any or all stages of their research (arts-based research) and for artists who use empirical data as a source of inspiration (research-informed arts). As such, it is an interdisciplinary text merging two genres of interpretation and portrayal. For the practicing researcher, through narrative and discussion, the book aims to open up a myriad of possibilities that are commonplace to a performing artist and playwright. For the practicing artist, the stories of devising scenes demonstrate how personal stories and the stories of others can be translated into a variety of dramatic media, and how one may gather information to guide one's work by focusing on a specific theatrical genre, known in Canada as Collective Creation (Berry and Reinbold, 1985; Filewod, 1987; Salutin and Theatre Passe Muraille, 1976) or Playbuilding (Bray, 1991; Weigler, 2002), a more generic term. The book highlights a genre of arts-based research. I hope that it will provide insights to all researchers and inform the practices of those in the visual and performing arts.

The book is about *participation*. A collaborative process inspired the scenes highlighted by the 11 middle chapters. Actors/researchers/teachers (A/R/Tors) generated data on chosen topics, told stories, and created and compiled scenes that were representative of their disparate and sometimes conflicting collective voices. The projects included many who were interested in a particular topic and/or participatory forms of dramatic representation. The scenes evolved through a rigorous process in which small working groups devised vignettes with the entire cast providing feedback and ultimately chose what scenes to include. The participants acted as researchers, playwrights, and performers and were involved in the research endeavor from data generation through to data presentation.

Audience members, too, became involved in data generation and interpretation of the topic under investigation, be it be bullying, addictions, human sexuality, the power differentials in teaching and learning, prejudice, or even qualitative research. They were asked to identify what they determined to be the central issues in scenes, to suggest courses of action, to provide the gathering with stories that they wished to share, and to dramatically explore all these as well. The performed scenes were created as evocative texts (Barone, 1990), not meant to didactically conclude or shut down the conversation (Smith and Heshusius, 1986) but to open it up, inviting other points of view. Hence, the research product was written to be fluid in nature, in anticipation of a reader's response (Rosenblatt, 1978). The consumers of the research re-informed it in a dialogic process.

The book is about *epistemology*. Through exemplars and discussion it challenges and extends the debate on how knowledge is defined, replacing the term *data collection* with *data generation*. It questions the concept of analysis, emphasizing the interplay between an event and one's internal processing. Data then is not interpreted but mediated, as both the knower and the knowing change (Heisenberg, 1927, 1983). Finally, through the acknowledgment that all research is a constructed narrative (Richardson, 1990), it advocates and celebrates the mediation of raw material into poetic (Butler-Kisber, 2002), artistic (Irwin and de Cosson, 2004), and fictionalized texts (Banks and Banks, 1998; Dunlop, 2002).

It is about *research dissemination*. Clearly outlining the participatory process, it transcends a dualistic style of interview in which a researcher (through observations, interviews, and questionnaires) attempts to understand the position of another, moving research to a dialogic encounter in which meanings of all parties co-emerge (Kieren, 1995) and are transformed. A variety of data generation processes are discussed, and a myriad of theatrical styles are presented.

As implied by the title, the book is about building plays, or *devising* theater (Jackson, 1993), as it is more commonly known. Through a vignette structure, it employs multiple forms, moving beyond the standard dramatic action. Voice collages, puppetry, narrated-mime, song, shadow screen, body sculpting, and other theatrical devices are a few of the possible theatrical elements that present social issues through metaphor, giving theatrical variety to any presentation. The book should also be of value to those researchers who wish to dramatize data, whether or not they intend to use the entire Playbuilding process, and theater practitioners who wish to expand their theatrical choices.

It is about *teaching*. The intention of the entire project was to create stories that evoke thought and to invite discussion. Using a social constructivist approach (Phillips, 1995), the theatrical research products are brought to the people whom the play/mirror reflects. Through discussions and audience participation, both audience and A/R/Tors deconstruct and reconstruct their understanding of the issues.

This book is a *narrative*. It tells "my" story of working with this emergent research form, predominantly as director with casts of Mirror Theatre. I say "my" with the recognition that other players would tell it differently. As a central player for well over 14 years, I have learned much about the various topics, how to theatrically stage them, how to work with audiences, and the organic participatory research process. Buber (1947) claims that the role of an artist is to make him or her the best that he or she can be, so he or she can be a better gift to others. In the spirit of this, I share my story of collaborative research and pedagogy.

Finally, the book is but "an" *example*, not "the" definitive Playbuilding process. There are many kindred Playbuilding processes, having similarities and differences, and no claim is made on the methodology nor the term. The book joins a polyphony of voices that employ theater as a form of inquiry and research.

The book need not be read in a linear fashion. It has been constructed so that each section stands alone. Consequently, there is some relevant repetition, connecting the content to philosophy and technique. For some readers, a vignette about a topic of interest may assist in understanding the theoretical discussion in Chapter 1. For those who wish an understanding of the Playbuilding process, Chapter 2 would be a good beginning. Chapter 3 provides a history of my work with Mirror Theatre and outlines the contexts that shaped this methodology. Chapters 4 through 14 provide scenes about social issues and represent a variety of theatrical forms. The matrix on page 91 can assist in finding appropriate scripts. The last chapter focuses on working with an audience and would be of primary value for those involved in applied theater. My vision is that each reader will find her/his own path through the book.

Acknowledgments

Coauthors and Cast Members

The following people have been involved in the performing and/or writing of the Mirror Theatre vignettes. Without their commitment, this collection and our expansive works would not have been possible. They are thanked, not only for this project but also for their support in using theater as means for human understanding and social change.

Stephanie Adams

Stephanie Alexander

Kerry Allchin

Lindsay Atkinson

Shonna Batke

Joel Bazin

Tara Beagan

David Berezan

Olenka Bilash

Vivian Blacklock

David Blades

Peter Bonnema

Valerie Bridge

Tara Brodin

Derrique Buchynski

Sarah Burghardt

Robert Burton

Jenna Butler

Trish Butler

Colin Byers

Chad Campbell

Gail Campbell

Anne Chiasson

Charles Chenard

Jim Cheung

Chris Wedman

Charlene Clarke

Diane Conrad

Jane Crowell-Bour

Jennifer Crumpton

Karrie Darichuk

Steve Davies

Nadine Dermott

Dianna Dollman

Deb Ebling

Michelle Fuller

Stacy Fysh

Cindy Gaffney

Robert Gallagher

Renee Gauthier, André Goulet

Lucy Goncalves

Regan Gramlich

Tina Green

Jeanie Greenidge

Sandy Greenslade

Chris Hanratty

Tonya Harris

Wade Hayden

Anne Hewson

Jodi Hodgins

Chantel Horon

Sean Horton

Karen Hotson (Westhaver)

Mike Hotson

Sarah Hoyles

Mike Hudema

Carl Irwin

Chris Janzen

Lisa Jensen-Hengstler

Kelly Johnson-Turnbull

Oliver Kamau

Vireo Karvonen-Lee

Laura Kennedy

Hayley King

Denny Lamoureux

Kendra Lanes

Cheryl Lepatski

Cheryl Rochelle Leipert

Jennifer Lindstrand

Jonathan Lindstrand

Yung Luu

Nuno Luzio

Sheri Lysyk

David Mallet

Dustin Maloney

Chris Martin

Melissa Mayville

Anna McCready (Janzen)

Kerry McPhail-Hayden

Michele Miller

Bryce Missall

Erin Mitchell

Karena Munroe

Jodie Murphy

Carmen Norris

Bali Panaser

Jillian Paschen

Esther Payne

Marcie Perdue

Rebecca Pickard

Chris Pethybridge

Cordelia Poczynek

Kris Ponto

Glen Pope

Jennifer Prestash

Asha Ram

Paulette Reese

Lisa Richter

Jennifer Roberts

Marnie Rutledge

Dane Sadownyk

Nisha Sajnani

Rob Schaan

Wendy Schaar

Deb Shinkaruk-Hobbs

Linette Smith

Fern Snart

Shannon Sookochoff

Susan Spence-Campbell

Dice Squires

Angela Stewart

Katherine Stewart

Jeff Strashok

Heather Taylor

Lisa Taylor

Peter Taylor

Jon Teghtmeyer

Reneé Thériault	Brent Voyer	Randy Wimmer
Yvette Timtim	Naomi Ward	Angela Wolfe
Kathy Tomnuk	Carolyn Waye	Lucie Wong
Josie Tong	Janice Weinberger	Norm Wong
Jon VanAlten	Todd Were	Philip Zinken
Rosanna Vanzella	Fiona Williams	

Organizations

The following organizations have been directly involved with Mirror Theatre's productions. They and their many staff members are thanked for their belief in and support of our work.

Alberta Alcohol and Drug Abuse Commission, Youth Services
Alberta Foundation for the Arts
Alberta Teachers Association
ASSIST Community Services
Canadian Brewers Association
Capital Health
City of Edmonton Community Services
Expecting Respect: Peer Education Program
Greater Edmonton Teachers Convention Association (GETCA)
HIV Edmonton
International Institute for Qualitative Methodology
Planned Parenthood TERRA Association
Sexual Assault Centre (Edmonton)
Society for Safe and Caring Schools and Communities
University of Alberta
Western Canadian Association for Student Teaching (WestCAST)
Western Canadian Conference on Human Sexuality

Transcribers

Gail Campbell and Yi Li assisted in transcribing scripts from our video-taped archives as part of their graduate assistantships. Their work in translating the spoken word in some of Mirror Theatre's archived videos to the printed word is much appreciated.

Colleagues and University Staff

Thanks also go to:

- Jan Morse, who has continually supported and advocated this research genre, first while director of the International Institute for Qualitative Methodology and more recently as series editor of the Developing Qualitative Inquiry series at Left Coast Press

- Joanne Reinbold, Glenys Berry, and David Barnet, who provided valuable support for my doctoral research, which provided the foundation for Mirror Theatre
- Stan Christie, who initially pointed me in this direction
- David Berezan, Diane Conrad, Anne Hewson, and Oliver Kamau, graduate students, who, through many conversations assisted me in rethinking and refining this Playbuilding process
- Olenka Bilash, David Blades, Fern Snart, Randy Wimmer, Josie Tong, and other faculty members, who joined me in various projects
- Betty Kiffiak and Herb Rupp, who continually supported the pragmatic dimensions of this work, from the booking of spaces to the procurement of equipment

The following people gave up their time to meet for a photo shoot for the pictures in this book: David Berezan, Olenka Bilash, Diane Conrad, Wade Hayden, Kerry McPhail-Hayden, Oliver Kamau, Carmen Norris, Glen Pope, Asha Ram, Mornie Rutledge, and Philip Zinken.

Thanks also go to Mitch Allen, publisher, Left Coast Press, who continues to foster the advancement of innovative research methodologies.

Last, but not least, thanks to my wife Pauline, who always patiently assisted me in bringing my thoughts to the printed page. Her writing suggestions and questioning skills are evident in this and my other works.

Bon voyage!

Joe

PART I

The Background

In the recent past, narrative construction has burgeoned, with researchers in the field of education experimenting with a variety of literary genres for plotting their data (Barone, 2007, p. 458). The history of qualitative research has been a short one, and the use of arts-based and narrative approaches even shorter. Although many advances have been made since the late 1970s, there still seems to be a need to justify why qualitative research is a legitimate approach to understanding our social world and to articulating those understandings to others. Perhaps that will always be the case, since many researchers take a postmodern approach (Giroux, 1991) to acknowledging the frame (Goffman, 1974) that underpins the research. As Janesick claims, "Qualitative researchers have the obligation to fully describe their theoretical postures at all stages of the research process, just as the choreographer fully describes and explains each component of a dance plan" (2004, p. 8). Part I is a description of the frame.

Chapter 1 questions the distinction between fact and fiction using literacy theory and qualitative research epistemology to challenge the false dichotomy of empirical and speculative approaches. Using Richardson's

(1990) claim that all research endeavors are constructed narratives differing in belief, styles, and forms, the chapter builds an argument for why the creation and the performance of plays on a given topic should be considered a genre of qualitative research.

Chapter 2 provides a thorough description of the methods used to generate data, how such data is treated, and the theatrical approaches used to disseminate such research, usually with a live audience, who engage with the researchers in a reconceptualization (Pinar, 2000) of the data presented. Although this chapter contains many details, they are provided more as a buffet than a prescriptive recipe. Researchers are encouraged to adapt as needed.

Chapter 3 provides my personal history with the method: (1) using Playbuilding as a theatrical genre with junior high students; (2) then moving to researching the theatrical approach as the topic of my doctoral dissertation; (3) employing this approach as a teaching tool with groups of university students who, with me, founded Mirror Theatre; (4) coming to the realization that the approach was a form of arts-based research; and (5) integrating theater and research approaches into a Playbuilding methodology. It is also a story of collaboration, as graduate and undergraduate students, faculty, staff, and members of the community participated in devising scripts that explored the human condition. The collaboration extends further into the community as partnerships are formed with a number of social agencies that wish to employ Playbuilding as a pedagogical approach to meet their mandates. Chapter 3 articulates my growth with the methodology over a 29-year period.

Part I articulates the epistemological, theatrical, and methodological features on which Playbuilding was built by providing my history with the methodology.

Introduction

Toward a Theory of Playbuilding as Research

CAPOTE: On the night of November 14, two men broke into a quiet farmhouse in Kansas and murdered an entire family. Why did they do that? It's been suggested that this subject is tawdry—it's not worthy of literature. I disagree. Two worlds exist in this country—the quiet conservative life, and the life of those two men—the underbelly, the criminally violent. Those worlds converged that bloody night. I spent the past three months interviewing everyone in Kansas touched by that violence. I spent hours talking to the killers—and I'll spend more. Researching this work has changed my life, altered my point of view about almost everything. I think those who read it will be similarly affected. Such a book can only be written by a journalist who has mastered the techniques of fiction. (Futterman, 2006, pp. 45–46)

Fiction and Research

Could *In Cold Blood* (Capote, 1965) also be considered a qualitative research project? Does it possess the necessary rigor of data saturation, an in-depth data analysis, enough thick description, and a cogent understanding of the lived-word of its participants? Clearly it does not have an extensive literature review, an explicit articulation of themes, indexing, and conclusions for future practice. But need it be thought of as qualitative research? Like phenomenology, it records the lived-experiences of others, and like biographical and autobiographical studies, it is a "truthful fiction" (Denzin, 1989, p. 23).

In Cold Blood falls under the classification of nonfiction novel (Koski, 1999) or literary nonfiction (Anderson, 1989) that blurs the distinction between fiction and journalism. Research has been conducted, systematically organized, and written in a narrative style. Applegate defines this genre as literary journalism, "a form of writing that combines the literary writing of fiction with the journalistic techniques of nonfiction" (1996, p. xi). The novel represents the lived-world of actual people.

Such writing is not uncommon. George Orwell's *Homage to Catalonia* (1938) was based on his militia experiences in Spain during its civil war. *Away All Boats* (Dodson, 1956) was based on his experiences aboard the *U.S.S. Pierce* and fictionalized as the *U.S.S. Belinda*. The movie version of the same name took on a pedagogical purpose, since it was used for naval officer training. *Up the Down Staircase* (1964), written as a teacher's journal, records the experiences of a beginning teacher. Its author, Bel Kaufman, drew on her own teaching experiences. Unlike the others who drew on their personal experiences, Arthur Hailey undertook extensive research of the automobile industry before writing his novel, *Wheels* (1971). Writers, directors, actors, and other production crew undertook extensive research in order to realistically create the film *I Am Sam* (Johnson and Nelson, 2002). Costumes, set, mannerisms, and dialogue were based on actual people and settings. The cast of *The Farm Show* (Theatre Passe Muraille, 1967), a Collective Creation (Canadian version of Playbuilding), visited the homesteads of Clinton, Ontario, and devised a play about that community. Literature, film, and theater have a long history of employing empirical data, and when they do so, they can be considered forms of "research-informed arts." Although they employ literary styles unique to their genres and take artistic license, they also maintain a high degree of loyalty to the actual.

"Arts-based research" has a shorter history than does literary journalism. Geertz noted:

> In the social sciences, or at least in those that have abandoned the reductionist conception of what they are about, the analogies are coming more and more from contrivances of cultural

performance than from those of physical manipulation—from theatre, painting, grammar, literature, law, play. (1983, p. 22)

Although he encourages the blurring of genres and the move to interdisciplinary research enterprises, he recognizes that such interdisciplinary work is no easy feat. Each discipline has its own set of canons, and hybridization can be held suspect.

> But my point is that some of those fit to judge work of this kind ought to be humanists who reputedly know something about what theater and mimesis and rhetoric are, and not just with respect to my work but to that of the whole steadily broadening stream of social analyses in which the drama analogy is, in one form or another, governing. At a time when social scientists are chattering about actors, scenes, plots, performances, and personae, and humanists are mumbling about motives, authority, persuasion, exchange, and hierarchy, the line between the two, however comforting to the puritan on the one side and the cavalier on the other, seems uncertain indeed. (p. 30)

It is as if one must completely please two disparate parents.

Barone notes that the social science community blurs the distinction between science and art, claiming that "scientific texts are as open to interpretation as literary texts" (1995, p. 171). Banks and Banks believe that fiction should not be considered the antithesis of truth.

> The opposite of fact isn't fiction but something like error. The opposite of fiction isn't truth but something like objectivity or actuality. Any genre or piece of writing that claims to be objective, to represent the actual, is a writing that denies its own existence, as David Lock said. In other words, no text is free of self-conscious constructions: no text can act as a mirror to the actual . . . . The imposition of fiction into the divide between fact and error doesn't negate the possibility of a real world: all it does is recognize the impossibility for others to be objective (1998, p. 13)

Consequently, theater, fiction, poetry, film, music, dance, and the visual arts that are grounded in reality should be considered empirical. Denzin recognizes that, since narrative research comes from a particular stance, it is, at best, a biased distortion. He calls stories and biographies "truthful fictions" (1989, p. 23). Richardson goes further, claiming that all research takes a narrative stance, albeit using different styles.

> Whenever we write science, we are telling some kind of story, or some part of a larger narrative. Some of our stories are more

complex, more densely described, and offer greater opportunities as emancipatory documents; others are more abstract, distanced from lived experience, and reinscribe existent hegemonies. Even when we think we are not telling a story, we are, at the very least, embedding our research in a metanarrative, about, for example, how science progresses or how art is accomplished (Lyotard, 1979). Even the shape of the conventional research report reveals a narratively driven subtext: theory (literature review) is the past or the (researcher's) cause for the present study (the hypothesis being tested), which will lead to the future-findings and implications (for the researcher, the researched, and science). Narrative structures, therefore, are preoperative regardless of whether one is writing primarily in the narrative or logico-scientific mode. (1990, p. 13)

The employment of the arts in research is therefore a question of style. Yes, each medium carries its own message (McLuhan, 1967), but to some degree the issue is more one of semiotics (Eco, 1976) and framing (Goffman, 1974) than of epistemology. Stories that reduce data to abstract definitions are of a different genre than those that display the particular. Neither should be hegemonic.

Barone takes a more ameliorative and perhaps more pragmatic stance. Rather than entering into the art/science debate, claiming the status of arts-based research as a social science, he does insist that "arts-based" is research. "While I decline to fight in the 'paradigm wars' to claim the title of science for arts-based educational inquiry, I *will* enter the struggle to demand the legitimation of educational storytelling of all sorts as *research*" (1995, p. 177).

The acceptance of the status of the arts as research is ongoing. Obtaining even the tenuous legitimacy held by literary journalism has not been easy. As late as 1997, Eisner, a pioneer in arts-based research, building on the optimistic "promise" of Geertz, argues for its place in the academy by tracing its roots and examining both its promises and perils. He outlines the advantages of arts-based approaches claiming that they:

> (a) shape experience and . . . enlarge understanding. Whether you use a story, create a film, employ a diagram, or construct a chart, what such tools have in common is the purpose of illuminating rather than obscuring the message . . . . (b) provide a sense of particularity that abstractions cannot render . . . (c) "productive ambiguity." By productive ambiguity, I mean that the material presented is more evocative than denotative, and, in its evocation, it generates insight and invites attention to complexity . . . . (d) increase the variety of questions that we can ask, . . . and (e) allow us to exploit

individual aptitudes. Neither the literal nor the quantitative are [*sic*] everybody's cup of tea. (Eisner, 1997, p. 8)

He concludes by inviting us to go to the edges, a better vantage point to see the stars and the seas.

Arts-Based Research

Saks (1996) moves to the specific, asking whether novels could be accepted as dissertations, a question debated at more than one American Educational Research Association's Annual Meeting. Dunlop (1999) and Sameshima (2006) pragmatically addressed the challenge by having their novels accepted as dissertations at the University of British Columbia. Both were subsequently published (Dunlop, 1999; Sameshima, 2007). The nonfiction novel is a recent genre in the research community.

In addition to the novel, theater and other performing arts have made similar gains in the research community. Mienczakowski's study of health workers and clients in a detoxification unit produced data that was represented in theatrical form. The participants validated the performance through preperformance observations of the play. The performance, *Busting*, "adapted verbatim accounts of informants into an authentic, validated, polyphonic narrative that expressed informant agendas of concern in their own words" (1995, p. 361). Portions of Meyer's research on principals (2009) were scripts, which were performed as part of his doctoral work. Bagley and Cancienne (2002), Blumenfeld-Jones (2002), and Snowber (2002) suggest "dancing the data." Saldaña (2005) has amassed a collection of studies that he calls "ethnodrama." He has compiled eight studies that dramatize the data. In all these cases, data was traditionally generated and translated into an "alternative form of representation" (Eisner, 1997). Although the scripts can be read like a nonfiction novel, they are written so that they can be performed.

Playbuilding as Research

Although Playbuilding shares similar epistemological underpinnings with the nonfiction novel and with ethnodrama, it is different in both process and intent. First, the intent is not to report findings but to provide evocative texts (Barone, 1990) that invite live audiences to engage in discussion for the mutual learning of all. Through audience participation, it takes both a democratic and pedagogical approach. It "dialogically inserts itself into the world, provoking conflict, curiosity, criticism, and reflection" (Denzin, 2003, p. 261). Second, its method does not follow a customary format. Traditionally, the research process is divided into three distinct, albeit overlapping, acts. First, is data collection (generation), followed by data analysis (interpretation), and concluded with dissemination (performance). Such is the case with ethnodrama, where data is traditionally collected, analyzed, and then disseminated through an "alternative" form of representation. With Playbuilding, data is generated and interpreted in a different manner, and, at times, these three phases are simultaneous.

The Method

Although this chapter focuses on the theories that underpin Playbuilding, it first provides a short description of the method, so that the abstract conversation can be connected to concrete experiences. Chapter 2 discusses the method in detail, and Chapter 3 provides a history of Mirror Theatre that supplies a context for the research. Some readers may find it useful to first read one of the script chapters (Chapters 4 through 14) to obtain an understanding of the theatrical research process that is being discussed.

PARTICIPATORY RESEARCH   In Playbuilding, as in a focus group or a "collective memory group" (Lesko, Simmons, and Quarshie, 2008), a team of actors/researchers/teachers (A/R/Tors) (Irwin and de Cosson [2004] use a similar term, a/r/tographers to define those who work in any of the arts) are assembled to discuss a topic of mutual concern. The topics are endless, but most often they focus on a specific social issue, such as prejudice, bullying, equality, and respect, conflict resolution, gender politics, or human sexuality. However, unlike most focus groups in which the participants consider themselves solely as data sources, with Playbuilding, they are collaborators who play an active role in the writing and the performing of the data.

   The first meeting/rehearsal typically begins with the question, "Why are you here?" Some are interested in the topic; some enjoy this genre of theater; and others are just curious. No particular experience in acting or research is required, and although some possess various degrees of experience and skill in each, the process is open to all who volunteer, because we recognize that we can learn from the various talents and understandings of every participant. An openness to learn from the "Other" (Barber, 1989; Levinas, 1984) is a prerequisite.

   For a period of about 45 minutes to an hour, the assembled participants provide personal beliefs and stories, each to his/her own degree of comfort. I have found that making potential undercurrents explicit tends to lessen their potentially negative power. I ask the veterans to make their former involvement with the process explicit, reminding them that a strength of a group rests in how it treats its newcomers. Having each member knowledgeable about former involvement helps to alleviate the tensions between insiders and outsiders. Trust is vital in any process of co-creation, and, since all participants are stakeholders, a respect for one another's position is vital. As director/researcher, one of my duties is to set the tone of our work. I assert that we are all in a state of "becoming" (de Chardin, 1969), and we, as pilgrims, have gathered to tell our stories (Kopp, 1972) not only to advance our current positions but also to change them, when personally deemed appropriate, as we listen to the stories of others. As dialogic researchers we must question everything, even our current positions.

During the next hour of this first rehearsal, I pass out blank recipe cards and ask us all to recall the initial conversation. On the cards, I ask the participants to write a catch phrase that would help them recall the stories that have been told and, in smaller print, to write their names in the bottom right-hand corner. As the stories are reviewed, we move to abstraction, asking "What themes are embedded within the stories?"

Although the cards could have been introduced at the beginning, I hesitate to do so for two reasons. First, for newcomers, the conversation is more informal without them. I want to keep the conversation open and relaxed. The veterans are comfortable with the process, but it can be intimidating the first time. Second, they function as a review. Our process is a spiral one, while we revisit the data again and again. It is important at this stage to keep all ideas as possibilities, and reviewing helps keep all things fresh.

We usually end with an interactive, physical drama game or warm-up that requires high energy and lots of laughter. "All work and no play make Jill and Jack dull children." Two hours of sitting and thinking needs to be balanced with other kinds of brain activities (action).

For the next eight to twelve rehearsals, we go through research spirals, first employing storytelling as research (Reason and Hawkins, 1988), then generating themes and translating both stories and themes into dramatic vignettes. At a given point, usually because of deadlines, we sort the scenes, choose those we collectively deem appropriate, then sequence, polish, and rehearse them for public presentations.

Suffice it to say that, owing to its participatory nature, Playbuilding's participatory method of generating and interpreting data, and its typical vignette structure, makes it different from ethnodrama in its methodology. True, its sibling also employs theatrical devises to present research findings, but Playbuilding's particular method of generating and translation of data, and its vignette product, make it a distinct genre.

DATA GENERATION   Can data be collected? Once amassed, does it remain pure or does it change, even slightly? Such questions were asked

in the physical sciences in the 1920s. Heisenberg (1927, 1983) claimed
that the act of research can intrude, and thus the data is mediated by
the research act. Even distant observations have different points of view
depending on the type of telescope used. It is my stance that data can
never be *collected*. The term is a misnomer that falsely separates the known
from the knower (Benjamin, 1990), the object from the research act,
giving it an undeserved pristine quality. What we do as researchers is generate data, not collect it. Even data generated for Likert scale is framed
(Goffman, 1974) by instructions and the order of the questions. What is
asked and not asked is also a matter of framing. The data cannot be separated from the research act; consequently, I consider "generated" a more
accurate term and use it throughout the book.

Playbuilding attempts to take an organic approach to data generation.
Although its outcome will be a formal product, and its method has much
structure, the tone of the data retrieval often resembles an informal conversation. A group of individuals assemble in a circle to tell stories and give
their opinions about a particular phenomenon that they have experienced
and/or witnessed. The project, then, is autoethnograhic (Ellis, 2004),
because each actor/researcher/teacher (A/R/Tor) draws on her/his
experiences. Each actor's story is partially embedded in the play.

However, Playbuilding escapes the danger of slipping into the master
narrative that can be found in autobiographies and autoethnographies.
Stories are told in juxtaposition with one another, providing multiple
perspectives. Rather than strictly being an autoethnographic study, Playbuilding is more like duoethnography (Norris, 2008a; Norris and Sawyer,
2004), whereby teams of researchers not only tell but also interrogate
their stories.

Collective storytelling is a rich data source. Stories beget stories, and
as conversations unfold there is a flood of information as one person's
account triggers memories in others. Declarative sentences in the form
of a narrative can yield more data than can an interview question. From
this research I am convinced that the traditional ethnographic interview
with a predetermined set of questions limits the research. The avoidance
of a researcher's disclosure, in fear of contamination, is a canon that needs
to be reconsidered. Storytelling may evoke stronger responses than a
well-designed research question.

Because of its collective nature, Playbuilding is a form of participatory
research. The distinct line between researcher and participant is nonexis-
tent. Not only are all involved in supplying data, they are all involved in its
treatment and dissemination. Consequently, all are cited as coauthors. We
have employed the common film citation with the director's name and the
name of the company. Each cast member inserts her/his name between
the director and the name of the company, citing her/his involvement

separately. (See an example in the "Cast Ethics" section of this chapter.) In this way, other cast members fall under the collective name, Mirror Theatre. In addition to authorship credit, all those involved also benefit from the process itself. Many have commented that they have gleaned insights from one another that better inform their daily living.

Playbuilding is a unique collaborative venture that requires a high degree of interpersonal skills from all its participants, something not required in a solo interview or in the filling-in of a questionnaire. As with any working team, one can expect moments of tension and times of elation. All participants are stakeholders who will eventually make their faces public. Participatory research has the added interpersonal complexity that many other studies do not have. Consequently, an ancillary but still vital aim of any Playbuilding project is to build positive working relationships. Without the necessary trust in one another that creates a sense of camaraderie, the project is likely to fail. Chapter 2 discusses in detail this interpersonal dimension of the process.

External Data Sources　　　　While cast members' histories provided the bulk of the empirical data, literature from research, prose, newspapers, and stories, as well as volunteered stories by previous audience members and others who were familiar with our work, provided other data sources. Usually Mirror Theatre's casts were large and diverse enough to provide a plethora of data; however, at times, we did search elsewhere. This external data came from both deliberate searches and serendipitous occasions.

In the case of *What's the Fine Line?*—our program/workshop on bullying—we did turn to the literature. Smith and associates' (1999) cross-national study was exhaustive and contained information about girl/girl bullying, so we began to search for that data as well. Our early work with student audiences informed us that female-on-female bullying takes place in the changing rooms. Our scene "The Girls' Locker Room" was based on these sources as well as experiences of our female cast members.

During Mirror Theatre's production exploring inclusion/exclusion, a series of controversial articles and letters to the editor appeared in our local paper. The owner and director of a dance company decided to exclude a young girl with Down Syndrome. Issues of safety, quality, and feelings became part of the debate. We used Readers Theatre (Coger and White, 1971) to present the scene with an array of actors providing sound bites of the various points of view. The public arena proved to be a rich source of relevant data, and, serendipitously, this event happened while we were in production.

What I found amazing was that some data sources sought us out. Individuals were aware of Mirror Theatre's work and came to us with their stories, which they wanted told. We became a voice of the people. While we were writing a video on student teaching, an assistant dean asked me if we would meet with a student who had concerns about sexual harassment during her student teaching experience. The student did not want to press the matter, since she wanted employment in the same small rural area, but she did want her story told. We listened, and after many improvisational interpretations she verified our emergent understanding of the event. We staged it in a quick series of four escalating scenes that she reported.

MALE: Miss Samms, let's go out for a drink after class. (*She stares at him, and he exits.*)

MALE: (*Male enters with a crate, turns his back to Female, gestures to his front pocket.*) Miss Samms, can you get my keys? The door's locked. (*She grimaces and he exits.*)

MALE: (*Enters and puts hand on Female's arm.*) Miss Samms, do you want to go to the baseball banquet with me? (*She turns away, and he exits.*)

(*Enter four actors. They sit on the floor facing the stage as if in a classroom. Male stands behind them, and Female mimes a lecture.*)

MALE: Okay class, we know Miss Samms can teach, but can she dance? Come on Miss Samms, stand up on the desk and show us how to dance. Class, take it easy on Miss Samms today. She and I were up late (*pause*) doing lesson planning, which we didn't get to 'til 2 A.M. (*He chuckles.*)

Although this series was based on a set of actual sexual harassment experiences, the data generation was more than that. The individual volunteering the information commented that through the retelling of the scene she felt that she had regained some of her power by raising the issue of sexual harassment for others.

In rehearsals for our program on prejudice, a cast member who worked with the University of Alberta's Aboriginal Student Services Centre brought an aboriginal guest to rehearsal to tell her story. In this instance, she was out shopping with a better-dressed white friend. Her friend was caught shoplifting, and she remained for support. When the police arrived, they took her, not her friend.

We asked them if either would like to perform it. Both declined, but they requested that we still include it in our video. In our devising of the vignette, we worked metaphorically with the story, making costume the key element. The friend arrested was the poorly dressed of the two. The story remained intact but lost its aboriginal element. Working with metaphor can provide a wider range of generalizability, but it also loses some of it particularity. The decision to perform the universal of "judging based on appearance" remained, but the particular of race was "lost." Such happens when one reduces any data, as is also the case when thoughts and opinions are reduced to numerical data. Data is always mediated by the medium chosen to present it (McLuhan, 1967).

Playbuilding has a unique characteristic that is not shared by most other qualitative research designs, because audience members are also data sources. During an early workshop of *What's the Fine Line?* an A/R/Tor lead a student discussion group that chose to perform a scene during the plenary summary. The vignette articulated the potential for sexism in coed sports. The males subtly and overtly exclude females through physical strength, ridicule, and ignoring. We adapted this situation and included it in subsequent iterations of the play. Owing to the immediacy of this form of presentation and conversational style, in the case of Playbuilding the act of dissemination can also serve as an opportunity to gather additional data from external sources. It is "dialogical data generation" (Denzin, 2003, p. 269).

Imagination as a Data Source   The A/R/Tors' collective imaginations also played a major role in generating data. For some researchers, this approach may be considered a move completely away from empiricism and deeply into the realm of fiction. Others, along with Harman and Rheingold (1984), may believe that the imagination underpins the empirical, recognizing that the formation of a hypothesis is a speculative, imaginary act. Those working in the field of drama are comfortable entering into the realm of the "what if." Here, one's experiences are building blocks to examine self and others through the safety of role. With full commitment to an improvisation, the A/R/Tors explore what is plausible in the context of the role. Some scenes grew from the question "what if?" For example, during rehearsals for a play on human sexuality the concept of innocence was raised, but we found it difficult to discuss. Our grown-up minds were layered with years of social mores and taboos. An improvisation was designed that had the A/R/Tors enter the stage area as young children on a playground (Chapter 5). Did our data happen "exactly the way that it was improvised"? No. Could it have? Maybe? Does it metaphorically represent the concept? Yes. Our actual life experiences influenced the improvisational "what if" situation and produced a plausible scene. The process was a blurring of the actual with the imagination.

As Banks and Banks (1998) have pointed out, the distinction between fact and fiction has little to do with truth claims. Fantasy is grounded in reality, and vice versa. Much of society's material, social, and intellectual worlds have been built on the imaginations of others. The paper in this book, a reality, has had many generations of imaginative thought to produce this iteration. Our present world has been created from the imaginations of our ancestors. As the Bard says, "We are such stuff as dreams are made on, and our little life is rounded with a sleep" (Shakespeare, *The Tempest*, 1972a, p. 1563). He recognized that our imaginations do influence our actions. Burniston (1972) reminds us that every word initially had an author. Originally sounds represented feelings, then meanings, and later, through their arrangement, thought and communication. Abstract thought has an empirical basis. Courtney (1980) claims that we are all playwrights. We often pre-live events, thinking, "what would we do if . . . ." These hypo-thetical scenarios are played and replayed, like a rehearsal, preparing us for what may ensue. Imagination is part of our lived-world; to deny it is to deny our very existence, part of what it means to be human.

In the creation of scenes, Playbuilding operates in the world of the plausible/possible; the vignettes are an integration of the actual and the imaginary. Scientific investigation also functions in this way. McGregor (1990) claims that scientific investigation begins with an understand-ing of the world that leads to a "hunch" and postulates on what is not known. The root of hypothesis is imaginative thought. Mishlove (online), in an interview with Willis Harman, makes the denial of the imagination explicit. "It's striking to me that scientists, who use their own conscious-ness, and very often their own deep intuitions, to develop their theories, have operated on assumptions that deny the very existence of those intu-itions." Like the theater, science is filled with "what if" scenarios.

The issue then is whether or not the event actually took place—that it is "documentable subject matter chosen from the real world as opposed to 'invented' from the writer's mind" (Lounsberry, 1990, p. xiii). If we agree with Banks and Banks that a "piece of writing that claims to be objective, to represent the actual, is a writing that denies its own existence" (1998, p. 13), we come to recognize that all knowledge is a social construction (Berger and Luckman, 1966) mediated by the author or researcher. Cer-tain details are focused on; others are left out. Known as the "Rashomon effect" (Werheane, 1999), the same "true" event told by two different people can be quite different. Merleau-Ponty (1962) claims that what we perceive is based on what we already know, and Jersild (1955) claims that knowing influences what we experience. If we recognize the subjectivity of perception, nothing would be considered empirical. The best we can achieve is a "contexture" (Norris, 1989), a texture of the context that is mediated by the observer/representer.

During an early rehearsal for a play on inclusion/exclusion, I cre-ated a warm-up activity to exercise the voice and explore the concept of exclusion more deeply. I asked the cast to move around the room while I sang a variation of the Sesame Street song "One of These Things." At certain times I asked the cast to freeze, and I chose one person to remain frozen while the rest relaxed. I asked the rest to find a characteristic of the person frozen that none of the A/R/Tors shared. The exercise continued until all but one were eliminated. It was always easy to find a distinguishing feature for each person.

During discussion we agreed that eliminating cast members by different characteristics was a potential scene, one that eventually opened *Fair Play Rulz* (Chapter 13). This scene was not empirically based but was plausible: "people are excluded because of differences." During our school tour of 2002, a female teacher approached me claiming this scene as her story. She informed me that her brothers would sing the song to her and run away, excluding her from their activities. On more than one other occasion an audience member reported a similar story. While the scene's roots were metaphorical, inadvertently it paralleled actual stories. Mienczakowski (1995) had his play verified with his data sources prior to public performance. In our case, audiences verified it during dissemination. After a preview of *What's the Fine Line?* the most common comment was that it was "too real." We had metaphorically represented the enormity of school bullying in an overwhelming manner.

During my doctoral research (Norris, 1999), I found that a vignette style of performance around a theme prevented the audience from identifying with the characters, a technique that Brecht calls the "alienation-effect" (1957, p. 91). Instead, the spectators focused on the issues, finding parallels in their own lives. The vignettes acted as evocateurs, eliciting the stories of others. I noted the vignette style's potential for dialogue with future audiences. These people were ready to discuss the issues imbedded within the scenes. This genre had the potential for pedagogical practice by warming-up students/audiences to the themes, by assisting them in memory retrieval. The non-alignment with the characters enabled them to find stories of their own. From this I deduced that the scenes, like the narratives that Barone (1990) suggests, must evoke other stories rather than seeking identification with the ones on stage. This student play was an evocative text through which the audience's histories merged with the A/R/Tors, creating a space for conversation.

Audience members' resonances with the piece confirm its plausibility. Does such audience verification make it empirical? Does it matter? Our audiences recognized how the metaphors paralleled their experiences regardless of whether it was an actual event. Although others may be concerned with this slippery slope, I am not. I am more comfortable living in the borderlands that Irwin and de Cosson recommend.

Artist-researcher-teachers are inhabitants of these borderlands as they re-create, re-search, and re-learn ways of understanding, appreciating, and representing the world . . . . They embrace a métisage existence that integrates knowing, doing, and making, an existence that desires an aesthetic experience found in an elegance of flow between intellect, feeling, and practice. (2004, p. 29)

Many of Mirror Theatre's over 200 vignettes have a strong empirical basis, and some are a composite of a variety of empirical data. Our "Party of Bigots" scene was devised from a list of bigoted comments that are often heard. We took artistic license and created a party scene that had each character making a comment. No, this party never actually happened. As with most qualitative research studies, we took isolated pieces of data and stitched them into a coherent whole.

Still other scenes were strictly from an imaginative source that was connected with the theme. All scenes merged the actual and the imaginative to create scenes with which our audiences would identify. Mirror Theatre does not make truth claims, but our plays are full of truths. They are "truthful fictions" (Denzin, 1989, p. 23).

DATA INTERPRETATION/VIGNETTE DEVISING

As discussed with the shoplifting scene above, the scripting of the data can be a conscious, deliberate act. In quantitative studies, researchers choose what numerical data is appropriate for the statistical formula that they will use. With Playbuilding, researchers make theatrical not numerical decisions. Donmoyer and Yennie-Donmoyer found that the scripting process paralleled the analytical stage of qualitative research.

Actually, we discovered-much to our surprise that at least in this case the processes of data analysis and readers theater script construction were really not very different from each other. Even in the process of staging the script—something that clearly is not done with social science reports—we can find some rather obvious analogs for procedures employed and techniques used in writing a social science research report. (1995, p. 409)

Scripting is also a "liminal" act (Neilsen, 2002). Intuition plays a major role as one's artistry emerges from what is known, creating new meanings and works of art. McNiff describes how his students' works assisted him in making a paradigm shift to art-based approaches.

Rather than jumping about from one exercise to another, there was a sustained meditation on a complex theme and the way it was played out within the medium of a painting. The artist-researcher's relationship with her mother was enacted within the material process of making a painting. Feelings and memories inspired expressions in paint, and the process of shaping the image in turn changed the nature of the artist's attachment to her mother. There was an ongoing correspondence and mutual influence between what happened with paint and the artist's inner relationship to one of the most significant figures in her life. As the picture unfolded there were many "finished" compositions which were covered over by yet another painting. These completed pictures were likened to episodes that come and go over the course of a long relationship. They were covered over but still present "underneath" the later forms of the painting. The painting became a physical embodiment of the phases we experience in our lives. What has impressed me most about this thesis is the way the inquiry was totally based in the material process of making art. (2000, p. 25)

Although data treatments can be conscious efforts, an openness to the liminal spaces through which meanings seem to magically appear is also an important aspect of Playbuilding. McNiff has little difficulty in accepting the value of both paradigms and perspectives. "I do not want to negate the value of scientific methods. I actually believe that scientifically orientated inquiries will be revitalized if we can create a more diverse research environment" (p. 21).

As director/researcher/teacher, my responsibility is to create spaces in which my research team can play. McNiff (2000) likens an artist's studio to a chemistry lab. So, too, with the rehearsal space; it is where A/R/Tors conduct their work. Besides creating opportunities for storytelling and translating those stories into dramatic forms, I look for ways to design improvisations that may better help us understand a phenomenon. As discussed earlier in our exploration of innocence on the playground, improvisation can be a powerful form of inquiry.

In a very early production that I directed, an A/R/Tor described his student teaching experience, claiming that people weren't giving him enough space. Intuitively, I went to a drama activity that I thought might help us achieve a deeper understanding of the comment. One form of "trust falls" has a person in the center of a tight circle of four to ten others who catch the person as he/she falls, keeping waist and knees tight. The catchers then restore the person to center, and she/he falls again. The falling could be forward, backward, to one side or the other. All points of the compass are possibilities. Two or more participants assist in the catching.

I entered the tight circle and fell. Once we achieved a rhythm, I asked, "Give me more space." As is done with this activity, the circle steps back, creating a space for longer falls. Again, once a rhythm was established, I asked for more space. This repeated a couple of more times. I am quite comfortable with this activity, and my falling was easy compared to the hard work of those catching me. When the activity concluded, I asked, "What did we experience?"

The student who wanted more space, discernibly tired, commented that he didn't realize how much work he was putting on his support group by asking for more space. This improvisation assisted him in seeing beyond his immediate position, creating a broader perspective of his lived-world and the meanings that he gave it. The metaphor acted as a mirror, an opportunity for reflection.

Throughout the years, I sought to create metaphorical activities that "may" provide insights to help us understand a concept. A precision activity that Jill Greenhalgh of the "Magdalena Project" (Goodman and Gay, 1996, p. 115) introduced to me helped us better understand the dimensions of trust. The exercise has people standing in a circle tossing a "stick" (a dowel 4 feet long and about 1¼ inches thick). Eye contact is vital as is the ability to throw the stick in a completely vertical position. (This activity is usually introduced later during the rehearsal process.) In our debriefing after the activity, we found that we did trust one another's intentions, but we did not trust one another's or our own abilities. Up until that point, we focused solely on intentions when we discussed trust. The stick exercise helped to elucidate other aspects of trust.

To understand "need," "want," and "desire," I cast three A/R/Tors as flowers and three as bees, giving a player in each group one of the three concepts (Chapter 5). The players did not know the terms that the others were given, and the rest of us observed, taking note of the differences in the interactions. Rutledge (2004), a cast member of Mirror Theatre, used gymnic balls to examine the experience of surrender in dance for her doctoral studies. In a pilot with Mirror Theatre, she led us through a series of activities and asked us for our thoughts. Through it I discovered an implicit aspect of my teaching, that I shared with the group.

When conducting these types of inquiry activities, I prefer that the participants do not know what they are about. In the past I found that such knowing predisposed them, framing the experience as Merleau-Ponty (1962) claims. The pre-knowing creates a pre-living that gets in the way of the experience. I ask them "not to think" but to experience. The thinking will come in the debriefing session (Norris, 1995).

As with McNiff's student described above, the process of inquiry changes the A/R/Tors' perspectives. They come to new personal insights as a result of listening to the stories of others and from improvisations that metaphorically examine lived-experiences. Playbuilding then is a form of transformative research and pedagogy for researchers and audiences. But it is not therapy, albeit possibly therapeutic. The intent is not to cure pathology but to provide opportunities through which people can create meanings that better serve them and their relationships with others and the world.

RESEARCH DISSEMINATION   Some of Mirror Theatre's scenes and their analyses have been published in print (Norris, 1998a, 1999; Norris and Mirror Theatre, 2001d); however, they are primarily designed to be performed and workshopped with a live audience. Unlike printed text, which is static, research disseminated through Playbuilding changes with each and every audience as the audience members rewrite the play through a technique called "forum theater" (Boal, 1979). This way audience members can make comments on the scene (simultaneous dramaturgy), make suggestions to the actors on how they might replay the scene, and/or actually go on stage, improvising their versions of the issue. The dissemination becomes a form of living research as the recipients of the research merge their opinions and stories with those of the A/C/Tors. Such a process makes the research dissemination dialogical.

From a theatrical perspective, the scenes are not completely polished, as is the case with scripted pieces. The raw edge of improvisation maintains a high energy for the actors and the audience. Thus the performance models a potential process in which the audience members can partake. Although the scenes are most often outlines and the underlying issues and intent explicit to the actors, in this form of dissemination a degree of openness and unpredictability is not only expected but also desired. The A/R/Tors are fully aware that a new director will take over shortly (audience members), turning their performances into invitations to dialogue. A well-polished piece can lose its raw improvisational edge, making it appear impermeable to change.

But this does not mean that improvisational theater is of lesser quality than mainstage productions; it is merely a different genre. Piirto (2002) in her discussion of quality in arts-based research makes a distinction between performance and workshop, with a workshop's intent being more about personal insights than performance skills. Her point is well taken. To paraphrase this chapter's opening quote: Such a play can be written only by a researcher who has mastered the techniques of theatre. The pedagogical nature of Playbuilding places it between workshop and performance as an intermediary ground. Chapter 15 discusses the workshop aspects of Playbuilding in detail.

As with any research or literary genre, there are stylistic choices that help define it. Pedagogical and theatrical decisions influence how the data is shaped into the structure of the play and the scenes within it. As with all research, it is necessary to make the data treatment of Playbuilding explicit so that others may understand how it has been "framed"

(Goffman, 1974). It can also be considered another form of "bracketing" (Gearing, 2009; Spradley, 1980).

Although Collective Creations and other Playbuilding projects can have a plot and central characters, the style chosen and the recommended form for research projects is a collage of vignettes. Like qualitative studies that categorize data into themes, Playbuilding performances that use a vignette style provide a range of issues experienced by many different people. The form allows for a greater range of issues, experiences, and perspectives. However, in the case of Playbuilding, the themes are not made explicit. Rather, they are imbedded into the story, respecting the theater adage "Show; don't tell." Playbuilding uses vignettes to phenomenologically reenact lived-experiences.

Owing to its constructivist pedagogical intent, the data is generated, constructed, and arranged to invite conversations. While information is provided, the aim is to move beyond the presentation analysis of that information through dialectical discussions. The first step to achieving this aim is to generate multiple, diverse, and often conflicting points of view. For example, in our program on substance use/abuse, we searched for reasons "to" and "not to" smoke; to fully understand the phenomenon, we needed to examine both reasons. For some individuals, "fitting in" could take precedence over health. Within either a scene or a juxtaposition of two or more scenes, a thesis and its antithesis are provided. Many issues are not completely developed, leaving spaces for the audience members to create their own synthesis.

Although participant voices are sought, they are neither affirmed nor denied. Rather, the discussions move into a quest for greater understanding. This form of research dissemination and generation does not work with fixed opinions; it is a collective lived-experience of meaning-making in flux. Even one's previous stories can be "reconceptualized" (Pinar, 1975, p. 396) as they are compared with the stories and opinions of others.

Greene encourages "teaching for openings" where we "break through the limits of the conventional and the taken for granted" (1995, p. 109). Rather than creating scenes that "preach," which can often put people on the defensive, this form thesis/antithesis/synthesis can create an ethos of exploration and an openness to change. To be pedagogical one must teeter on the totter of accepting the participants' perspectives on the one side and the questioning and challenging of them on the other. Such is the paradox of teaching; we must simultaneously welcome and disrupt student knowledge if growth is to occur. Gallagher and Riviére claim "we wanted to both capitalize on and complicate the students' adamant opinions by placing us within an embodied, theatrical context. Dialogue, in theatre, is more than mere dialogue; it is the action of the play" (2007, p. 323). This form of research dissemination is structured so that dialogue is possible.

A criterion that we use when creating a scene is its "jokerablity." Using the concept of the "joker" (Berezan, 2004; Boal, 1979; Bowman, 1997, p. 139; Hewson, 2007; Smith, 1996), an MC acts as an intermediary between audience members and the cast (discussed in detail in Chapter 15) facilitating conversation and/or dramatic explorations. Such explorations might be a new scene, taking place the day before, the day after, or with other characters that influence the scene as suggested by the audience. Prepared scenes that reach a resolution usually "dead-end" as the text becomes closed. The data is disseminated in an exploratory format that makes "jokering" or "teaching for openings" possible.

As a mathematician uses formulae to shape numbers and the meanings we take from them, so does an artist, albeit with the tools of the artistic genre chosen. For Playbuilding, the range of performance possibilities is broad. A number of dramatic research presentations have underutilized this resource relying predominantly on the forms of Readers Theatre and monologues. Over time these can get repetitive and boring, missing the rich resources that the art form has to offer. This Playbuilding process is enhanced by the use of a wide theatrical brush, utilizing many dramatic forms (discussed in Chapter 2). The A/R/Tors take the generated data and judiciously take artistic license, using metaphor, composites, and theatrical styles to create a verisimilitude of lived-experiences to create texts (theatrical vignettes) that evoke conversation.

ETHICAL ISSUES   Working with "human subjects" is delicate work at the best of times. The process of Playbuilding is far more complex than traditional qualitative research studies, because the roles that the participants play differ from the typical participant/observer, interviewer/interviewee, and questionnaire designer/responder relationships. With Playbuilding, the data sources are primarily A/R/Tors and audience members. Moving to a far greater participatory form of research requires a different set of ethical considerations. This section first discusses the ethical issues that have emerged from working with cast members and then those of working with audiences.

Cast Ethics   Since cast members are considered coresearchers and coauthors, no formal ethics review has been needed. Like any cocreated piece in which the authors disclose part of their backgrounds to "bracket out" (Geertz, 1974) or "bracket in" (Norris and Sawyer, 2004), they have final say on what to include or exclude. The degree of participation with a voice in the shaping of the final product and the responsibility of co-ownership provide a role very different than that of passive participants. Instead of research that is done "on" a human subject, it is research "with" others, changing the category "subject" to "partner." Adapting the Collective Creation tradition of Rick Salutin (Salutin and Theatre Passe Muraille, 1976), we cite the director and the name of the theater company, because to list all co-authors would be cumbersome. For example:

> Norris, J., & Mirror Theatre. 1997. (Director, MC, actor and coauthor). *What's the Fine Line?* **Keynote** performance presented at the 1997 Conference for Safe and Caring Schools. Edmonton, Alberta.

In the citation, the roles are provided in parentheses. When another coauthor cites the piece, she/he adds her/his name to the citation and change the roles played:

> Norris, J., Hotson, M., & Mirror Theatre. 1997. (Actor and coauthor). *What's the Fine Line?* **Keynote** performance presented at the 1997 Conference for Safe and Caring Schools. Edmonton, Alberta.

Such a process clearly defines the cast members as coauthors, not subjects.

As discussed in the history of Mirror Theatre (Chapter 3), in an agreement of membership, cast members give the cocreated scenes to Mirror Theatre, a not-for-profit registered company with a board elected by its members. The board authorizes performance and distribution rights. This enables all to function efficiently, eliminating the need to track down all the previous participants.

But the cast members do have an ethical relationship to one another, and this is established during the first two rehearsals. An informal "nondisclosure" rule applies throughout the data generation/rehearsal process. We are asked to keep one another's stories and opinions confidential. First, the stories are meant as exploration, and, until shaped, they are provided as possibilities. Without such a rule, trust is harder to establish, and valuable stories may be withheld. Second, we try to look at all opinions as emergent ones, as temporary placeholders. To define one another based on our initial opinions and then discuss them with others destroys all hope of a collaborative, trusting relationship. Until performance, all is confidential to the cast, unless a cast member makes it otherwise explicit.

This ethical stance of the cast extends beyond its members. Bloom notes that "I will be telling other people's stories as well—whether they like it or not, whether they know it or not" (2003, p. 277). During rehearsals we wrestle with this. In most cases the reference to others who have participated in our lives is obscure enough that no particular individual could be identified. When it is not, we explore other possibilities, such as searching for a universal metaphor to portray the essentials of the event, having another cast member tell or play the story, or portraying it without anonymity—but only if the A/R/Tor agrees.

Before her grade nine graduation, my daughter told me that her Asian friend explained to her that if they went to a particular high school they would not be able to "hang out," because she would be expected to be in the "Asian hallway." This was a school that publicly boasted that they had no prejudice. We used this story in "Respecting Diversity and Preventing Prejudice" (Norris and Mirror Theatre, 1999a). One at a time, cast members entered a cafeteria wearing green, blue, and red sweatshirts. Through mime it was made clear that each color had to sit together. Its root, my daughter's story, was never revealed—until now. While the consequences are minimal, if any, I take the responsibility involved in portraying it.

Although the majority of our scenes have a strong empirical basis, through theater they are presented under a thin veil of fiction. This can provide the anonymity needed to protect cast members and associated others.

Finally, we recognize that we are dealing with sensitive issues and that our work may trigger memories of disturbing events. Cast members are made aware of this, and we all agree to take responsibility for ourselves. What we ask is that if such things do arise, the affected individuals seek professional help. The research team can support as friends, but our project is not to be a therapy session. We have no such expertise, and it would be unethical to pretend to have it. One cast member reported a date rape. She wanted the story told, and she wanted to tell it. It was staged as a diary. She sat center stage, writing it as it was mimed in a shadow screen on stage right. She claimed that she didn't require counseling. To the best of my knowledge, no cast member has required such a service. However, a few A/R/Tors have noted benefits in telling their stories. Our rehearsals, although not therapy, have been therapeutic, bringing participants to what they deem a better state of mind about a prior event.

A safe and caring community has been an aim of many of our projects, and we have attempted to practice what we encourage. Although we have the normal hiccups experienced with most group situations, we aim to treat one another with respect and care. This type of ethical stance is necessary to achieve the degree of data generation and public display that are expected from involvement in such projects.

Audience Ethics   Audiences are seldom considered formal data sources. This is not the case with Mirror Theatre's form of Playbuilding, since we enter into dialogue with those in attendance. There were only two instances when formal research was conducted with a student audience. In one case, ethics approval was granted and consent forms obtained (Appendix A). Two school administrators were also interviewed. The other was a program review (Appendix F).

In other cases, we provided permission slips to attend the performances, similar to those in Appendix A, but with the research portion removed. We wanted to keep parents informed. It is not often the case that the recipients of the research are asked permission to receive it. We went beyond standard ethical protocols with our request for dissemination permission.

Unsolicited data, however, has been noted and recorded. Audience members have approached cast members and me after an event with comments about the performance/workshop. These occurrences were at public events and were volunteered to the company. Those who commented cannot be identified. Small portions of our data come from these sources and are incorporated into our work; so, too, with our vignettes. During the workshops, stories are told that add to our understanding of the phenomenon. Sometimes scenes are created in our discussion groups that can be reworked into a subsequent program. They are coauthored by the audience under the direction of an A/R/Tor. Informal permission is requested and granted.

A last note on ethics also demonstrates going beyond standard protocols. This has to do with relationships. Often research separates the data source from those generating it and those receiving it. In these instances, the researchers act like Hermes, translating what is given for their readership. Research is conducted "on" certain individuals "for" others. Those generating the data frequently never receive it. In the case of Playbuilding, the prepositions "on" and "for" are replaced with "with," redefining the researcher/researched relationship. Those generating the data are involved in all stages of the research. Those receiving it are not removed from the lived-experience presented but are directly related to it. Dissemination is grassroots. Those receiving it also are provided an opportunity to add their voices. Consequently, all those involved work "with" the researchers. A dialogical position is a political and an ethical one.

In summary, Playbuilding's purpose, like that of literary journalism, is to "deepen understanding, not to arrive at totalized truth" (Hartsock, 2000, p. 12). Using both empirical and imaginative data, vignettes are devised using a variety of theatrical forms that serve as "evocateurs," inviting live audiences into the quest for meaning about the social issues that face them. Rather than being declarative, dissemination is interrogative, as A/R/Tors and audiences participate in situations where they question their present stances based on listening to the Other. Playbuilding is an attempt to operationalize dialogic research.

CHAPTER 2

"A" Research to Performance Process

> The open texture of the form increases the probability that multiple perspectives will emerge. Multiple perspectives make our engagement with the phenomena more complex. Ironically, good research often complicates our lives. (Eisner, 1997, p. 8)

Group work isn't easy. Creating a common product can be a difficult task. The act of negotiation is a mastered art, and the ability to merge one's own vision with the disparate visions of others requires a unique balance of personal integrity and humility. Looking back at the history of Mirror Theatre, I am amazed that we accomplished as much as we did. We had our moments of difficulty as we struggled to create harmony out of polyphony and sometimes settled with a dash or two of cacophony. The particulars of our group interactions are reserved for private conversations, but many generalities are provided as guideposts for those who choose to venture down a similar path.

Unlike many research methods, the Playbuilding process is a collective venture with a variety of players acting as data sources, coresearchers, and actors. It is a form of participatory research in the extreme. Besides having a team of A/R/Tors working toward a product of human understanding, the method of dissemination involves a live, participating audience. All stages of the research are collaborative and open to the possibility of new insights from other participants.

The early stages of study of this process began with my doctoral research (Norris, 1989a, b, c, d, and e), in which I observed a drama teacher and her grade-eleven students work ninety minutes a day, five days a week for three and one-half months devising a play. I was interested in the concept of student voice and asked, "What do we do as teachers that fosters student creativity, and what do we do that inhibits it?" I believed that the drama class, in which students cowrote a play, would be a good example of a democratic classroom. I was familiar with the process from my teacher experiences and followed the steps outlined by Berry and Reinbold (1985). Although they are a useful guide, I believed that there was something missing. Berry and Reinbold provided the technical steps (Table 2.1), but from my experience, there was a second process, an interpersonal one (Table 2.2). My doctoral research portrays the journey of one group of individuals "devising" (Jackson, 1993) a play about growing up and the theatrical choices made. It is both an example of a curriculum in which students take a highly active role and an exploration of the interpersonal dimensions of collaboration.

This chapter is a collection of my cumulative insights on the Play-building process, which I gleaned and applied as I directed theatrical projects of coauthorship. The technical and the interpersonal dimensions of

Table 2.1 • Collective Steps (Berry and Reinbold, 1985, p. 8).

PERFORMANCE

REHEARSAL

SCRIPTING

REFINING
(making choices, deletion and inclusion of scene work)

EXPLORATION
(ideas translated into dramatic form)

SYNTHESIS
(grouping, organizing, and eliminating ideas)

RESEARCH
Gathering

TOPIC CHOICE

Table 2.2 • Norris's Interpersonal Steps (Norris, 1989a, p. 108).

FOCUS

(Public Meaning)

BELIEF

OWNERSHIP

IDEAS ACCEPTED (coauthorship)

RESPONSIBILITY

COMMITMENT

PURPOSE

CHALLENGED

(Collective Meaning)

ENGAGED

INTERESTED

ARTICULATION: Work/Play = Discipline

TRUST

PERSONAL MEANING

(Personal Meaning)

STIMULATION

DISCIPLINE: WORK/PLAY

Can't work together without trust
BUT
Working together builds trust

Playbuilding work in tandem. The technical dimension outlines a series of steps that other researchers may wish to follow, but alone it fails to provide an understanding of the lived-experiences of individuals in collaboration. The Playbuilding process requires attention to both dimensions.

This chapter first outlines the technical processes employed in this version of Playbuilding, as I integrated qualitative research principles and practices with the established Collective Creation or Playbuilding processes. It then discusses the interpersonal dimensions of collaboration, noting how the establishment of a functioning team is essential for the successful completion of this type of research project. But, as the chapter title implies, it is "a" process. The description of this process is not meant to be prescriptive for others to follow verbatim. Each group of A/R/Tors will bring their own talents and perspectives to the project. As Barbossa says in *Pirates of the Caribbean: The Curse of the Black Pearl* (Verbinski, 2003), "They're more like guidelines."

The Technical

A group of A/R/Tors is gathered in a circle discussing their upcoming project. It consists of an experienced Playbuilding director (in these cases, me), a few cast members who have worked with me before, and a few new A/R/Tors who have expressed interest in either the topic and/or the process. I begin by informally "contracting" with the assembly, outlining a few rights and responsibilities (discussed in detail in the section "The Interpersonal," below). Short introductions are made, and we begin to discuss the topic. Usually I outline a few themes and tell a personal story. I then invite others to join in. Using a version of a talking stick (for example, a small, soft, stuffed toy, my keys, a sponge brick, or a leather pouch), I toss it to a person who has indicated a willingness to go next. So begins our journey.

Data Generation

The assembly wants to be here. The members have stories that they want to tell, beliefs that they want to share, and questions that they want to address. They enjoy the collaborative process and theater both as a means of meaning-making and as a form of presentation. The cast members are rich in data and willing to spend considerable time examining themselves and others to better understand the phenomenon we have chosen to investigate.

STORYTELLING   The stories of others are strong evocateurs for one's own stories, and the conversations cascade as the participants take turns articulating their similarities and differences. The process, grounded in the qualitative research methodology storytelling (Reason and Hawkins, 1988), is quite simple. As when one drops a pebble in a pond and watches its ripples, a story naturally eddies, creating unique nuances as it encounters the stories of others and its own ripple of ripples. It is an unfolding process that is contextually bound, because the data generated is dependent on the individuals involved. The process is thick with rich data.

For example, in a conversation regarding reverse discrimination, a black man from Africa noted that he experienced an interesting behavior while out in public in Canada. Often when he encountered another black man, that stranger nodded as he passed. Eventually, he deduced that it was an affirmation of similarity and nodded back. A white female then told a similar story. When traveling in China, she found that Caucasians nodded to one another. His story had evoked hers. It seems, that, when in the minority, racial commonality needed to be affirmed. This phenomenon was performed in our scene "Party of Bigots" in a video about prejudice (Norris and Mirror Theatre 1999a), with two black men unknown to each other nodding to each other. Confusion ensued when a white friend of one the black men also nodded to the other. In this way, a large collection of stories on a wide range of subjects emerged over the years, not as a result of structured questions but of the power of storytelling.

GUIDED IMAGERY   Another strong data generator has been guided imagery (Norris, 1995a), a powerful tool in evoking memories. Early in the rehearsal process for a production later named *Warts or Beauty Marks?* (Norris and Student Company, 2005), I informed the cast (students enrolled in a six-credit graduate course called "Playbuilding as Pedagogical Inquiry") that the next day would be a BYOB day (Bring Your Own Blankee). After a couple of warm-ups that introduced them to the topic and established emotional safety parameters, I took them back in time.

> Today we will be going back in time to an early memory, your first day of school. If you can't remember, that's fine. Try to recall your first day of high school or teaching. Go to the moment of first waking up. What did you feel? Were you excited? Nervous? Neutral? Explore the range of emotions that you experienced. (*Pause*) Now look around the room. Can you remember its color? How it was decorated? What furniture was in it? Did you share it, or was it your own room? Where were the windows? What was the weather like? Where was the door? Were there sounds or smells coming from another part of the house? (*Pause*) What did your blankets look like? What were you wearing? What did you plan to wear? Get out of bed. Did you get dressed first or after breakfast, if you had any? (*Pause*) Don't worry if you can't think of everything or if it might not have been that exact day. What is important is that you have a collage of memories that approximate that particular day. (*Pause*) What else did you do before leaving? Did you have breakfast? Do the dishes? Clean up? What were your daily "going to school" rituals? (*Pause*) Now, leave your home. How did you travel to school? Walk? Bike? Drive in a car? Your parent's car or a neighbor's? Take a bus? What did you bring with you? In your mind's eye, take your time and travel to school, but don't go in. Wait outside. (*Pause*) Look at the school. What were your impressions and anticipations? What did going to school mean to you? (*Pause*) Now go inside. Do you remember the location of your first classroom? What it looked like from the inside? How

the seats, tables, and desks were organized? How was it deco-
rated? Where did you sit? Do you remember anyone's name? Your
teacher's name? What activities did you do that day? Whom did
you talk to? Play with? Work with? Or did you spend a lot of alone
time? (*Pause*) Now travel home? How did you get there? Do you
recall what you told others about your first day at school?'

The scripting of a guiding imagery is meant to evoke thoughts and be
open enough to accommodate a variety of differences. Overly structuring
the details would work for those who had had the given experience but
would be confusing to those that hadn't. Still, in the work that ensues,
such discrepancies can provide additional information. Questions, rather
than declarative sentences, tend to keep the process open.

The cast is then divided into groups of three or four and asked to
tell the parts of the story that they feel comfortable sharing. As director,
I circulate, listening to what unfolds, making notes of possible discussion
starters for later. Participants' reports to the entire cast, however, won't
be a recounting of what they have told; rather, they will be reframed as
dramatic presentations that could either be one person's story or a composite. The aim is to present an ethos of the first day of school. Like a
caricature of a celebrity, certain features are highlighted for emphasis and
recognizability. The presentation is no less truthful. It merely tells the
story using a different artistic style. Here are some suggestions from a list
of possibilities:

- The group mime key events with a narrator telling the story.
- The group mime key events with a narrator telling the main characters' inner thoughts.
- Perform a slide show of tableaus/frozen pictures emphasizing the
  key events. The audience members close their eyes after each picture
  so that the cast set can up the next one.
- Perform a slide show of tableaus/frozen pictures metaphorically,
  emphasizing the key emotional experiences.
- Present using a traditional dramatic style with conversation and
  action.

Each scene is presented and discussed for both content and form.
Typically, the scenes evoke even more stories from the A/R/Tors, and
these are also recorded for possible use. The guided imagery provides rich
data that could easily be translated into dramatic forms by the cast as they
collectively and simultaneously integrate the data generation, analysis,
and dissemination stages of the research. The groups are asked to record
key elements of their scenes for future discussion. To polish now would
be a waste of time, because it would be premature to decide which scene,

if any, or a composite will be used. It is much too early in the research to determine its focus. We use an internal hermeneutic approach (Werner and Rothe, 1979) that stalls dissemination decision making until we reach a high level of data saturation. Only then are particular scenes and themes chosen for inclusion.

IMPROVISATION   Improvisation is an excellent way to assist in the articulation of what we know/believe when we can't find the words. Often, when a conversation spins its metaphorical wheels, I spontaneously create an improvisational scene that may, through a simulation, help us to get beyond our abstract doldrums. This approach, too, simultaneously integrates data generation, analysis, and dissemination, because the improvised scenes include all three functions.

While trying to understand the differences between the words "need," "want," and "desire," I cast three A/R/Tors as flowers and three as bees (Chapter 5) and had them interact. This resulted in a lengthy discussion about types of attraction. To explore innocence, the cast created a playground (Chapter 5), concretizing innocent behaviors, with me observing, trying to discern where guilt may appear. I resorted to a trust fall activity to metaphorically help us understand the needs of student teachers (Chapter 1). Appropriateness of clothing was explored by having a male adjust his belt while carrying on a benign conversation with a female (Chapter 6). The politics of student teaching and sexual harassment was explored with a non-cast member (Chapter 1). These and other scenes employed improvisation to assist cast members in articulating their thoughts theatrically, rather than employing the hegemonic discourse of expository conversation. Like Kostera's work with fictional narrative (2006), improvisation became a medium through which the A/R/Tors could articulate their underlying beliefs through concrete representation. The role-play was not fiction, but it brought the A/R/Tors closer to themselves, as the medium enabled them to examine themselves differently (Norris, 1995b).

EXTERNAL SOURCES   Although storytelling, guided imagery, and improvisation were the primary methods of generating data from this motley crew of diverse A/R/Tors, as reported in Chapter 1, we did occasionally require and utilize external sources. Literature on bullying informed a number of our plays; a series of a newspaper's letters to the editor was compiled for a scene on inclusion; individuals approached us asking that we tell their stories on racism and harassment; and audience members, as a result of workshops and interactive drama, provided us with more ideas and actual scenes (Chapter 15). What is noteworthy is the grassroots element of our data generation. How often do individuals contact researchers to informally supply data, and where are the opportunities for consumers of research studies to respond with stories of their own? Playbuilding is a participatory dialogic form of research that seldom remains static. A/R/Tors and their audiences analyze and re-create data in real time.

CARDS AND FOLDERS   During the second rehearsal, a data recording system is introduced to the cast. A set of approximately ten blank recipe cards and a marker are passed out to each cast member. The cast members in a circle facing one another and begin to recount our last rehearsal. This acts activity as a form of review as well as a record of events. As the conversation unfolds, other stories that were told during the last rehearsal, as well as new ones, are noted. The cast is also asked to move to abstraction, noting the themes within each story. This theme analysis also evokes new stories as the abstractions trigger other connections. The rehearsal moves into an organic spiral of collaborative storytelling and analysis. As stories are told, the A/R/Tors write story titles and themes on cards with the originator's name in the bottom right-hand corner and placed in the center of the circle.

At the end of the evening, the cards are collected and placed in a file folder labeled "To Be Filed." During the fourth or fifth rehearsal, I bring out the folder that, by this point, holds a large number of ideas. We collectively sort them into newly introduced folders (Norris, 2000) as follows:

- Scene Ideas
- Rehearsed (Devised) Scenes
- Quickies (short scenes and/or phrases)
- Themes/Issues
- Metaphors
- Props/Costumes/Music needs
- External Resources
- Potential Titles
- Keepers

The act of sorting cards in folders acts as a review of what has taken place and as a springboard to what is still to be done. It provides newcomers with confidence that we are indeed getting somewhere. Near the end of this process, I ask: "Based on what we have articulated, what do we want our play to be about? And "What haven't we focused on that still needs exploration?" For the final few rehearsals, new cards again find their way into "To Be Filed" and are sorted at a later date. Near the end of the

Photo 2.1 • Writing themes and scene ideas on cards.

data generation phase, we return to all the folders to determine our final structure (discussed in the section "Keepers" below).

The following sections outline the technical process of "devising" (Pammenter, 1993), the term commonly used to discuss the act of translating raw material into theatrical forms. Since the card system plays a major role in the Mirror Theatre Playbuilding process, a discussion of the contents of the folders provides a detailed outline of how our research-based performance/workshops were devised.

Scene Ideas   All stories are regarded as scene ideas, and a short note summarizing each story is placed on a file card with the name of the storyteller in the bottom-right corner. In addition, there are often multiple scene ideas within each story. All are noted, as well as comments on how they might be theatrically staged. These summaries are revisited throughout the process, and some are chosen to explore theatrically. At any stage of the devising process, new scene ideas can be added to the "To Be Filed" folder and later find their ways to the "Scene Ideas" folder.

Rehearsed (Devised) Scenes   During each rehearsal, I determine when the conversation has reached an optimum degree of content saturation. Then, by reading the cards, I ask cast members what themes or scene ideas they want to work on. A few make choices and others join them, breaking up into small groups to generate scenes. As with the previous stage, there is a spiral of data generation and analysis as the small groups discuss both the content and the most appropriate way to present it. Usually the originator whose name is on the scene ideas card accompanies the group, to assist in translating the story into dramatic form. Having the original storyteller present insures that additional details not found on the card will be added to provide richer details. Like a series of incrementally smaller sieves, a large number of scene ideas are reduced to a much smaller number of rehearsed scenes that will be even further reduced to the chosen scenes, or "Keepers." During rehearsals, a program emerges piece by piece, with the devising of scenes being a major part in Mirror Theatre's process.

The act of devising is more than the construction of theatrical scenes. As Donmoyer and Yennie-Donmoyer have found, the act of structuring data into a script is a sophisticated form of analysis.

> Actually, we discovered—much to our surprise—that at least in this case the processes of data analysis and readers theater script construction were really not very different from each other. Even in the process of staging the script—something that clearly is not done with social science reports—we can find some rather obvious analogs for procedures employed and techniques used in writing a social science research report. (1995, p. 409)

Before the first small group working session, I give a short lecture on theatrical conventions (Norris, 1995b) or dramatic elements (Schonmann, 2006). Similar to using a variety of ways to translate participants' memories (data) of their first days of school into theatrical forms, I encourage the groups to explore other dramatic structures. The chart (see Table 2.3)

Table 2.3 • Theatrical Conventions: Three Dyads and Eight Arrangements (Norris, 1995b, p. 292).

	Light/Dark		Movement/Stillness		Sound/Silence	
	Light	Dark	Movement	Stillness	Sound	Silence
Dramatic action	x		x		x	
Mime	x		x			x
Narration	x			x	x	
Picture tableau	x			x		x
Stereo radio		x	x		x	
Blackout (time)		x	x			x
Mono radio		x		x	x	
Blackout (no time)		x		x		x

that I hand out provides an outline of possibilities. It outlines the eight possible arrangements of the three dyads, light/darkness, movement/ stillness, and sound/silence and the labels that I have assigned them.

"Dramatic action" is the most common; lights are on, movement can be detected, and sounds (voices) can be heard. Usually it is realistic and the basic form that is chosen. My aim is to expand the repertoire of choices, abandoning the hegemony of this form by providing other pos- sibilities. The chart helps to make this clear. However, rather than refer- ring to silence as the absence of sound, and so forth, I prefer to make both sides dominant by indicating that silence is on and movement is off, thereby questioning the logocentrism (Culler, 1982) of dualisms.

"Mime" can be seen, and movement is detected; however, silence replaces sound. With mime, attention is drawn to the significance of the movement. Usually it provides more metaphorical interpretations that

Photo 2.2 • Body sculpting characters into tableaus.

eventually lead to lively discussions with cast members and audiences. Although in a classical sense mime is silent, we have used background music to provide mood and "gibberish" (Chapter 8) without the denotative meanings of words to convey inflection.

With "narration," an actor usually stands still or moves periodically without dramatic action. The narrator, in plain view, speaks directly to the audience. Sometimes it is expedient not to use dramatic action to provide information; rather, a narrator can quickly and efficiently move a story along. Brecht uses a narrator in *The Caucasian Chalk Circle* (1961) to break the dramatic action and create the alienation effect (Brecht, 1957). Saldaña (1998) casts the narrator as a qualitative researcher to provide the research information about an individual he had interviewed. In *What's the Fine Line?* (Norris and Mirror Theatre, 1995d), we used a narrator in the "New Kid at School" scene to bridge transitions in time. Narration, discriminately employed, can economize time and provide distance from the dramatic action.

I refer to light, stillness, and silence as "picture tableau." At times, a still actor can convey more meaning than a moving one can. In "Pressures" (Chapter 4) a young male and female are frozen on stage and sculpted into different positions by other characters. Their stillness signifies their passivity to the pressures that surround them. The scene is not realistic but acts as a metaphor, highlighting the pressures one experiences relating to sexuality.

One may think that darkness, sound, and movement are not possible, since an audience cannot detect movement in the dark. However, one can hear footsteps crossing the stage while "watching" a murder mystery and hear voices coming from various locations. These are auditory movements that I call "stereo radio." In a junior high Christmas production that I helped direct, the students uttered certain phrases: "Open mine first"; "Just what I always wanted"; and "Pass the gravy" were some of the sound bites. The performance began with the cast scattered throughout the audience. The lights were out, and, one at a time, cast members started walking to the front while saying a phrase. Our working metaphor for the tone of the scene was "a gentle snow fall," and this stereo radio scene enabled the audience focus on the major element, the expressions themselves, not the visuals.

There can also be movement with darkness and stillness. I call this "blackout (time)." A common use of this is during an intermission. Act I ends with a room in disarray and the dead body on the floor as the detective searches for clues. The curtain comes down, and the house lights come up. When the audience returns to their seats and the curtain rises, they find that the room has been restored sans body. There has been movement in time not seen or heard by the audience.

In *Warts and Beauty Marks* (Norris, and Student Company, 2005) a series of tableaus that take place during a first day of school were shown with a blackout between each one. Like a slide show of events, the audience detected passages in time that took place in the dark. This visual collage utilized blackouts to indicate time shifts. When involved with audience participation (Chapter 15), sometimes a student would suggest a fight scene to resolve a conflict. Accepting the suggestion, I would ask one character to throw the first blow in slow motion and freeze before contact. I would then have one of the characters lie on the floor, fast-forwarding time. Although seen, fast-forwarding would serve as a pseudo blackout. I would explain to the audience that to do a safe fight would take hours of rehearsal with actors experienced in stage fighting. Our conversation would focus on the consequences of the physical fight. Blackouts can be an effective way to fast-forward and sometimes rewind time.

Sound can also come from a single dark place. In the example of the slide show, the inner dialogue of one of the characters in the photo was given off stage through a microphone. Here, there was no movement in the sound. Besides being an example of "mono radio," this scene demonstrates that two or more conventions can be pared with each other; in this case, blackout (time) with mono radio.

Blackout (no time) is often used during audience participation. The characters are frozen, and the audience discusses what they would like to hear or see next. Such a convention slows down the action, giving the audience time to process. In traditional theater, this technique is also used during acts. After the intermission, the audience returns, and the play resumes where it left off.

These eight variations offer limitless possibilities. Light comprises everything that can be seen, including set, costumes, and props. Sound, in addition to the spoken word, could include sound effect, music, and natural sounds that are made on stage, such as the clinking of glasses, the stirring of tea, the clashing of swords, and footsteps in the dark. Movement can be realistic or stylized in dance and mime. These conventions need not stand alone, nor are they prescriptive canons. They are a pallet from which the A/R/Tors mix form and content to create vignettes that appropriately convey their desired intents.

In addition to the conventions, other factors are considered while participants are devising scenes. What is paramount is that those creating the scene defer ownership to the larger group and consider themselves as playwrights. The devised scenes could have more or fewer characters than the devising group, and they should not limit their ideas based on number. This approach provides more flexibility in generating scenes.

Although not necessary for every scene, the devising process should also look for performance ideas that may eventually lead to audience participation. Often, didactic scenes leave little room for discussion, whereas open-ended scenes that make the issue problematic invite points of view from audience members. For example, in rehearsal for *What's the Use?* (Norris and Mirror Theatre, 2000c), we explored both the pros and cons of taking the first cigarette. Such an approach keeps the scene open for conversation. The question asked is "Is it jokerable?" which means, is there a strong likelihood that audience members can discuss and possibly rewrite the scene. Either within a scene, or as a result of two or more scenes, we wished to perform data that provided both thesis and antithesis, enabling audience members to construct their own synthesis. This process moved away from a didactic text and toward a pedagogic one.

Recording of the rehearsed scenes for later use was also an expectation; however, detailed scripting was not expected at this point, because the entire cast would be involved with revisions. We employed a notation system that defined the characters and their motivations and then listed the key events and changes in the scene. By using "beats," a theatrical concept for small, focused, emotional segments of a scene, we were able to efficiently record the essential elements of a scene. Often these were used to improvise scenes, and the actual scripting was a transcription of a videotaped performance. An early version of *What's the Fine Line?* contained a mimed scene called "Territoriality," as did "The Party" scene (Chapter 9) in *Coulda/Shoulda*. Since there was no dialogue, the beats were the only way to script the scene.

After devising a rehearsal's scenes, the A/R/Tors reassemble to present their works in progress. After each presentation, all present make comments

Photo 2.3 • "Party of Bigots"—quickie collage.

and give suggestions; a spirit of co-ownership is expected for the entire piece (discussed in the following section on "The Interpersonal"). These scenes are not polished during this stage, because they may not make the final cut. However, this feedback can produce more detailed notes both on the form and content of the scene. The scene ideas cards and their addition notes would now be filed in the "Rehearsed (Devised) Scenes" folder.

Quickies (Short Scenes and/or Phrases)   Many scene ideas are short in nature and are often sound bites. However, they are not substantial enough to carry a scene, but neither are they to be discarded. They are filed, and over time a number of them, like emergent themes, can coalesce to form their own unity. In *Respecting Diversity and Preventing Prejudice* (Norris and Mirror Theatre, 1999a), the scene "Party of Bigots" consisted of a number of one-liner prejudicial phrases such as "time of the month" and "gypping someone"— a composite of quickies collected over time.

In *Mirror Mirror* (Norris and Student Company, 1993a) quickies were used as transitions. Quick set changes needed to be made. Rather have the audience wait in darkness, participants aimed spotlights at both sides of the stage. Actors would recite lines as a phrase collage, filling the empty space and progressing the play. The quickies folder provided both structural and content elements to the program.

Themes/Issues   Besides concrete lived-experiences, abstract coding occurs throughout the process. Such themes as innocence, harassment, identity, relationships, decisions, territoriality, risk, consequences, and fear are just a few of the many themes found in an assortment of "themes/issues" folders in Mirror Theatre's archives. These cards did not have any details but were meant (a) to assist in insuring that our research covered a wide range of issues relative to the phenomenon and (b) to act as triggers for stories and scenes.

The value of themes is that, rather than being specific, they invoke a variety of stories and suggest a number of scenes underneath a universal heading.

"Drama ideas usually begin with a general area of interest, narrowed to a particular, then, if the experience is to be related to the person's own experience, are universalized to draw in the unique experience of the group at work on the idea. This dropping of the particular into the universal is the digestion process of the arts, creating the opportunity for reflection. This is what education is all about" (Heathcote, Johnson, and O'Neill, 1991, p. 35).

The interplay between themes (universals) and scenes (particulars) can generate a lot of data from which the research performance can evolve. For example, the theme "fear" yielded "Preparation Paranoia" in *Great Expectations* (Norris and Student Company, 1994a), and the theme "innocence" led to the "M Word" (Chapter 5) from *Complexities and Contradictions* (Norris and Mirror Theatre, 1998c).

Metaphors   Similar to themes and issues, metaphors enable us to look beyond the particular to the bigger picture (universal). "Bursting bubbles" was a metaphor in *The First Frontier* (Norris and Student Company, 1994a), and "Heard It through the Grapevine" examined rumors in *Great Expectations* (Norris and Student Company, 1994a). The metaphor "pass the baby" grew from two scenes in *Great Expectations* to become a major component of *Shadowing* (Norris and Mirror Theatre, 2004).

Since metaphors suggest many particulars, they enabled the A/R/Tors to explore a variety of avenues of the phenomenon, and, as performance pieces, they created openings for the audience members to search for their own particulars. The metaphor cards were playful abstractions of the emergent stories and themes.

Props/Costumes/Music Needs   In earlier productions, this folder was missing, much to our chagrin. During scene generation, certain objects would emerge that would be necessary in order to perform the scene. For *Complexities and Contradictions*, a play on human sexuality, we required covers of magazines that depicted war and others that were seductive in nature in order to examine society's attitudes toward violence and sexuality. Each year, during remounts of *What's the Fine Line?* we updated our music for the school dance scene. For *Fair Play Rulz* we required a decorative pencil with a fancy eraser, and for *Great Expectations* we required green, blue, and red sweat- or T-shirts to distinguish among student teachers, cooperating teachers, and university faculty. Without an adequate record of these and many other items, we found ourselves scrambling at the last minute to obtain them. So, this folder was revisited from time to time and items checked off when a cast member procured an item. Attention to these details alleviated some unnecessary last-minute stress.

External Resources   As discussed earlier in this chapter, although most of the research was generated in a theatrical focus group atmosphere, external resources were also utilized. Data collected from these sources were placed in the "External Resources" folder. In addition to stories from individuals and audience members, academic literature, newspapers and magazine articles, poetry, and fictional pieces were also collected. For example, after it had been read to the cast, the children's picture book *First Grade Takes the Test* (Cohen, 1995) was placed in the folder. Later, a short excerpt was used in *One of These Things Is Not Like the Others; One of These Things Just Doesn't Belong*' (Norris and Mirror Theatre, 1998a). The folder was a visual reminder that, although our diverse stories were collectively rich data sources, other points of view also existed that could inform our work.

Potential Titles   Throughout the process we looked for potential titles for the production, knowing full well that they could change as more data was processed. Still, the activity added additional focus to our work. At times, themes and metaphors could be also be used for titles, and, when this was the case, the theme/metaphor/title was written on a separate card and placed in the "Potential Titles" folder. For example, the play *Mirror/Mirror* had other working titles, including *Reflection, What If...*, *Who's on First?*, *Uncertain/Uncomfortable/Unbecoming*, and *When You Cut to the Core of the Onion, You Cry*.

Keepers   The Playbuilding structure may be considered to be a kite shape.

Once a topic is chosen, a focus is found that excludes other possibilities. However, from this narrow point, the work expands like the bottom of a "V." During the devising stage, more and more data is collected, expanding the possibilities. There does come a saturation point when this process concludes and a refocusing occurs. Here the "V" inverts, forming the shape of a kite as the research takes form. The "Keepers" folder contains the items from all other folders that have been chosen for inclusion, which involves a painful discarding phase.

Approximately three-quarters through the process all researched scene titles are written on 8½- by 11-inch paper in large letters and stapled to the top of each scene's notes and spread out on the floor. The cast wanders, looking at the material that we have amassed. I ask the questions "Based on what we have collected, what do we want this play to be about?" and "What issues do we want to address that are not present?" Some scenes are rejected, because they seem tangential, and a few new scenes are suggested. Cast members choose either to work on a new scene or to take one of the rehearsed scenes and begin to polish it. Those who choose to work on the rehearsed scenes will more than likely be cast in those roles, although some recasting will take place once a sequence is determined.

A number of variables are taken into consideration when choosing and sequencing scenes into a final product. They are both pragmatic and theatrical in nature, and their interplay requires a high degree of flexibility. Initially, a sequence is determined by both content and tone. Usually a high-energy scene that frames the production is chosen for the first scene. This approach serves to introduce the topic to the audience and "arrest their attention" (Heathcote, 1971). Still looking at the floor, we ask, "What's next?" For fifteen minutes to one-half hour, scenes are arranged and rearranged on the floor until a potentially satisfactory sequence is achieved.

A hard-hitting emotional scene is often followed by a light but enthusiastic scene. In *What's the Fine Line?* a powerful and disturbing scene of testimonials about bullying is followed by a school dance with up-beat music. A roller-coaster metaphor is used to structure the vignettes of the play. Too much pensiveness can become boring, like the rollercoaster's assent, and long periods of frenetic energy can become tedious, like the coaster's decent. Energy balance is sought.

Subthemes can be clustered or separated. For example, all scenes dealing with homophobia could be strung together or separated by scenes on different aspects of the topic, for dramatic effect (Chapter 5). We tried both approaches, each being effective.

Casting then is over-layered onto the sequence. Some cast members may be in two scenes in a row, playing two distinct characters, necessitating a costume change. Choices are (a) modify the sequence, (b) insert a transitional quickie, or (c) recast. We have used all these techniques in our sequencing.

Actor choice is another component. Although some participants were involved in the writing of specific scenes, they did not necessarily need or want to act in them. This can affect scene sequence, as can having one person act in a number of consecutive scenes in a row followed by a long absence. Again, a sequence may change, or recasting could occur.

When we toured schools during the university term, we used multiple casts, because different cast members had different university schedules. In these cases, the same A/R/Tor could end up playing different characters during different performances of the same play. To make this situation efficient, we always used the A/R/Tors real names. This minimized confusion for the performers, because the real names aided in the identification of fictional characters. The scripted scenes were written with roles A, B, C, D, and E always played by females and roles V, W, X, Y, Z played by males. Thus in our scripts, the beginning letters of the alphabet indicated female roles and the ending letters male roles, which made for easy distinction. (The male letters were chosen because of the male X-Y chromosome sequence.) Table 2.4 shows a tentative casting of our tour

Table 2.4 • Tentative Casting of *Last Call, Your Call* (pseudonyms).

	Monday Stettler	Tuesday Drumheller	Wednesday Valleyview
J	Joe	Devon	Joe
A	Demi	Lavender	Demi
B	Samantha	Samantha	Fergie
C	Lavender	Cherise	Cherise
D	Lulu	Yasmin	Yasmin
E	Melanie	Melanie	Dasha
X	Phoenix	Phoenix	Phoenix

Table 2.5 • List of Scenes Posted Backstage for *C5: Civility, Citizenship, and Community Construction on Campus* (pseudonyms).

1	*Prologue/How Rude*	Joe
2	*Campfire*	Joe, Phoenix, Shelia, Melanie, Aria
3	*Nice Shirt*	Aria, Phoenix, Fergie
4	*Envelope*	Shelia, Melanie
5	*Field Experience/Chain of Command*	Lavender, Paul, Samantha
6	*What's Your Major?*	All
7	*Group Work*	Melanie, Martha, Shelia, Detroit, Dasha
8	*Cafeteria Racism*	Lavender, Walter, Bernie
9	*Classroom*	Samantha, Fergie, Lulu, Phoenix
10a	*Exam Criteria Late/Talking/Cell Phone/Early*	Walter, Dasha, Bernie, Lulu
10b	*Do You Know Me?*	Phoenix, Aria, Fergie
11	*Course Evaluation—Score Cards*	Paul
12	*Epilogue/How Rude*	Detroit

of *Last Call, Your Call* (Norris and Mirror Theatre, 2001c). "J" indicates the MC, or joker. A list of scenes was posted backstage so that cast members could keep track of the sequence. Table 2.5 shows the scene-casting list for *C5: Civility, Citizenship, and Community Construction on Campus* (Norris and Mirror Theatre, 2002).

The "Keepers" folder then became the source of all scenes that needed to be polished for the performance, as well as their sequence and casting. Information about costume, props, and set details for each scene were included, as well as possible lighting. Usually the cast wore a black shirt and blue jeans and used an accessory that indicated a sense of character. For example, a lab coat and stethoscope were used in one scene of *ReSearch: RePlay* (Norris and Mirror Theatre, 2000d) and surgical masks in another. Minimal costumes and/or props gave the essential impressions needed and were listed with the rehearsed scene details.

The Interpersonal

As can be deduced from the technical explanation, Playbuilding demands a high degree of interpersonal skill. Tuckman (1965) claims that small groups go through four developmental stages: forming, storming, norming, performing. In the forming stage, the participants get to know one another, recognizing individual differences and their emergent group identity. During the storming stage, participants begin to assert themselves, creating natural and healthy frictions between them and others. Once a few storms have been weathered, the rough waters become tranquil as the group members begin to know one another's boundaries. When this occurs, the group settles into the tasks at hand; this is the norming stage. Once group members norm, they can effectively perform. I have found Tuckman's stages to be generally true not only when I begin a new collective process but also when I assign group work in any class.

From many similar experiences, I have concluded that the time taken for a strong forming stage better prepares group members for the inevitable storms. It may seem counterproductive, but as with a bow-and-arrow, the effort taken in properly pulling back guarantees a better shot (Herrigel, 1989). Through a number of orientation drama games and icebreakers at the beginning of rehearsals, I foster a sense of play and camaraderie. This approach helps us to laugh and interact without the pressure of the product in mind. They act as warm-ups to performance skills, the topic, and to one another.

Over the years, through trial and error, I gleaned a number of insights into the process that I present to the group as conversation starters. They are by no means absolute but are indications of the disposition necessary to work in this manner and to avoid some problems. I present these insights to the assembly, and we discuss them. Often others add their insights, which both affirm and question mine. Agreement need not be reached; rather, the discussion raises our collective awareness of the interpersonal dimensions of this work. In total, this discussion aims to provide us with the spirit of the process. Without this, trust will not be established, and the personal sharings necessary for this unique form of focus group will not be articulated. Both the icebreakers and the conversation lay the foundation necessary for the work ahead.

Following are a few of the major items discussed.

ACTORS MUST CHANGE   One of the most difficult aspects of the collective process to achieve is to tell one's story while being open to the diverse stories of others. For our research to be productive, an attitude of openness of heart and mind is required. As Kopp (1972) claims, we are all pilgrims on our own journeys, and we can vicariously learn by listening to other pilgrims. Yes, our stories have merit, but they cannot remain stagnant. In Playbuilding, we revisit them not merely to affirm them but to question them as well. A lecture or performance that preaches preset ideas can be deadly, creating in one's audience resistance rather than a state of listening. If Playbuilding is to be dialectic, then many stories will change when they encounter the stories of others. We cannot expect our audiences to enter into transformative pedagogy if we don't practice and model it. Consequently, the data generated does not give primacy to the accuracy of the past but enters a temporal rift in which former stories intermingle with a present process to include the stories of others that will be reshaped into a future event that will also be reshaped with new participants.

There will be times when one goes through a self-indulgent phase. This is natural and to be expected. We are intricately tied up in the stories we tell ourselves. The danger is to remain there. The juxtaposition of our stories with others enables us to detect our personal framing that obscures parts of our own stories from us. We tell them and give them away for others to reconceptualize with care and respect. Both our process and the research performance itself will reflect a struggle for meaning rather than a meaning discovered.

Watson's poster (1994) claims that liberation work is reciprocal:

> If you have come to help me, you are wasting your time. But if you have come because your liberation is bound up with mine, then let us work together.

Such a stance encourages humility in all parties.

Buber (1947) claims that artists' role is to make themselves the best they can be so that they can be better gifts for others. By entering into the Playbuilding process, one both expects and invites renewal. By examining oneself, one refines one's gift. Playbuilding programs that do not encourage change remain at the self-indulgent stage, which is immediately transparent to an audience. Thus, for epistemological, pedagogical, and performance reasons, an attitude that supports change is required.

SPIRIT OF PLAY   Playbuilding is a process of exploration. As I often say: "I don't know where we are going, but I know how to get there." Nachmanovitch (1990) claims that an artist works with the givens. With Playbuilding, the data generated and the A/R/Tors that provide them are our research and artistic givens. As with all research, conclusions materialize from the generated data. By using an internal hermeneutic approach (Werner and Rothe, 1979), the framing of the scenes emerges from such data. Thus the outcomes and structure cannot be predetermined. Consequently, the director and A/R/Tors must be willing to play with the data, exploring it for possible performance ideas.

This situation does not mean that the process lacks rigor; far from it. Cottrell (1979) claims that play is the work of the young child, and I extend this to the work of all creative activity in all people (1998b). Cloke and Goldsmith state:

> Research at the University of California at Berkeley regarding key insights that lead to successful scientific discoveries found in interviews with scientists that the main activity that seemed to influence successful results was play. The more these scientists were able to enjoy light, seemingly off-purpose games and activities while engaged in research, the greater were their successes at breakthrough discoveries. (2002, p. 11)

To play means to allow one's intuition to emerge no matter how silly it may seem at first. Root-Bernstein and Root-Bernstein (1999) document the lives of the "world's most creative thinkers" and claim that Fleming's discovery of penicillin was due, in part, to his playing around with drawing figures in Petri dishes using different color molds, at first, a seemingly frivolous activity.

I ask the A/R/Tors to articulate their half-baked ideas and trust that the community of researchers will accept them as works-in-progress and help to fully bake them. As reported in Chapter 6, it took a number of casts before the scene "Funky Shirt" emerged as an appropriate way to examine the ambiguous messages of clothing.

By playing, we push our own conceptual boundaries as we (re)look and (re)search our lives. The spirit of play supports an openness to the unknown, to change. But such work/play is not easy. If we want gems, we must recognize that there will be much mill tailings in the process. Play, like science, is experimental. There will be many explorations before the final product is ready.

TRUST IS CENTRAL   The ability to play with others requires a high degree of trust. One will not articulate her/his works in progress in a hostile atmosphere. Icebreakers can take a group only so far. Slowly, as the A/R/Tors disclose their stories, opinions, and thoughts, the state of trust grows. Over time, it can spiral to greater degrees; however, it remains forever fragile. An openness to the Other is required (Levinas, 1984). If those gathered recognize that we all enter as learners, needing the Other to expand our understandings, a research community is created. However, if one enters insisting that he/she has already found the truth, no research can take place, because ideas are fixed. Trust, play, and change are intricately bound.

To enable growth, all participants make an informal pact of confidentiality. We agree not to discuss the personally disclosed information outside the rehearsal, with the exception of scenes that are eventually performed for a public. Even then, the identity of the source remains private. Through both explicit and implicit means an atmosphere of trust is generated that enables collaborative research. Trust enables us to do and say things that we might otherwise not. Chapter 5 makes this evident, describing a production on human sexuality.

SAFETY AND RISK   We live in the tension between safety and risk. Although we want to play/work in a safe environment, we do not want to be shackled by fear. The desire for safety can be as limiting as leg irons. Research means testing the boundaries, and there are risks to self and others as a result. As we examine social issues through ourselves with an openness to others, we can expect a degree of personal discomfort. Playbuilding can generate much cognitive dissonance, but rather than avoiding it, we must embrace cognitive dissonance as a necessary, albeit risky state. As Kuhn (1962) claims, scientific breakthroughs occur as a result of anomalies, and cognitive dissonance makes the anomalies within social constructs explicit. Here lies some of the epistemological power of the Playbuilding process. Many A/R/Tors claim that they see the world differently as a result of the process. And we discuss that change/learning is risky business.

Another aspect of safety stems from the interpersonal aspects of play and improvisation. Half-baked ideas can hurt others even when they are not intended to do so. We can unintentionally offend and hurt one another (as we do in living). Some researchers and directors understandably shy away from this degree of personal risk. We each have a comfort level. If we clearly articulate risks, as research ethics boards require, participants enter with certain information. This, however, is not enough. Creating a collaborative community means creating safety nets for all.

One such net is the ability to give one another some latitude. If we recognize that we are all pilgrims, then we recognize that each of us is struggling, in our own way, to achieve new meanings. Like the play, we, too, are works in progress and will change. I have found that A/R/Tors who accept their peers as pilgrims create the necessary environment. This acceptance, however, does not mean that there are no challenges—merely, that we treat one another with respect. Even so, harm can occur. I ask that the offended seek reconciliation, because the offender may not be aware of an unintentional harm. Most often the issue is between the message sent and the message received. We each have a comfort level regarding different issues, and different comfort levels alone can create discomfort among individuals.

Finally, early in the research rehearsal process I comment that sometimes a personal sensitivity may arise that is bigger than the collective purpose. I request that if this occurs, the individual seek professional services. Although it's important to make this requirement clear, to my knowledge the use of professional services has never been necessary.

Collaborative work is fraught with personal and interpersonal issues. It requires a high degree of trust, and those involved need to know to be aware not only that some risk is involved but also that they have some responsibility in dealing with it. Such is their informed consent, be it formal or informal.

NO UNFINISHED BUSINESS

Connected with safety is a time issue. As director, I am never fully aware of what can arise at the last minute. A scene by one group may spark a strong reaction by another A/R/Tor. I prepare the cast for such a possibility, and if it does occur, I ask that those who can, to remain. Stewing permits certain individuals to work through an issue that excludes other members. Unfinished business can fester, leading to unnecessary negative spinning between rehearsals. While extending the rehearsal time owing to emergent difficulties has been rare, it is a safety net for the group process and needs to be articulated and employed when needed.

ENTIRE GROUP FOCUS

As implied above, I ask that we discuss our process as an entire group rather than holding informal conversations with smaller segments. In my early stages of this work, I found that certain groups who naturally socialized would reach a conclusion of position between rehearsals only to return with "their" answer. I discourage this, although it is well intentioned, because it creates an informal clique within the group. During one production, a cast member had general conversations with his wife during breaks and returned with their worked-out positions. Eventually we asked that either she join the company or the conversations stop. It was extremely difficult to have a dialogue with a nonpresent member. I request that thoughts be raised with the entire group, not within a subset.

However, this approach has raised some questions, because some participants do like to continue conversations, and they can sometimes be productive. I also recognize that I do not want to restrict voice. The corollary to this guideline is to recognize the problematics of such an act. My understanding of the complexities of collaborative work has been a long-term evolving journey.

OWNERSHIP/CO-OWNERSHIP

During my doctoral research, one student described the Collective process as "brainsqueezing":

> We're kind of thinking what we have to do first and then putting it all together kind of smunching it up and all of our brains get squeezed in together. The Collective is like that, our brains are just squeezing in together. (Norris, 1989a, p. 138)

The term that I use to describe the basis of our process is "offers," which implies that what is suggested is fluid. Stories, opinions, scenes, and their critiques and extensions are all provided as possibilities that are expected to be transformed by another person and yet another in a spiral-like process. Consequently, ideas and scenes are co-owned, since one person's ideas are usually evoked by thoughts of other A/C/Tors. With collaboration, ownership cannot be determined as half-baked ideas are transformed by the group process.

I once heard a Bachelor of Education student say that she liked Collectives, because you get your own way. From my extensive collaborative research experience, I would have to qualify that. Yes, all voices are attended to, but that does not mean that you get your own way. Collaboration implies that meanings are negotiated, and/or conflicting meanings are performed to encourage audience members to find their own synthesis. In a sense, all get their voice by way of inclusion.

Over time, there came a need for a formal contracting of co-ownership (Appendix B) in order to enable scenes to be reused in the public arena. Mirror Theatre became the infrastructure to manage the use of scenes.

In summary, the Mirror Theatre process emerged over time. Pammenter claims that "the devising process has differed much from company to company and cannot be discussed as there were one definitive method" (1993, p. 53), and this book makes no such definitive claim. It is one example of some of the technical and interpersonal considerations that this large collective group encountered over a number of years. Pammenter continues: "Before TIE had established itself there was clearly no extant body of work for the teams to draw on" (1993, p. 53). This book's aim is to add to this emerging body of literature (now commonly referred to as "Applied Theater" [Ackroyd, 2007]).

CHAPTER 3

History of Mirror Theatre

> Be not afraid of greatness: some men are born great, some
> achieve greatness, and some have greatness thrust upon them.
> (Shakespeare, *Twelfth Night,* 1972b, p. 893)

Applied to Mirror Theatre's history, "greatness" would be an overstate-
ment; however, this history was certainly not planned—it was thrust upon
us. The needs of the community beckoned us into being. Our beginnings were small and informal and over time grew from touring provincial
schools to giving performances in schools at major national and international educational, theatrical, and research conferences and becoming
a registered not-for-profit society. There was no strategic planning or
advertising campaign, but each year we received more requests than we
could handle. Our projects were grassroots, with every program being
a commissioned one, as schools, conference organizers, and community
organizations contacted us with specific projects in mind. The company
grew as those outside the field recognized the powerful educational and
research tool that theater can be.

This chapter provides an abbreviated story of Mirror Theatre's birth and growth in which I was actively involved as a director, researcher, instructor, and administrator in all but two projects. The intent is to provide the context of this emergent research genre. Similar to qualitative research studies in which researchers describe the setting from whence their data came, this chapter outlines approximately twenty years of work with many A/R/Tors, organizations, and schools. Its compilation comes from the archives of Mirror Theatre and my recollections, as triggered by those documents and artifacts. Boxes of file folders with our rehearsal records and computer files of contracts, performance programs, Board minutes, and correspondence were reexamined. Much was ignored as irrelevant; however, what is presented in underpinned by pillars of stories beneath the stories that enabled the social-issues theater troupe to flourish and this research genre to emerge.

The intent is also to provide stepping-stones to assist others who may wish to embark on a similar or partial venture. I had no such guide to assist me when I began using Playbuilding as a research and teaching method, and so I ended up "re-inventing the wheel," using Collective Creation sources (Berry and Reinbold, 1985; Filewod, 1987; Salutin and Theatre Passe Muraille, 1976) and theater-in-education literature (TIE) (Jackson, 1993). One caught glimpses of the genre in the qualitative research literature (Donmoyer and Yennie-Donmoyer, 1995; Mienczakowski, 1995), but I longed for materials that would provide details on data generation, its analysis, how to shape data into dramatic forms, and the logistics of dissemination through tours and conferences presentations. This book is, in part, my response to that need. It reports experiences in devising research findings into theater. However, it is meant to be more fluid rather than fixed or prescriptive. It is Mirror Theatre's story, not "the" definitive story on Playbuilding as qualitative research and participatory social-issues theatre. Its history provides a foundation on which the remaining chapters are based. I hope that readers will shape and morph its contents into approaches unique to their particular contexts.

For beginners, this chapter documents a starting place. Mirror Theatre had humble beginnings, and our learning curve was steep, but with appropriate partnerships and allies it did become a highly recognized theater-in-education troupe in western Canada. Our history can assist those wishing to begin such a troupe by providing details on building partnerships with community organizations from which they can begin their work.

For those who are experienced in TIE work, more recently referred to as Applied Theatre (Ackroyd, 2000, 2007; O'Toole and Stinson, 2009; Taylor, 2003), this chapter may provide fresh ideas, as these readers juxtapose their histories with ours, exploring new possibilities. Such is the nature of stories, as we borrow from the lived-experiences of others

(Donmoyer, 1990). In time, I hope that more theatrical and research histories will be shared to enable others to benefit from a rich diversity of directions that different companies take as they share their research findings in theatrical, research, educational, and community venues.

For researchers, this chapter provides a genealogy of the methodology. Since "the role of the qualitative researcher is of critical importance, because the researcher is the research instrument" (Janesick, 2001, p. 533), we must understand the development of the instrument/methodology and the factors that influenced its shaping. My work and expertise have been cumulative, growing with every Mirror Theatre project and building on the previous ones. Over time, the research methodology was refined— for example, through record keeping, building videotaped archives, and creating waivers and contracts—as a deeper understanding of this collaborative form emerged.

For directors and artistic directors, this chapter provides a glimpse at the theatrical processes, organizational structures, funding opportunities, and touring equipment that brought our work to audiences internationally, from New Orleans to New York, nationally, from Vancouver to Saskatoon, and provincially, from Medicine Hat to Slave Lake and Grand Prairie. As at a buffet, readers can pick and choose what they wish to apply to their contexts. The early stages were informal, but once money was exchanged, a legal infrastructure involving incorporation and performance contracts became necessary. The history demonstrates the importance of partnerships in establishing and maintaining research-based educational theater programs.

For university instructors, the chapter is an example of how teaching, research, and service can be integrated into a cohesive unit. It is also about course development, since the initial collaborative extracurricular projects became a course with a service-learning component. This development was an emergent one that slowly fell into place.

Other readers may wish to skip this chapter. Although the history does provide a context for the chapters that follow, its reading is not completely necessary for their comprehension.

Prehistory: The Conception

Secondary Teaching

My personal history was scattered. I was introduced to Playbuilding (Bray, 1991, Weigler, 2002) by its Canadian name "Collective Creation" (Berry and Reinbold, 1985, Filewod, 1982, 1987; Salutin and Theatre Passe Muraille, 1976) while I taught in secondary schools in Nova Scotia in the 1970s and 1980s. As a director of extracurricular drama clubs, I led the students through a rudimentary process of cowriting plays based on their collective interest. I found that students became invested in the roles created by them, and so line memorization was far less difficult, because as coauthors, they knew the scripts intimately. In addition, a large number of theatrical skills can be taught within scripts construction. These productions were presented to parents and at local educational theater festivals.

Doctoral Research

During my doctoral studies, I was struck by the lack of concrete examples in curriculum theory that professed the value of student voice. I sought "a model of socialization in which meaning is made interactively. That is, meaning is 'given' by situations but also created by students as they interact in classrooms (Giroux and Penna, 1981, p. 213)." Asking myself, "Where in the school system are examples of teaching that foster student voice?" my response was, Collective Creation. I enrolled in a Collective Creation course taught by David Barnet, a Canadian leader in this process (Filewod, 1987), and I designed a participant/observation study of a high school drama class that focused on Collective Creation. For ninety minutes a day, five days a week, over three and one-half months, I observed and professionally video-recorded Joanne Reinbold and her twenty-five students cowrite a play that they titled *Merry-Grow-Round*. It was indeed a curriculum in which student voice was essential, and from this study I produced a dissertation (Norris, 1989a) and four instructional videotapes (Norris, 1989b, 1989c, 1989d, 1989e). This work laid a solid foundation on which Mirror Theatre would later be built.

Drama in Teacher Education

Owing to my initial teaching load during my first university position, I placed Collective Creation on the back shelf, since my duties took me elsewhere. However, like a heavy book, it kept falling off. It would not let me be. Each year, cooperating teachers came to campus for an orientation and to meet the student teachers. In the fall of 1990, with one year under my belt coordinating these meetings, I wanted to move beyond the typical didactic presentation and create a coauthored performance with my students. In past years, these meetings were somewhat stifled, so I asked the students if they would be interested in creating a short series of vignettes on their fears and concerns regarding student teaching that we would perform for the cooperating teachers as a conversation starter.

During the rehearsal stage, I discussed my plan with the coordinator of field experiences, who expressed excitement over the approach and requested that her graduate students enrolled in her Analysis of Teaching course attend the session as a class assignment. From here, the collective work evolved quickly and began to take on a life of its own. Although the initial project remained intact, the coordinator of field experiences suggested that we remount it as a presentation at The Western Canadian Conference for Student Teaching (WestCAST) that winter.

Snapshots of Playing Together (Norris and Student Company, 1991) became my first university production. Students who were willing to attend WestCAST conference met with me outside class hours to devise the program. Approximately twenty-five short pieces were generated, and scene titles included "Teaching Is Like a Fairground," "Teaching Is Like an Old Sneaker," "Give Me More Space," "Baby Makes Three," "Brick Walls," "Post Practicum Depression," and "Mirror." The presentation was well received by conference delegates, with requests to perform at other institutions. Owing to costs and time considerations, the program was remounted only twice, once at a neighboring college and once on campus.

A second year's cast, now including an adjunct faculty member, named themselves "No Spare Time." Their presentation, entitled *Paradise Lost*, performed at the 1992 WestCAST, represented the move from naiveté, as the student teachers began to understand the complexities of teaching. Scene titles included "Grinding Gears," "Teacher Motivation Pack," "Practical Utopia," and "Seduction, Hats, and Sculpting." The major scene was a series of body sculptures with the actors shaped into ideals. Time was allotted to allow for audience discussions and a reworking of the scenes based on their comments.

In July of 1992, I moved to the University of Alberta, but before I arrived, the 1992 conference chair of WestCAST, Andrea Borys, who was Assistant Dean (Practicum), University of Alberta, asked me to work with students to generate a performance for faculty members and support staff as an initiative of the Faculty of Education's Equality and Respect Committee. She valued the manner in which the theatrical presentations evoked meaningful discussions on student teaching and was convinced that the presentations would do the same with other social topics. Consequently, based on reputation alone, my Collective Creation/Playbuilding transition from one institution to another was made. This reinforced my claim that our best practices are our best forms of advocacy (Norris, 1994).

This program on equality and respect was entitled *Mirror Mirror* (Norris and Student Company, 1993a). The lecture classroom was slightly raked and acting space was minimal. Wing areas on both sides of the stage were created with portable blackboards draped with butcher paper on which "graffiti" of the themes and expressions from the devising stage were written. It was lit predominantly by photography lights as no budget was given. Luckily a cast member from the community was able to borrow a dimming board from his school. Fortunately, power failures occurred only during the dress rehearsal. Minimal props were used, and scene changes took place quickly in the dark. The performance opened with groups of two conducting the mirror exercise where groups of two faced each other and mimed basic movements in unison, while I read a poem on reflective practice (Norris, 1993). Scenes explored issues of political correctness, sexual harassment, misunderstandings between faculty and support staff, status, how one deals with a "no," rumors, the disrespect of last minute notices, library conflicts, and a variety of gender issues. All were based on actual stories collected from faculty, staff, and students and adapted for the theatrical medium.

Mirror Mirror was presented twice to a mixture of faculty and staff over a one-day period and consisted of the performance, break out discussion groups, and a plenary session for reporting, improvising, and role-playing of some issues discussed. The response was positive with the number one comment on evaluation forms being that this should be taken to schools.

During rehearsals for *Mirror Mirror*, plans were made to attend the 1993 WestCAST in Vancouver. *The First Frontier* (Norris and Student Company, 1993b) was an entirely new show. For this work I changed my focus. As director I now took the position of a qualitative researcher who was both participant and observer. While I did have some previous knowledge about student teaching I did not want to merely remount the previous shows. Using storytelling as a form of inquiry (Reason and Hawkins, 1988), I elicited the thoughts and experiences of the new cast members. The play focused on the politics of the student teaching experience and our program cover listed our major themes and scenes (Appendix C). This program format has been used for all our performances.

Shortly after the event, the Faculty of Education's Assistant Dean (Admissions), Anne Marie Decore, approached me with the request to create a video about student teaching experiences to be used in our teacher education classes. During discussions we agreed to have a live studio audience and tape the conversation as well. *Great Expectations* (Norris and Student Company, 1994a) was professionally videotaped and from my knowledge it is still being used in at least one Bachelor of Education course.

In previous productions, the scenes were discussed and generated through improvisation. Little record keeping was conducted as our focus was on performing, not archiving. During the devising of this play I decided to formalize the process, merging two recording genres into one. Joanne Reinbold, the teacher in my doctoral study (Norris, 1989a) used large sheets of paper on which students recorded their thoughts. These were placed around the room as constant reminders and referred to when the time came to choose which scenes to include. I had found recipe cards and file folders useful in my doctoral research to code and identify themes. The cards were easy to sort and sequence. As I discussed in Chapter 2, during the cast's focus group discussions we would write down our individual thoughts on cards with our names in the bottom-right corner. Thoughts could include themes, metaphors, and scene ideas. These would be used later to generate scenes. This activity was the beginning of our systematic recording process, which still continues. All subsequent research was archived in such a manner and most performances were videotaped.

The video *Great Expectations* (Norris and Student Company, 1994a) extended *The First Frontier*, focusing even more on the politics among student teachers, cooperating teachers, and faculty consultants. The opening three scenes after the credits depict each person caught in the middle of the other two. First, the cooperating teacher and the faculty consultant chant their "expectations" to a frozen student teacher; then the cooperating teacher and the faculty consultant each receive expectations from the other two in the triad. Based on data that indicated that not all cooperating teachers, student teachers, and faculty consultants are in agreement, we created two characters of each representative group to portray a variety of sometimes conflicting expectations. Thus a total of twenty-six scenes were generated. The video was remounted as live-theatre for an international curriculum theory conference (Norris and Student Company, 1995a), with most of the original cast attending.

Social Issues Theatre

Throughout 1994 and 1995 other smaller projects also took place. *Rules of the Game* (Norris and Student Company, 1994b) was performed during the University's International Week and explored how the rules of one culture can clash with the rules of another. *If We Offend* (Norris and Student Company, 1995b) examined political correctness and humor, making both problematic. But our first major turning point, unknown to us at the time, was *'clusions* (Norris and Student Company, 1995c). One drama major, who had worked with me since the *Mirror Mirror* project, was now a high school teacher and requested that we create a program for her school. We merged scenes from *Mirror Mirror*, *Rules of the Game*, and *If We Offend*, rewriting them into a new performance and making it relevant to this audience. This was to be the first of many school tours that focused on Safe and Caring Schools.

During the summer of 1995, I was contacted by Maureen Palmer from the Canadian Broadcasting Company (CBC) and asked if I would be interested in remounting *'clusions* for their upcoming documentary on sexual harassment called *Boys Will Be Boys* (Palmer, 1995). I met with her and compiled a cast of old and new members. We decided to do a major revamp and called the new show *What's the Fine Line?* (Norris and Student Company, 1995d). Although only two performances were to be videotaped by CBC, we volunteered to do five at the school. We decided to have small breakout discussion sessions lead by the A/R/Tors. Approximately sixty students assembled for each performance and met in groups of ten after the performance, each led by an A/R/Tor. During one summary session, one group performed a scene on how males systemically exclude females in coed sports and gave us permission to incorporate it into our play. This demonstrates how Playbuilding with audience participation not only disseminates data but also generates it simultaneously. A live performance is an example of dialectic research.

EQUIPMENT   During this time, I sat on the Faculty of Education's technology committee, and lengthy discussions were held concerning exactly what could be regarded as instructional technology. Clearly, it was more than computers. A broader definition was accepted, and during the next funding period I requested a two-scene preset dimmer board, eight mini-elipsoidal lights, two lighting trees, cables, and storage boxes. Funds were granted, and our performance for CBC at Steele Heights Junior High School marked our first road trip with the portable lighting system. No longer did we need to borrow makeshift systems from others, and the lights provided a strong theatrical focus to the performance. I believe that our performance/workshop with faculty on equality and respect in the workplace contributed to the success of the funding of our lights.

An Unplanned Birth

Incorporation

Until the CBC production, little thought was given to the longevity of this work, but with a growing history behind us, and more projects in the offing, logistics needed to be formalized. A series of events led to the incorporation of Mirror Theatre as a not-for-profit society. First, the chair of the 1996 WestCAST made a request that I mount a play to be the opening keynote for the conference. There was no infrastructure to pay us for expenses. Second, one of the cast members, a guidance teacher at a local junior high school, wanted the *What's the Fine Line?* program at her school. Again, payment of expenses and small honoraria for the actors needed an infrastructure. Banks and funding agencies required incorporation to open an account, and we also needed incorporation to receive funds from the Alberta Foundation for the Arts. Third, although cast members enjoyed the process, they requested course credit. Some claimed that they learned more about teaching from Playbuilding than from other teacher education experiences. From the performance workshops, a few reported that they learned how to talk "with" their students rather than "to" them. They requested formal documentation through a course credit. Fourth, in addition to the large amount of time spent directing, the administrative time, including the logistics of booking arrangements with venues, the hotel bookings, the transportation arrangements, the casting with multiple casts, and so on were huge. I longed for the day when I would no longer be the hub of the projects but would just share the responsibility for keeping the work going.

As the scattered parts of our work began to coalesce, a single entity needed to take shape. The debate for a name is not an easy one, as described by Papin (1985), but eventually we settled on Mirror Theatre, based on our show *Mirror Mirror*. It emphasized our belief that we were reflecting life to our audience who expressed their meanings to us. In 1997 we incorporated as a not-for-profit society, with board members elected from previous cast members. Six board members would serve staggered three-year terms, with two positions expiring each year. This would guarantee a degree of consistency yet make room for "new blood." Membership was conditional during the first year. Those wishing permanent membership requested it, and requests were approved by full members at the annual general meeting. Membership agreements were signed (Appendix B) and archived.

Incorporation also addressed another logistical detail. Since the scenes were coauthored by many, so, too, was ownership. Some scenes could be remounted in future years by different casts. It would be impossible to continually obtain permission from all the coauthors, so the membership agreement defined the relationship. Mirror Theatre would own the rights, and its Board would grant permission to remount or publish. In this way, all scenes remained collective property, with an infrastructure for fair use. The Board did grant permission for the scenes published in this book.

University Relationship

Mirror Theatre's relationship with the university was an informal one. Its existence provided an infrastructure for my research/scholarship and community service. When we reached a point where funds were collected and cast members were paid (Appendix D), I did not take a share. Rather, at the end of each year the board donated funds to the university. This offset some of the operation costs, enabling me to buy new bulbs and other equipment. Some funds were allocated to my professional development account, which I used to attend conferences in order to disseminate the work of Mirror Theatre.

Course Creation

Based on the requests of previous cast members, in the fall of 1998 an official course, Theory and Practice of Drama/Theatre in Education, was offered. Eight undergraduate and two graduate students were enrolled, and the class work became one source of material for Mirror Theatre's programs. The course contained an outreach component, and we targeted our work to our local community's needs. Each spring, students from the course with other interested A/R/Tors mounted a May tour to schools using our growing collection of scenes. Later, we formed a partnership with Expecting Respect, a peer education program (discussed later in the chapter), and students in this course prepared and delivered a program. When funds were provided for the program, students were paid a small honorarium.

It has been my longstanding belief that artists should be paid for their work. These often underpaid citizens are the first to be asked to volunteer a piece of their work or to perform at a fundraiser or social event. During holiday seasons, student groups flock to the malls to sing, while their adult counterparts remain underemployed. Although I appreciate the educational value of this activity, I question practices whereby store-owners—refusing to employ professionals—profit from increased business because family and friends attend student presentations. If we "value" the arts, we should pay for them. I also advocate payment for student performances, be it a donation to the school or a free lunch for the performers. Such a stance was taken with students in this course.

The course was listed as a lecture/lab, with the school tour being part of the lab section. Students enrolled were asked not to schedule classes immediately before or after our class, because we required some transportation time. Owing to the collective nature of the course, I obtained permission to grade students using a pass/fail system instead of the norm-referenced grades, which can inhibit collaboration through the competition. The course outline (Appendix E) contained explanations for changes from the norm. In total, the course is an example of the combination of teaching, research, and service into an integrated whole for both instructor and students.

The Tours

The 1996 performances of *What's the Fine Line?* at École J. E. Lapointe School in Beaumont, Alberta (Norris and Mirror Theatre, 1996a), were the beginning of our official school tours. In the spring of 1996, I met with the school council and staff, and I invited them to a preview performance of *What's the Fine Line?* Just before the performance I was asked if students from the school could attend, and I agreed. Later that decision proved invaluable. The guidance counselor informed me that she was told that the engagement of the students convinced the committee. We were booked to perform in the fall.

COMMUNITY INVOLVEMENT   In addition to our student performances, we always offer a no-charge evening performance for parents and community members. This is our gift to the community. This has a two-fold purpose. First the invitation to "come and see" helps alleviate any suspicions parents may have about the program. Second, we want to mobilize the community, inviting its elders to help address certain issues. After one evening's performance, a woman approached me and said that she was a grandparent. She stated that it was about time schools addressed these issues, because they had existed in her era as well. Such comments were common throughout our tours. An RCMP office claimed that our interactive program was far more effective than his didactic presentations. Parents informed us that their children, after they had seen it during the day, insisted that their families attend. One woman who had not seen our program emailed the school principal with thanks. She claimed to have had a meaningful conversation with her daughter based on the program. Evening performances for the community became an integral part of our tours.

Mirror Theatre's Programs

From 1996 through 2004, Mirror Theatre had two major thrusts. Its school-based work focused on Safe and Caring Schools, with research topics including identity, homophobia, various forms of bullying, human sexuality, substance abuse, gambling, unwritten rules, and rumors. Its teacher-education research focused primarily on relationships, including those with students, cooperating teachers, and faculty. In 1999 a third focus emerged as it became evident that the Playbuilding process was a form of empirical narrative research. Presentations of compilations of our school tours were subsequently made at research and theatrical conferences, and the play, *ReSearch Reprise,* was written at and presented as a keynote at a research conference (discussed later in the chapter).

FORMAL AND INFORMAL PARTNERSHIPS: MUTUALLY SUPPORTING GROWTH   In keeping with a birthing/rearing metaphor, Mirror Theatre did not reach adulthood alone. Over the years, a series of partnerships were established that provided the company with an assortment of clients with needs that social-issues theater could address. The West-CAST relationship was informal and was reestablished each year with new conference committees in different provinces. Following are the names of longstanding partners within the province that enabled us to hone our performance craft, pedagogical approaches, and research skills.

WestCAST   We continued performing at WestCAST conferences until 2004. Our keynote performance at WestCAST (Norris and Mirror Theatre, 1996a) solidified our relationship with that organization. Since the opening keynote concluded with no discussion, we volunteered to write a performance based on the conference sessions and present it as a closing keynote, complete with audience participation (Norris and Mirror Theatre, 1996a). The discussion, in addition to its interactive pedagogical approach, added to our repertoire of ideas. Again, our program was reflexive, being both a form of data dissemination and generation.

Our 1998 keynote, *One of These Things Is Not Like the Others* (Norris and Mirror Theatre, 1998a), was devised around the conference theme of inclusion. We explored the hidden and null curricula of schooling (Flinders et al., 1986), noting how discrimination is taught. Our 2004 keynote, *Shadowing* (Norris and Mirror Theatre, 2004), was a short metaphorical piece that expanded the scene "Pass the Baby" from the Vancouver conference and the "Shadowing" scene that was in *Great Expectations II* (Norris and Mirror Theatre, 1996b). "Pass the Baby" now had three variations. In the first, the teacher is reluctant to give up authority. In the second, the teacher quickly gives up the difficult class. In the third, the student teacher takes control without negotiation. As a triad, they show a variety of power relationships. The three "Shadowing" scene variations, mimed to the song "Me and My Shadow," depicted a strong cooperating teacher who believes that "his" way is "the" way, a student teacher who is reluctant to take authority, and perhaps the ideal relationship, in which power and expertise are shared. The play lasted about fifteen minutes, giving ample time for audience involvement.

Safe and Caring Schools   At the time of Mirror Theatre's conception, Alberta Education and The Alberta Teachers Association formed a committee for Safe and Caring Schools. Its mandate was to address bullying and other socially undesirable behaviors. The belief was that, in addition to physical and psychological harm, emotional stress could impede the academic growth of both the victims and the perpetrators. In 1997 they launched their first conference, and Mirror Theatre's *What's the Fine Line?* (Norris and Mirror Theatre, 1997a) was a keynote piece. Topics included clique warfare, the new kid at school (based on a story told by an audience member at a previous show), rumors, put-downs, peer pressure, misreading signals, bullying, and youth-culture rules.

The show was a hit, and principals from the audience wanted to hire cast members when they graduated. I am aware of at least two cast members who were employed as a result of this performance. One principal claimed that he wanted teachers who understood students, and the cast members clearly demonstrated that they could. This fact confirmed the validity of our research, because he and other faculty members recognized their students throughout the performance. During another performance, a vice-principal came to the school to preview the program. She called the following week, stating that, since viewing the play, in her school she had experienced every single scene. The validity and the generalizability of our research have always rested where they belong, with our readers/audiences.

The conference solidified Mirror Theatre's presence in the province. Schools and community agencies were not only aware of our existence but also applauded the performances' credibility. Our research was solid, and our performances representational. The back cover of our program contained our contact information, and many requests grew directly from that performance or through word-of-mouth reports based on this exposure. *What's the Fine Line?* was presented fifty-eight times, including the CBC taping and its preview, with a number of schools booking us as part of their Safe and Caring school initiatives.

Traditionally, one thinks of research dissemination as being accomplished through printed publications and/or online journals. Although *What's the Fine Line?* has been published (Norris, 1999) as a book chapter appendix, the adage "the play is the thing" is appropriate here, because the effect of a live performance is much stronger than the printed word. In addition to its research dissemination merits, the program also has a pedagogical purpose. Its aim is to stimulate conversations on how to better one's lived-world. As Denzin challenges, "performance ethnography is more than a tool of liberation. It is a way of being moral and political in the world. Performance ethnography is moral discourse" (2003, p. 258). Its pedagogical intent does not detract from its academic merit; rather, it enhances it. Although touring is more costly than publishing in an academic journal, it is the appropriate means to present research to those it directly affects, because "the use of art-based representational strategies brings academic scholarship to a wider audience" (Leavy, 2009, p. 14). Through the audience participation component, which obviously is not possible with the printed page, the interaction both invites and mobilizes the participants to action. The willingness to cover transportation, travel, meals, and the cost of a small honorarium attests to the value that discerning communities place on this form of research dissemination, perhaps in a manner stronger than that rendered by a double-blind jury.

What's the Fine Line? was not the only tour we brought to the Safe and Caring Schools programs. *Under Construction* (Norris and Mirror Theatre, 1998b) was written by students in the first class of Theory and Practice of Drama/Theatre in Education during the fall of 1998. This program explored concepts of identity and status, asking the question "Who has the power?" It was originally performed for an Expecting Respect program but was remounted for a nine-day tour in May of 1999, supported by the University of Alberta's Emil Skarin Fund, a university program focusing on humanities and arts. *Under Construction II* was presented at the 2nd Conference for Safe and Caring Schools.

Coulda/Shoulda was a composite program that merged scenes from *What's the Fine Line?*, *Under Construction*, and *Crossroads*, a performance devised during the second offering of the course, Theory and Practice of Drama/Theatre in Education. Since this program offered a wider range of scenes, it replaced *What's the Fine Line?* as our main program for our Safe and Caring Schools tours. It included homophobia, status, sexuality, peer pressure, bullying, and rumors. The performance ended with a challenge that was based on an actual experience of a student in the *Crossroads* class.

During the course, the student told a story about being at a bus stop and overhearing a group of adolescent males bragging about what they did to another boy. In their recounting of the story, which they knew she could hear, they recalled dragging the boy into a girl's washroom, beating him up, and stuffing a tampon down his throat until he "puked." In her recalling, she asked, "What could I or should I have done?" Hence the title *Coulda/Shoulda*. The story was scripted into a conversation of adults and used as the opening scene of our video, *Dealing with Bullying* (Norris and Mirror Theatre, 2000a).

Fair Play Rulz was also devised during this time and went on tour with *Coulda/Shoulda*. Some schools requested an elementary program similar to our junior/senior high productions, and middle schools wanted a combination of both for the different grade levels. Using a drama activity that exemplified the effects of implicit cultural rules, we asked, "What rules do elementary students practice that create conflict and alienation?" In our research, we brainstormed a huge list (Chapter 13), and these rules became the focus of our scenes.

For three seasons, we presented these two programs a total of fifty-five times. Of note was our relationship with St Joseph's High School in Edmonton. A former student of mine, now a religion teacher at the school, wanted to use the program to create an ethos of caring in the school. After our first year, we returned to work with the current year's tenth-graders. The *Coulda/Shoulda* program was meant to create a common history. After three years, they anticipated that all students would have seen the play, and the school could build its own safe and caring school discussions from the scenes in the play.

In addition to our six years of community outreach supporting Safe and Caring Schools and our presentations at the Safe and Caring Schools Conferences, Mirror Theatre was commissioned over a three-year period to create three videos for the Safe and Caring Communities program, funded by Lions International.

In 1999 we researched and devised our first program for the video medium, *Respecting Diversity and Preventing Prejudice* (Norris and Mirror Theatre, 1999a). We began by asking the questions "What examples of prejudice and discrimination have we experienced or witnessed?" and "How have we been victims and villains in these acts?" In keeping with Mirror Theatre's tradition, the cast was open to examining the problematics of their exclusive behaviors.

In 2000 we were awarded the contract to devise *Dealing with Bullying* (Norris and Mirror Theatre, 2000a). We took scenes from a number of past programs, creating a representative collage of examples. They were restructured for the video medium and focused on put-downs, teasing, the new kid at school, how spectators can reinforce bullying, and bus politics. In 2001 we made our third video with Safe and Caring Schools: *Resolving Conflict Peacefully* (Norris and Mirror Theatre, 2001a) was a departure from the previous two, because live audiences partook in the shooting. Since the focus was on "resolving," we wanted to highlight the "forum theater" (Boal, 1979) aspect of our programs, demonstrating how the audience members can rework the scenes by making suggestions to the characters or by performing themselves. "The Pencil" (Chapter 14) was taken from *Fair Play Rulz* and workshopped with a live audience of elementary students. "To the Movies" was a scene taken from our performance at the 2000 Safe and Caring Schools conference (Norris and Mirror Theatre, 2000b). It, too, was workshopped with a live audience, albeit secondary students.

Our contracts for these videos stipulated that Mirror Theatre retain the performance rights and that the videos not be released for general distribution. Our concern was that the videos would replace our tours. Although discussions could take place with teachers and students, they were no substitute for improvisational interactions with a troupe of A/R/Tors.

Expecting Respect: A Peer Education Program   Through Mirror Theatre's early exposure at the first Safe and Caring Schools conference and a conference on teen wellness, representatives from Expecting Respect: A Peer Education Program (ER) contacted me to determine how a Mirror Theatre program might assist them in the training of their peer educators. The group was a consortium of government and social agencies (The Alberta Alcohol and Drug Abuse Commission's Youth Services, Alberta Teachers Association, Capital Health, City of Edmonton Community Services, HIV Edmonton, Planned Parenthood, TERRA Association, and the Sexual Assault Centre) that wished to animate youth in addressing issues that concerned them.

Each fall ER would have three to four senior and junior high training days. The senior high school students would be introduced to curricula that examined sexual harassment, conflict, tobacco, social injustice, healthy dating relationships, and sexual boundaries. The junior high school students would be introduced to media advertisements, bullying, healthy relationships; and tobacco, alcohol, drugs, and gambling addictions for the junior high program. Both would receive instruction on presenting skills and leading discussions; members of the ER committee believed that a play such as *What's the Fine Line?* would be a strong orientation kick-off to their training sessions.

Their timing was perfect. We were able to remount *Shadows* (Chapter 7) for their 1997 program. In 1998, the first year of the establishment of the course, the class agreed that we would target our efforts to the needs of the ER group. *Under Construction* (Norris and Mirror Theatre, 1998b) was Mirror Theatre's first commissioned piece for Expecting Respect. Like the previous programs, it was a series of vignettes. Unlike other pieces, the vignettes were not performed in their entirety and workshopped at the end. Rather, after each scene was performed, we conducted miniworkshops with the entire audience.

Our first scene, "Who's who?," used gibberish. A party scene (Chapter 9) opened the program, and after the scene the audience was asked to create a status hierarchy, indicating who was the most and the least popular. The scene quite effectively addressed the theme of "healthy relationships." This generated a lot of discussion, and following that, suggestions were made to the characters about how not to abuse their power. New scenes were improvised using the audience suggestions. Often, we never went beyond the first couple of scenes. Since the audience helped us build the play, we called it *Under Construction*.

The Expecting Respect committee was pleased with our work and invited us back for the next year's training session. To keep communication lines open, I was asked to sit on the steering committee. Our second program with Expecting Respect was *Crossroads* (Norris and Mirror Theatre, 1999b). We used the ER curriculum list to help guide our work. We asked "What pressures face adolescents?" "What are some natural uncertainties in their lives?" "What roles do teachers and parents play?" And "What responsibilities can they and should they take?" Because of the choices they would be making, they were at the "crossroads." Of all our programs, this one focused the most on sexuality.

Each year the peer educators filled in an evaluation form of the entire program, including the training session. The Mirror Theatre program was highly regarded (Appendix F). The performances were considered realistic, engaging, and more powerful than being just spoken to. Some believed that it had given them a better understanding of the situations, and they wanted more. One peer educator became a member of Mirror Theatre once she entered university and eventually became our president. During these assessments, students were polled on the topics that most interested them and ones that were missing. Drugs and Alcohol was a popular theme. At one time, there was a saturation of theater troupes doing plays on drugs, so this theme was avoided—in error. We forget that every three years, a new group of students makes up an entirely new high school population. Based on the evaluations, the 2000 class was invited to explore drugs and alcohol.

What's the Use? (Norris and Mirror Theatre, 2000c) could be considered our substance use/abuse programs. Based on our philosophy of providing thesis and antithesis, so that the audience could process their own synthesis, we avoided creating scenes that preached. We asked "What are reasons to and not to smoke, drink, do drugs, and take risks?" Scenes were built on such themes as dares, permissive parents, peer pressures, and "natural" highs.

Whereas *What's the Use?* focused on substance use/abuse, *Friends, Family, and Foreigners* (Norris and Mirror Theatre, 2001b) explored the complexities of relationships. "To the Movies" was reworked, with each character given a motivation. The debate was over a betrayal, whereby one friend went with another friend to see a movie the night before a planned group-of-four event for the same movie. The scene took place in a car with the group driving to the movie, with the driver being hurt by the betrayer but the betrayer thinking she had a good reason to go the night before. In the back seat, there was a peacekeeper as well as a "my way or the highway" personality. This scene had many jokerable possibilities. Reshuffling the personalities to the "driver's seat" made a big difference in the power of the relationships. This scene is a good example of improvisation as research, since each shuffle assisted us in better understanding the concepts of power and reconciliation. Other scene topics included computer harassment and name-calling; these included the A/R/Tors' personal testimonials, explaining how certain comments hurt them. We have used testimonials sparingly, because such use borders on preaching, but connecting the issue to actual people can have a strong impact. Personal testimonials that underpin a scene make explicit the scene's connection to the actual, which can open up a deeper dialogue through the creation of empathy. Owing to my change of employment, this program was Mirror Theatre's last program with Expecting Respect. Recently I heard from one of the Expecting Respect team and she reported that our contribution was greatly missed.

International Institute for Qualitative Methodology   The International Institute for Qualitative Methodology (IIQM), while under the direction of Jan Morse, was a strong supporter of Mirror Theatre. The institute's openness to advances in qualitative research through their programs, conferences, and publications provided a new venue for our work. Whereas our previous emphasis had been primarily on the use of theater as a pedagogical vehicle for social change, our work with the institute took a methodological focus.

In 1999 Mirror Theatre performed *What's the Fine Line?* at IIQM's Advances in Qualitative Methods conference. This marked our first official foray into "Playbuilding as research." Although we had always asserted that our work had been largely empirically based, we now found a research community that accepted that. The follow-up discussion after the performance focused on the research process. IIQM provided fertile ground from which the methodological and epistemological dimensions of playbuilding could be explored.

I served on the Institute's advisory committee and promoted a variety of arts-based presentations. An arts-based research strand was proposed, and I encouraged the keynote performance of *Finding My Place: The Brad Trilogy* (Saldaña, 2001, 2002) and provided technical support, including operating the lights. Although not an official Mirror Theatre program, an arts-based research piece on desire (Campbell et al., 2001) was proposed and performed at that same IIQM conference by a number of Mirror Theatre members. I attended a few rehearsals and made comments after the presentation but remained on the periphery of this event. What I did observe was an emergent process of how one can come to a deeper understanding of a phenomenon through a variety of drama activities. Drama has much to offer data generation and analysis.

The highlight of Mirror Theatre's involvement with IIQM was at its 2000 Qualitative Health Research conference. The conference committee was willing to try a different form of evaluation based on Kieren's concept of "envaluation" (1995), in which the evaluator's stance is made explicit, and the comments are cocreated mutually by the evaluator and those being evaluated. The committee accepted that a performance written and workshopped at the conference, about the event, would be a novel way of reporting on the conference. It was videotaped and is in both IIQM's and Mirror Theatre's archives.

ReSearch: RePlay (Norris and Mirror Theatre, 2000d) was similar to the weekend novel-writing marathons that novelists sometimes attend. Although we came prepared, having had a couple of rehearsals based on the conference program, the bulk of our devising took place from the Thursday night keynote to the late Saturday afternoon keynote, which was to be our performance. We arrived with a few boxes of props as potential working materials and the knowledge that the Banff Center would be supplying their technical crew to create a set and lighting design in the Eric Harvie Theatre. As we devised our performance on the stage on the Saturday morning and early afternoon, the crew watched and intuitively designed around us. Our closing keynote performance was based on the opening keynote and the conference sessions that the cast members attended (Chapter 14). Mirror Theatre's involvement with IIQM helped make explicit the research dimensions of Playbuilding as a qualitative research genre (Norris, 2000, 2008b).

Alberta Alcohol and Drug Abuse Commission   The Alberta Alcohol and Drug Abuse Commission (ADDAC) is a major Alberta government agency that is involved in operating and providing funding for addiction prevention and intervention programs. They have had a long-standing history of utilizing theater as a means of achieving their goals (Berry and Reinbold, 1985, Selman, 1986a, 1986b). Mirror Theatre was directly involved in three regional and one provincial program.

In 1998 we were commissioned to present at an ADDAC program in the Drayton Valley community. I invited drama education majors from my methods course to develop a program that used process drama (Neelands, 1984; O'Neill, 1995). *Wishes* was designed around a story, "Yallery Brown," introduced to me by Jonothan Neelands. It is ideal for exploring the phenomena of addiction, codependence, and ecology. In it a young man, Tom, is granted wishes, causing his world to change in unpredictable ways. Tom eventually is alienated from friends and family and finds it difficult to get rid of the "magic bag."

Our program started with a *Readers Theatre* performance (Coger and White, 1971) version that we had adapted from the original text. The lights were dimmed, and we were lit by an overhead covered by a red gel. The mood was like that in a haunted house, and a number of participants reported that it was like listening to a ghost story. At an appropriate point, the story was interrupted, and the students were broken into discussion groups. Rather than a standard program, we utilized a variety of workshop formats, including teacher-in-role (Wagner, 1976), town hall meeting (Neelands and Goode, 2000) and general discussion. The focus was advice for Tom. In this way, the audience would also be giving advice for themselves and their peers. The program ended with us finishing the story.

Based on the success of this program, we were invited back to explore issue of risk. We were informed that the number-one cause of youth deaths in that area was snowmobile accidents. *Where's the Risk in That?* (Conrad, Zinken, and Mirror Theatre, 1999) was one of a few programs in which I was not personally involved, owing to other commitments; however, I was thrilled to see others take responsibility and put their own spin on a program sans my direct influence. The program had the actors take risks with eggs. Sometimes the eggs remained intact, and on other occasions they fell to the floor and splattered. The consequences of risky behaviors were made explicit. The audience then compared the excitement of the activity with the possible negative results. The program was informed by research on "edgework" (Lyng, 1990); Lyng claims that the emotional high of risky behaviors is a factor that should not be underestimated. Eventually, connections were made to snowmobiling.

In 2001 ADDAC requested that Mirror Theatre submit a proposal to design a program and tour funded by the Canadian Brewers' Association (CBA) that examined the issue of under-age drinking (18 is legal age in Alberta). After a series of meetings with members of ADDAC and the CBA, we were awarded the contract. Some representatives from ADDAC and CBA also attended rehearsals, and one observer initially raised a concern over the constructivist rather than didactic approach of *Last Call . . . Your Call.* This concern wasn't completely dispelled until members of the CBA saw us work with a live audience, where they could see how our approach engaged the youth in deep conversations.

We researched ourselves for these scenes and amassed a number of complex issues around alcohol consumption at an early age. Themes included being cool, popularity, deception, risk, consequences, experimentation, rite of passage, and responsibility. On this occasion, we abandoned our small audience with break-out discussion groups for a one-performance discussion with approximately three hundred students in each of the three audiences. Those cast members who were involved in other programs reported a lack of intimacy and a more superficial level of conversation. Although it was effective, we knew that the format diminished the quality. There was, however, still an audience participation component, albeit with large groups.

After my departure, Mirror Theatre devised and presented, *I Bet You Can't Do That* (Zinken, and Mirror Theatre, 2003) for two years, funded by ADDAC and organized by the ASSIST Community Services Center of Edmonton and the Chinese Cultural Society; it was our first program to address gambling. Our clients requested that we focus on students at the upper elementary level, because their research sources reported that this is when the behavior begins and attitudes form. Although the company still exists, this was the last program of Mirror Theatre.

Other Programs   Other agencies occasionally commissioned Mirror Theatre for specific purposes. These programs were usually performed once in their entirety; however, their scenes were recorded, and some found their way directly or indirectly into other productions.

Shadows (Norris and Mirror Theatre, 1997b) was devised for a Teen Wellness Conference held at the Grey Nuns Hospital, Edmonton. Originally the conference was arranged for high school females, with a focus on body image, and we conducted our research with that topic in mind. Upon our arrival, we were informed that a number of males would be attending owing to requests of the high school teachers, who wanted to bring their entire classes. Their presence drastically changed the tone of the day.

The play was given the name *Shadows* to represent the specter of body image that permeates much of Western society. To emphasize the metaphor, shadow-screen scenes opened and closed the play as well as being used throughout. "Cattle Call" was the beginning scene, in which male directors debated which females to cast to the play, based on body image. The female cast members stood between a back stage light and the

Photo 3.1 • Shadow screen used during "Cattle Call" scene.

shadow screen that displayed them in shadow to the audience. It is easy to determine that this set-up would play differently to an all-female audience than to a mixed one.

The scenes examined clothing, dating, gender politics, miscommunication, pressures, mores, and labeling. The shadow screen was placed on stage left, and its scenes were used as transitions when a set change was required at center stage. While center stage was dark, the lit screen attracted the audience's attention while the next scene was set.

Break-out discussion groups followed the performance, and later we met as a whole and for a final discussion. One scene that was chosen for reexamination focused on a male/female conflict. One of the rowdy males volunteered to play the male, and each time, it escalated into a frenzied state. Finally the male threw up his arms and left the stage. After the event, as we were packing up, he came up to me and said, "You know, sometimes the best thing to do is walk away." His comment reinforced the pedagogical aspect of our programs. Although the males presented some difficulty, they needed to be involved. At least one got part of the concept. We learned not to be lulled into a comfortable and easy path of presenting only to the converted.

A personal friend who was aware of my work with Mirror Theatre was on a committee that was organizing an inter-provincial conference on human sexuality. He was intrigued by our work, eventually inviting us to be a keynote at that conference. Throughout our history at the University of Alberta, every production contained some sexual and gender-politics issues. Longstanding cast members would ask, "When are we going to do our sex show?" noting that these issues underpinned many other themes. *Complexities and Contradictions* (Norris and Mirror Theatre, 1998c) met the need of both the conference committee and the cast members.

For this project, we decided to steer away from the typical biological aspects of sexuality, focusing more on the social and the psychological. Themes included sex education, experimentation, expectations, pornography, attention seeking, homophobia, and innocence/guilt. A few relevant scenes from earlier shows were remounted, but the play was mostly new material. "The 'M' Word" (Chapter 5) was a series of three miniscenes that grew from our improvisational research and that explored the fall from innocence to guilt.

This performance was immediately followed with an entire audience discussion. The focus, which came from the audience, was prepubescent sexuality. The discussion raised more questions than answers as we asked "How do we introduce sexuality to our young when society at large is suspicious when we do?" The question is an unbounded one (Henderson, 1992) that guides future action, rather than prescribing it. Such is the aim of all our programs.

C5: Civility, Citizenship and Community Construction on Campus was devised for the University of Alberta's University Teaching Services (UTS), who requested that we create a program for faculty, graduate students, and part-time instructors on university teaching issues. We sent out a call to the university community for interested parties to participate or to offer suggestions. A few undergraduate and graduate students volunteered to participate. I provided a faculty member's perspective, while the students provided theirs.

Rudeness by all parties, appropriate assessment criteria, course evaluations, judging one another by university major, bullying for grades, and political correctness were a few of the emergent themes that were chosen to be performed. Approximately thirty students attended the performance, some requiring a signature, as attendance was part of a UTS accreditation certificate. The conversation was lively, and discussion centered on the lack of collegial relationships between instructors and students.

In addition, Mirror Theatre had an assortment of other smaller projects and remounts. *Fair Play Rulz* was remounted for the 2002 Fringe Festival in Edmonton. *What's the Fine Line?* was presented at the 2000 American Educational Research Association's Annual Meeting, in a few University of Alberta classes, and portions were presented at the Safe and Caring Schools' Your Voice, Your Choice Youth Forum and the Let's Talk Conference. *Shadowing* (student-teaching politics) was performed at the 2002 Greater Edmonton Teachers Convention and for call-back sessions with student teachers at the University of Alberta. An earlier version of *To the Movies* was also presented at the 2000 Safe and Caring Communities Conference, and in 2003 Mirror Theatre presented a compilation of scenes at the American Alliance for Theatre and Education preconference on theater-in-education in New York. This piece was a collection of our strongest vignettes. "Examining social issues through forum theatre" (Norris and Mirror Theatre, 2003) could be considered the best of Mirror Theatre.

From 1992 to 2004, Mirror Theatre researched and devised thirty different programs and collectively presented them between 190 and 200 times. Three programs were produced as instructional videos. Much of the work was done after hours and during class time with little or no financial recompense. Eventually, an honorarium was provided for off-campus presentations. For out-of-town trips, travel, meals, and accommodations expenses were also covered.

Mirror Theatre's programs represent the exact opposite of the phrase "If you build it, they will come." In our case, they came and asked us to build it. Our programs were grassroots, as we worked in and with communities (schools, universities, conferences, charitable organizations, governmental agencies, and industry) in quest of better ways of living together. Our research was both empirical and imaginative, basing scenes on the lived-experiences of cast members and others, and working with metaphors to represent the concepts. And, our approach was a form of pedagogy called "enactivism" (Kieren, 1995). The casts and audiences entered as colearners, listening to each other as they collectively coconstructed meanings. Mirror Theatre's research, programs, and pedagogy attempted to move from a didactic to the dialogic (Bakhtin, 1981) style of research in all its stages. In our case, research dissemination meant bringing it directly to the people that the research was about, expanding its audience range beyond traditional academic circles.

PART II

The Scripting

The play's the thing wherein I'll catch the conscience of the king.
(*Hamlet*, Shakespeare, 1972c, p. 935)

The following 11 chapters are representative scripts selected from a range of Mirror Theatre's performance/workshops. They cover a variety of issues and are examples of a number of dramatic forms or presentational styles. They act as a buffet, not prescribing a particular form of presentation; rather, they are examples from which other A/R/Tors can pick and choose.

Each chapter follows the same format. First the history of the scene is provided, describing the context and the processes through which data is generated and translated into dramatic forms. Paralleling a traditional qualitative research process, this section makes the framing of the data explicit.

Second is the script itself. It is written in a play format with both dialogue and stage directions. In a couple of cases, two versions of the same script are given (Chapters 7 and 13), demonstrating how the same content is reworked for different contexts and audiences. The performed scripts are design to "bring academic scholarship to a wider audience" (Leavy, 2009, p. 14), and, like poetry, the written script is "not simply an alternative way of presenting the same information; rather, it can help the researcher evoke different meanings from the data, work through different set of issues, and help the [academic] audience receive the data differently" (p. 64).

The third section (Content Analysis) makes explicit the themes embedded within the script. This parallels a discussion section in traditional research. However, making things explicit is not the purpose of a live-performance form of dissemination. For pedagogical and political reasons, we chose to invite our audiences into analysis rather than superimposing our own meta-narrative (Chapter 15). The analysis is provided here (1) to demonstrate that the scenes do have a substance of thought that underpins them and (2) to offer a potential style of integrating a literary, thick description with discussion for academic consumption, similar to that of Frank (2000).

The fourth section (Form Analysis) makes explicit the dissemination style chosen and the reasons behind it. Content cannot be disassociated from form (McLuhan, 1967), and an understanding of this intricacy can be of assistance to those who are considering presenting their data through drama. The 11 chapters of scripts offer a variety of forms from which one can choose.

The following matrix of these chapters allows readers to choose what to read next based what they deem relevant. For some, the choice may be theme-based; for others, it could be based on the dramatic style; still others may wish to target a particular age group. Although some chapters make reference to earlier ones, their arrangement is not necessarily chronological. These chapters can be read in any order; the matrix facilitates readers' choices.

Note that the letters at the beginning of the alphabet denote female roles and those at the end, male characters. Owing to multiple casting, the A/R/Tors use their real names in all scenes for ease of memory. Refer to "*http://www.joenorrisplaybuilding.ca*" for videos of each of the vignettes.

Chapter Scene, Theme, Dramatic Form, and Source Matrix

	Scene	Theme	Dramatic Forms Used	Source Play	Audience
4	"Pressures"	Peer pressure	Sculpting & readers theatre	*What's the Fine Line?*	14 up
5	"The M Word"	Sexuality	Improvisation testimonials	*Complexities & Contradictions*	14 up
6	"Funky Shirt"	Gender politics/clothing	Voices off	*What's the Fine Line?*	14 up
7	"Cattle Call"	Body image	Shadow screen	*One of These Things*	14 up
8	"Great Expectations"	Student teaching	Voice collage	*Great Expectations*	Teachers
9	"The Party"	Status	Gibberish	*Coulda/Shoulda*	14 up
10	"Dares"	Substance abuse	Surrealistic drama	*Last Call Your Call*	14 up
11	"Are You Really Listening?"	Alienation/judging others	Inner dialogue	*Understanding Prejudice*	14 up
12	"Who's with Whom?"	Prejudice	Mime	*Understanding Prejudice*	10 up
13	"Whose Pencil Is It Anyway?"	Dealing with conflict	Realistic scene problem plays	*Fair Play Rulz*	6 up
14	"Distillation"	Qualitative research	Machines & metaphors	*ReSearch RePlay*	Academic

CHAPTER 4

Pressures

Understanding Peer Pressure and Sexual Activity through Sculpting and Readers Theatre

History and Method

"Pressures" was a scene generated for Mirror Theatre's first touring show, *What's the Fine Line?* Two years previously, the cast wrote a show, *Mirror Mirror*, for the Faculty of Education at the University of Alberta examining issues of equality and respect on campus, and the evaluation of the half-day workshop included comments from faculty and staff that it should tour schools. One of the cast members from that show was now teaching in a high school and requested that we bring the show to her school. We called this edited version *'clusions*.

An invitation was sent out, and a group of new and old members assembled to examine the *Mirror Mirror* script and its archival video to determine what scenes might be relevant to high school students. Some scenes were taken from *Mirror Mirror* and some from another show, *If we Offend,* which was devised for the 1995 Education Week at the University of Alberta. Together, with a major restructuring and additions, a set of scenes addressing the question "How are people are included and excluded in schools?" was devised. This was our first foray into the school system.

Until this time all the shows were designed for special events, and the thought of touring had not been really considered. The casts were predominantly Bachelor of Education drama majors and minors, and their heavy on-campus workload and student teaching placements throughout greater Edmonton precluded any thought of a workable tour. But word began to spread. The news department of the Canadian Broadcasting Company (CBC) approached us to work with them on a documentary entitled *Boys Will Be Boys* (Palmer, 1995). We agreed and began to devise a performance workshop for a group of junior high school students.

Our research question was broader than CBC's. We chose to focus on the wider issue of power and asked, "How do adolescents cross the line and inflict physical and emotional pain on one another?" Gender played a role, but we expanded our perspective in our story circle (Reason and Hawkins, 1988) and sought stories about situations in which power was negatively used. Peer pressure was one topic, and we brainstormed the various forms of peer pressure. Smoking, drinking, and drugs were the initial examples listed but had become clichés during that time period. Sexuality was another topic that the cast listed, and we chose this. It was relevant to the age group but not overdone by guest speakers and theater troupes. A few years later, we received requests about substance abuse and were surprised. As mentioned earlier, we had forgotten that as a new group of students comes of age they may not have been overexposed by other presentations. We realized that when one is working with specific age groups, the clientele changes quickly.

For our scene on sexual pressures we went into our data-collection phase with a product/form in mind. This is not the same as a quantitative researcher entering a study knowing that she/he will use a t-test, chi-square, or ANOVA or a qualitative researcher planning to use some found poetry (Butler-Kisber, 2002). The medium is the message (McLuhan, 1967), and we wanted to demonstrate the barrage of messages young teens receive about sex. A "quote collage" of things said that pressure adolescents would be a useful form.

On file cards we listed a large number of comments on sexuality that we recalled hearing. In keeping with our belief of exploring both thesis and antithesis (Boal, 1992), we looked at statements for and against premarital sexual activity. We also looked for pro and con statements from both teens and adults. We did not want to fall into the stereotype that all teens are pro sexual activity and all adults against it. With a list in hand, I privately constructed a script of collective thoughts to bring back to the cast.

I chose six characters, two representing a male and a female being pressured, who would provide some of their thoughts about the onslaught of comments; also one male adult and one female adult and one male teen and one female teen, whose comments would both promote and discourage sexual activity.

This production was staged with the pressured couple in the middle, the adults on one side, and the teens on the other. The characters were caught in a verbal tug of war. Later, we added a body-sculpting element to the scene as a form of exposition. After taking their positions, the four pressurers took turns sculpting the pressured teens. Initially, we did not script the sculptors' words, but I asked the actors to improvise their beliefs while sculpting. The result added to the methodology. Improvisation can assist individuals in articulating some of their thoughts in a way that even open-ended questions may not. Usually we think of generating data and translating it into a dramatic form, as was the case with the Readers Theatre portion of this scene, but through the improvisation, other phrases and insights emerged. The improvisation itself was a form of data generation and collection.

Script

From *What's the Fine Line?*—Commissioned by School Tour

PART ONE —SCULPTING WAR
Parents and adolescents sculpt two figures into relationship poses.

Cast:
Male Teen (MT) and Female Teen (FT) are center stage.
Male Adult (MA) and Female Adult (FA) are on stage right.
Male Peer Group (MPG) and Female Peer Group (FPG) are on stage left.

MA: (*sculpts MT and FT while talking*)
(*looks at the couple*) Don't you look like a nice couple. But you can be friendlier than that. You're young. Enjoy your age.
(*while moving MT*).
You can face her. Let her know that you are interested.
(*while moving FT*) And you can face him.
(*the couple is facing each other about 1.5 feet away from each other. MA steps back and looks*)
Something's missing. (*pause*) I know,
(*moves them both*)

Photo 4.1 • Body sculpting characters into tableaus.

you can move a bit closer, and so can you. Maybe a bit farther
back. But you can touch.
(*puts MT's hand on FT's shoulder*)
Now gaze lovingly into her eyes. Lovingly, not lustfully.
(*moving FT's head*)
and you look into his eyes and tell him that you care.
(*MA steps back and looks*)
There, now don't you two look nice.
(*returns to stage right*)

FPG: (*sculpts MT and FT while talking*)
Come on! You can do better than that! Closer.
(*pushes them together so that they are touching*)
That's better.
(*sculpting FT*)
Put you arms around his neck.
(*sculpting MT*)

and you put your arms around her waist. That's getting bet-
ter. What's the matter with a little lust?
(*MA steps back and looks*)
Something's missing. (*pause*) I know.
(*goes behind sculpture, so they won't be blocked and takes the
FT's downstage hand and places it on the MT's butt*)
There!
(*returns to stage left*)

FA: No, No, No!
(*separates the two and faces them front*)
This is completely inappropriate behavior.
(*sculpts FT first and ends her by placing her hands in the
"prayer" position*)
Think pure thoughts.
(*faces head up*)
Think heavenly thoughts. And you young man,
(*places his hands over his crotch*)
don't even think about it.

MPG: (*sculpts MT and FT while talking*)
Yeah!? (*sarcastically*) Right!? You can move closer together,
closer. Hold hands
(*places their hands in each other*)
and look at each other. Smile. That's much better.
(*returns to stage left*)

PART TWO—READERS THEATRE
MPG gives MT and FT Readers Theatre scripts and says to male:

MPG:	Do it. Go on and do it.
	(*returns to stage right*)
FPG:	Yeah, everyone's do it
MPG:	You're a nerd if you don't.
MT:	Yeah, the guys will finally respect me.
FT:	Do I really want to do this?
MPG & FPG:	(*chant softly*) Do it, Do it, Do it.
FT:	I'd like to but . . .
MT:	I want to but . . .
FT:	Maybe, but what would mom and dad say?

Photo 4.2 • Readers Theatre of Sexual Pressures.

FA:	It's wrong.
MA:	It's natural, but make sure you use protection.
FA:	It's dirty.

FA & MMPG: (*chant softly twice*) It's dirty. It's wrong. Use
              protection.

MT:	I don't want to, but . . .
FT:	No, but I do want to kiss him.
MT:	What if she thinks I'm chicken if I don't?
FT:	What if he thinks I don't like him if I don't?

MPG:	Virgin, Virgin, Virgin.
FA:	Tramp, slut.

FPG:	He's a girly man.
MA:	Show women some respect.

MT:	What should I do?
MA:	Son, we should talk. (*pause*) Later.

FT:	What should I do?
MPG:	Do it or you'll lose him.

MA & FA: Read a book.
MPG & FPG: We wish we could do it.

MT/FT: Who can we talk to?

FA: You're not old enough.
MA: 16 is a good age.

MT: I'm 14.
FT: I'm 14.

FPG: Wait for marriage.
MA: Sex is natural, let them go.

MT: What if she gets pregnant?
FT: What if I get pregnant?

MT: If we do it, I'll have to tell Jack.
FT: I hope he doesn't tell . . . . . but I'll have to tell Sheila.

MA: Remember sexually transmitted diseases.
FA: I don't want you to bring home that trash again.
FA: Remember AIDS.

FT: What if I smell?
MT: What if I'm not good?

MPG: Get her drunk first.
FPG: Whore.
MPG: Do it, you'll love it.

MT: Maybe.
FT: Maybe.

FA: I can't condone this behavior.
MPG: Go for it!

(*Both choruses softly chant some of their slogans while circling the statues.
The statues come alive turn and look at each group, face the audience.*)

MPG & FPG: Stop pressuring me!
               (*all freeze*)

Lights: blackout.

Content Analysis

Building on one of our basic tenets, we sought data from multiple perspectives in order to avoid polarizing or stereotyping. We asked, "What comments do adults say to adolescents about sexual behavior and what comments do teens themselves say?" Ancillary questions were "What messages from each group promote sexual activity? What messages discourage it? What messages make it healthy? What messages make it 'dirty'?" Our intent was not to deliver a conclusion to our audiences but to evoke thought enabling our audiences/readers to examine the thesis and antithesis and form their own synthesis (Barone, 1990). The scene was called "Pressures," because we did not want to preach about sexual behaviors but bring into focus some of the external and internal pressures that are experienced. Following are some of the themes embedded within the scene.

Coming of Age

Through our discussions we recalled that while we were adolescents we debated the appropriate age to engage in sexual activity. As teens we were anxious to grow up. Sex wasn't just a physical thing but a social status symbol, like the car keys, voting, cigarettes, and alcohol. Engaging in rites of passage led to being mature and grown up. Some rites of passage involve legal ages, but there are also social ones. Setting one's boundaries rather than accepting imposed ones was not so much an act of defiance as taking control over life and body. Taboo breaking and establishing an age engendered a sense of power and permission to respond to one's body. "16's a good age." "I'm 14." "I'm 14" reflected this dimension. However, the script did not contain all the information imparted in the production. The inflections of the two instances of "I'm 14" differed. The first was said as "I'm 14—old enough and ready." The second was said sheepishly: "I'm ONLY 14." "I'm 14" was repeated to show the ambiguity of any statement and the difference of opinions regarding any established formal or informal boundary.

Harm/Danger/Risk

Sexual behavior comes with physical, emotional, and social risks. Physical risks are real, but these risks have been used as threats—for example, "Don't do it, or else" or "Do it, or else." Sexual activity has been socially defined as risky behavior, making it, for some, a thing to be avoided; however, for others, the challenge is part of its lure (Lyng, 1990). Note that although the scenes are based on focus-group research, they are written with pedagogical intent. The scenes are meant to outline issues for possible discussion with an interactive audience. Discussions about sexually transmitted disease and pregnancy could be discussed in the context of precautions but also in the context of how the risks themselves are perceived.

Reputation/Bravado

Loss or gain of reputation is another form of risk, but it depends on the situation and era. The old standard of "males are studs and females tramps if they engage in sexual behavior" was articulated in the scene, but often there are double and triple standards. Through discussion we found that rather than pressure always being in the form of either/or messages, it could also be all and none simultaneously. As being was for Hamlet, both the "to do and not to do" were problematic, both bringing potential positive and negative consequences at the same time. A change in reputation can be both a loss and a gain as a new identity emerges. The first sexual act with another person is a passage over a threshold. And, although reputations may change, the relationship is also affected. The reputation of each of the two parties is also articulated as one wonders how the other will perceive the act.

Bravado is an extension of reputation when one believes that his/her identity is connected with the act and does the act with the belief that his/her status will improve. Telling or not telling is a crucial element of sexual activity. Both individuals want to share their new identity with others but recognize the ambiguity of telling; one reveals not only a new side of self but also a new side of another person. Telling to gain reputation could have a negative effect on another.

Morality/Ethics

It's clear that, although private, sexual activity is also a social act that affects and is influenced by a larger venue. One's acts of doing and telling have implications for others. Pregnancy and disease are the typical two possibilities, but the emotional and social well-being of self and the other are also ethical concerns. The scene highlights the responsibility one must assume when acting with another. Moralizing, in our analysis, seems to have a negative effect. Mandating "pure thoughts" as an antithesis to sex can make sex dirty. Secrecy and taboos make it a vulgar act. Sex is not merely a physical act but one that has major interpersonal, social, and emotional implications. The ending plea of "Stop pressuring me!" questions the ethics of pressures, whether they be moral or social.

Form Analysis

Positioning (Blocking)

Staging, blocking, and picturization are all terms that apply to the visual aspects of a live performance, from the movement of actors to the scenery on stage. Determining the visuals for an audience is an important element of translating a written script into a living act. Where one stands, who stands next to whom, the proximity of location to others, and furniture all send visual cues and meanings to an audience. For pressures, we wanted to portray both internal and external pressures as well as adult and peer pressures. Three clusters were chosen to visually portray these dimensions.

The partners were placed close to each other at center stage. Stage right had the adult cluster and stage left the peer cluster. Each cluster's proximity to the couple was the same, and each cluster was some distance away, to demonstrate that the pressures were external. They remained fixed for most of the scene, demonstrating a backdrop of beliefs about sexual involvement, but at the end they moved closer, circling the couple to show that the cumulative effect can be a violent and confusing barrage of impositions. Implicit and overt messages are imbedded in the blocking of a scene and require careful attention.

Sculpting with Inner Dialogue

Body sculpting is a powerful way of visualizing concepts (Boal, 1979). It has been used to sculpt emotions and to portray abstract concepts. In this case, the external pressures sculpt the main characters as they passively respond to the touch of others. As in the 1960s song, "Child of Clay" (Rodgers, 1967), they are "shaped and molded." The sculpting raises questions of systemic violence as some people impose their belief systems on others. The act of physically moving a person makes explicit the external forces at play.

The use of inner dialogue is also an effective theatrical technique. Like an aside, it permits the audience to hear what a character is thinking, as action takes place. The dramatic impact of the sculpting is enhanced by superimposing words with actions, layering meaning and complexity. Having the couple remain silent during the sculpting adds to the dimension of voicelessness, as rules are ambiguously built around them by competing ideologies. Such a situation could be generalized to many aspects of growing up.

Choice of Characters

Choice of characters and their points of view are always major decisions in scripting. At times a narrator can be more effective than a character, and decisions about representative groups need to be taken into account. In the sexual pressure scenes, having adults but no peers would have sent a message different from that of a scene including peers, and vice versa. This particular scene was heterosexually focused, thereby excluding homosexual characters. (A scene in our restructuring of *What's the Fine Line?* into *Coulda/Shoulda* does explore other sexual orientations. No one scene can do it all.)

Readers Theatre

The use of Readers Theatre (Coger and White, 1971) had both pragmatic and theatrical reasons. During our first tour, we had multiple interchanging casts, and for a given performance an actor might play a different part from the one she/he played on the previous day. The scripts in hand enabled the actors to take on different roles on different days. The scripts were put in color-coded folders; the adults were one color, the peers another, and the main characters a third. This system communicated that they were distinct groups and made it easier for cast members to be given their appropriate scripts. But the Readers Theatre scripts also added a performance quality. Since the actors were reading from a "finely tuned prepared script," the overarching meaning was that they also were told what to say and think. Social norms and mores, not they, were driving the scene. Whether all audience members detected this implied meaning is not important, since there were many other issues imbedded in the scene. This was but one that could be taken.

Dialogue

The dialogue was structured in a thesis/antithesis format in which thesis statements always engendered a retort. The characters in the middle were the metaphorical rope in a tug of war as they were pulled to one side and back to the other. Readers Theatre was an alternative to the typical realistic theatrical style of conversation and acted as a voice collage, providing a wide range of opinions. Although organized around issues, the assortment of comments economically provided a range of issues and perspectives. Audience members were able to form their own synthesis in thought and through discussion. The scene was constructed to encourage this possibility.

Chanting

Chanting and choral speech can have a powerful effect; collective voices tend to magnify the intensity of an issue. As the peers and adults circled the couple, the volume increased. Pandemonium ensued, because the chant was not in unison; instead, each chanter strived for supremacy, which brought an emotional conclusion to the piece, since one could imagine the feeling of being pressured on many sides. Ultimately, the scene was not about sex, but, as the title made explicit, about being pressured. Smoking, alcohol, drugs, and drinking and driving could be easily be substituted. The chant, in which the concepts are lost in the confusion, articulates the lived-experience of being pressured.

CHAPTER 5

The "M" Word

Understanding Sexuality through Improvisation and Personal Testimony

History and Method

In 1998 the Western Canadian Conference on Human Sexuality approached Mirror Theatre to provide their closing keynote. As was the case with a number of other commissioned pieces, Mirror Theatre did not go seeking the work; rather, those who had attended other conferences spread the word, and the Western Canadian Conference organizers asked us to write a show specifically for them. Mirror Theatre told the organizers that the performance would be a series of vignettes on a variety of aspects of human sexuality and would conclude with audience participation. Mirror Theatre was given the conference theme and a list of potential conference sessions. These were used to begin the rehearsal discussions with the cast.

As usual, a call for actors was made and was open to anyone who wished to participate. Former and new cast members assembled, and after the preliminary guidelines were set at the first rehearsal (as discussed in Chapter 2), a list of specific issues were brainstormed and personal stories were told. For a few of the former cast members, this was a long-awaited project. In a number of previous productions, individuals claimed that we needed to do a "sex show," because sex was a theme than ran through many of our performances, including bullying, body image, and the politics of student teaching. The scenes, "Pressures" and "Funky Shirt," from *What's the Fine Line*, were integrated into this show, called *Complexities and Contradictions*.

This sequence of three vignettes makes up the scene "The M-Word," short for the taboo of masturbation. During one rehearsal, as emergent themes were recorded on file cards, the concept of "innocence" arose. We discussed it for a while, but the conversation failed to yield significant insights. As adults we had become so acclimatized by our own baggage of guilt that we could not easily unpack the multiple layers of imposed morality that we had learned over time. As director/researcher, I believed that an improvisation might help us to return to a state of innocence in order to reveal our tacit understandings. I asked all cast members to go to the stage section of our rehearsal studio and imagine that they were on the playground. They were to both play alone and interact. I observed and made notes for the discussion that followed.

Some people skipped, others played hopscotch, others marbles. The scene was a high-energy one and a delight to watch, as a playground emerged out of their imaginations. One female cast member wore a long flowing skirt, and as she twirled, it billowed like a large tent. I noticed one male cast member, who had been watching her, move forward and then stop. From that action, I knew that we had both discovered a central insight and the beginnings of the scene. I stopped the drama and asked the male what impulse he had had and why he stopped. After a few denials, he admitted that he wanted to go under the dress.

Here was a strong example of the juxtaposition of innocence and guilt. As the character, he wanted to go into the beckoning billow; as an adult actor, his own well-established value system prevented him from doing so. As director, I witnessed this conflict manifested physically and used it for discussion that led to the first of three vignettes.

Four important research aspects are worth noting here. First, performative inquiry (Fels and Belliveau, 2008) was used as a means of data generation and analysis, Our discussion brought us to a particular point, but we had reached an impasse. We needed another medium to continue. The playground improvisation enabled us to bring to the surface what we could not say. In traditional research interviews, we ask our participants to recall events and experiences. In this case, we asked them to imaginatively reenact, to explore their tacit knowledge of the issue. The role-play enabled us to uncover a dimension that was difficult to articulate through words alone.

Kostera uses a narrative collage in a similar fashion. She believes that the imagination has a role to play in eliciting implicit beliefs and understandings. She instructs her informants to create fictional stories. Narrative collage is this:

> a method that consciously goes beyond realist storytelling. Its purpose is to play with ideas and discover the cultural context and the actors' creativity. It is aimed at encouraging the respondents to invent stories about a given topic or beginning with a specified starting line. The respondents choose the genre themselves and construct the plot as they wish. The researcher acts as a collector and editor of stories. Their role is not so much to analyze the material, as to see what whole can be made up of the stories and what it says about the cultural context of organizing. The goal is to enter the domain of the social imagination. (2006, p. 9)

The imagination has its roots in reality. In fact, every retelling is a reconstruction that uses a variety of literary devices (Richardson, 1990). The distinction between fact and fiction is an ambiguous:

> The opposite of fact isn't fiction but something like error. The opposite of fiction isn't truth but something like objectivity or actuality. Any genre or piece of writing that claims to be objective, to represent the actual, is a writing that denies its own existence, as David Lock said. In other words, no text is free of self-conscious constructions: no text can act as a mirror to the actual . . . . The imposition of fiction into the divide between fact and error doesn't negate the possibility of a real world: all it does is recognize the impossibility for others to be objective. (Banks and Banks, 1998, p. 13).

Second, when moving into improvisational scenes for data exploration, one must have one or more members be observers, to record the details (beats) of the scene. The actors thus provide an "experience-near" perspective and the recorders an "experience-distant" one (Geertz, 1974). When an actor experiences "metaxis" (Boal, 1995), a sense of simultaneously being both within the character and outside the character, the dramatic action happens too quickly for the A/R/Tor to lock it from short-term recall into permanent memory, since authenticity is achieved when the character, not the actor, is in control of the scene. Having a recorder frees the improvisational A/R/Tors to enter into the present, knowing that others will record what they found to be of significance.

In an early version of the play *Mirror Mirror*, an actress and I used mime to create a scene on territoriality. I established a space; she entered, and we interacted. The rest of the cast observed and commented after the scene was completed. We made a list of the important aspects of the scene. The parallel to participation-observation is obvious: the researcher(s) observe and use those observations in follow-up interviews to extend the discussion. In our case, the follow-up was an immediate debriefing, with a discussion of both the content and the theatrical elements.

In rehearsals of *Mirror Mirror*, I cast three members as flowers and asked them to remain on the spot but allowed them to move. I whispered the motivating factors of need, want, and desire, one to each person. I cast three other members as bees and gave each person one of the same three motivations. One at a time, the bees entered the scene and interacted with the flowers, while other cast members watched. The rest of the audience did not know the words or context and were asked after the event to analyze what they had witnessed. The discussion was thick with insights into the lived meanings of those three concepts. It reinforced the knowledge that improvisation can be a powerful tool of inquiry. The discussion produced some additional themes, and, although we used them a couple of times, they were considered too obtuse for a general audience. As with most creative works and research, certain paths and products end up on the metaphorical "cutting room floor."

The third research aspect is that stories beget stories. As researchers, we typically rely on questions to evoke our participants' stories and meanings. But there are many other useful evocateurs, improvisation being one. In the discussion of innocence, one cast member related a story about masturbation. I asked her to tell it as a monologue to an audience. She related how she discovered masturbation at the age of 4 and was excited to tell her father about her self-discovered, newly found pleasure. His reaction taught her the beginnings of guilt and shame, the fall from innocence. The improvisation was the catalyst, helping the actress to recall and to feel comfortable in relating her story.

We modified the playground and the masturbation vignettes into the script shown below and rehearsed them for future use. At the end of our rehearsal of these two scenes, I was compelled to tell a story. I had previously set one light as a spotlight for monologues and decided to use it for a follow-up third scene. I instructed a cast member to bring it up after the masturbation vignette was completed. This was the first time that the cast had heard the story, and it was an experiment for me to translate an idea directly into a theatrical convention. It was a story about autoerotic

asphyxiation ("scarfing") and the secrecy surrounding it. This story punc-
tuated the previous two, both of which dealt with innocence and taboo.

Fourth, while the last two parts of the scene were based on fact, the
first scene had its root in improvisation. Although not grounded in an
actual event, the scene was plausible, acting as a metaphor for the fall from
innocence and the guilt that accompanies it. As Bank and Banks (1998)
suggest, fiction does play a legitimate role in the construction of a text.

Script

From *Complexities and Contradictions*

COMMISSIONED BY THE WESTERN CANADIAN CONFERENCE ON
HUMAN SEXUALITY
The "M" Word—Part 1: Play Doctor

Note that the letters at the beginning of the alphabet denote female
roles and those at the end, male characters (as described in Chapter 2).

High energy, delightful tone of children at play

Catch (upstage right and left): X and Y improvise lines while playing
catch.
Playing with Doll (downstage right): A dresses and talks to dolly.
Hop Scotch (downstage left): B plays hopscotch.

Lines are heard on top of one another.

B twirls and her skirt billows.
She crosses to down center stage and sits spreading her skirt while
the others play.

X waves to Y and exits.
A still plays with doll.
Y crosses to B.

Y: What are you doing?
B: I'm playing princess.
Y: Can I play?
B: Sure, help me to spread out my gown.
Y: Yes, you majesty. It is such a pretty gown.
B: Why, thank you kind sir.
A: (*crosses to Y and B*) What are you playing?

Y & B: (*in unison*) Princess.

A: Can I play?

Y: Help me straighten her gown.
   (*they smooth the gown*)

A: Let's pretend she is having a baby. (*she takes her doll and stuffs it under B's dress*)

B: (*pats her belly and starts moaning*) It's coming, its coming. Help!

A: (*to Y*) You be the doctor.

Y: (*goes under B's dress*) I can see the head. Push harder. Harder. It's coming. Push harder.

Z: (*During this Z enters from up stage right. He looks stern, hands on hips. He crosses to action and calls Y by name.*) What are you doing? That's no way your mother and I taught you how to treat girls. You go straight home and into your room. Young lady, you should be ashamed of yourself. I am going to have a long talk with your parents.

blackout

Part 2: I'd Rather be a Robber Than a Rubber

SET: A shadow scene has been previously set up center stage. It is moved forward so that it can be lit from behind. The shadow A/R/Tor stands between the light and the screen, making the shadow.

PROPS: Doll and a stick rocking horse

B: When I was only 3 years old I discovered the most miraculous thing! And I knew that I invented it because I'd never even heard the smartest people in the world talk about it. Not even my Mom and Dad!
   I found out (*pause*) that if I took my dolly's head and put it between my legs just so, it tickled. Not just any tickle. A special, deep tickle that I never knew before.
   Sometimes it would take longer to find the right spot— but those times the tickle was even stronger when I did find it.
   I decided that before I showed the world my new invention I should practice really hard and learn as much as I could about this new pleasure before I chose a name for it.

W: (*stern voice from behind the screen as it is lit up; his shadow is seen; calls B by name*) B, what are you doing?

B: Here Dad! Let me show you! (*W comes out from behind the scene*) I figured that if I could tell anyone I could tell my Dad. (*she places the doll between her legs*) It feels good . . . and kinda tickles.

W: (*clearly flustered*) Honey, that's called m . . . , it's m . . . It's called (*pause*) rubbing. If you keep doing it you could break your doll's head. And if I ever catch you doing it again, I'll take all your dolls away.

      (*W leaves, then, on second thought, returns, grabs the doll and leaves. We see his shadow behind the screen. He remains for a few seconds, like a conscience. Then the light dims.*)

B: I knew I wouldn't stop. I couldn't stop. It was okay that he took my dolls. Because by that time I had already discovered lots of other things that could give me that sort of . . . "pleasure." (*goes around the screen returning with the stick rocking horse*) My number one back up was my rocking horse. I was glad that I didn't tell Dad about him.
      The best time to get away with it was during quiet time when my mom made me and the neighbor kids that she baby-sat stay in the living room and play quietly while she took a nap. Then I could sneak away. (*plays with the horse*)

Y: (*walks up and watches her wearily*) What are you doing now?

B: With my new found terminology I proudly responded, "I'm rubbing!"

Y: (*disgusted*) Who are you robbing?

B: No, I'm rubbing.

Y: Then whose horse is it?

B: No, I'm rubbing.

Y: You're a robber?

B: No, I'm a rubber.

Y: So why do you steal things?

B: Because (*turns to audience*) . . . I told him that he was right. My family stole things, because by this time I had learned that I'd rather be thought a robber than a rubber.

blackout

Part 3: Shhhhh

V: (*in the dark upper stage right*) Shhhhhhhhhhhhhh. (*crosses to spotlight down center stage*) Shhhhhhhhhhhhh. (*looks around suspiciously and puts finger to lips*) Shhhhhhhhhhh. My father told me not to tell this story.

Last summer when I returned home for a visit, my father took me away from the crowd, asked me to sit down, and told me this story. "I am going to tell you what really happened to your uncle Leroy," he said. "But, shhhhhhhhhhhh, don't tell anyone."

I nodded, not in agreement but to communicate my understanding. "I already know." I told him. He looked shocked, as if no one could figure out such a dark secret. That previous Christmas season, my mother's cousin, uncle Leroy [*pseudonym*], was found dead of an apparent hanging. At first it was labeled a suicide. He was in his 70s, had lost his mother and brother within the previous few years, and it is a common fact that there are more suicides over this holiday period.

But the facts didn't add up for me. He was highly religious, self-sufficient, and had recently acquired a girlfriend. He had never married, and now was the time to spread his wings, or so I thought. Suicide didn't suit him.

During one of my many calls home, I was informed that the police had relabeled his death "accidental" and that he was granted a church burial. From this I deduced what had really happened, but (*placing a finger across his lips*) shhhhhhhhhhhh—my family doesn't want you to know.

You see, my uncle was a scarfer. He liked to masturbate while choking himself. The proper term is autoerotic asphyxiation. Sadly, he didn't release himself in time and died. But shhhhhhhhhhhhhhhh. My family would prefer you to believe that it was suicide, not masturbation.

Lights: blackout.

Content Analysis

From our collective stories and personal meanings a number of themes emerged. Entering into the project, we focused on adult issues of sexuality and the socially constructed meanings attached to them. Sexual orientation, prostitution, body image, and pornography were some of the social dimensions that we explored. Intimacy, the differences among needs/wants/desires, attraction, and pleasure were some of the emotional dimensions chosen. We deliberately steered away from typical physiological/biological aspects, such as reproduction/birth control and STDs, which were a major focus of the conference. Our approach was both to complement and to add to the conference's themes. The play, *Complexities and Contradictions,* addressed a variety of issues.

Prepuberty Sexuality

The three scenes described here were not on our original list but emerged during improvisation and discussion. In these scenes, we entered into a realm that is full of taboos, "pre-adolescent, prepuberty sexuality" being one. As a society, we tend to define childhood as an asexual period, but from our discussions with cast members and the audience, we knew that such is not the case. Although children are culturally aware of sexuality through media exposure and peer conversations, they are also very aware of their bodies and feelings. Of all the scenes presented, it was the one on preadolescent sexuality that became the focus of our discussion with the audience.

Null Curriculum

Flinders and colleagues (1986) discuss the role that the null curriculum plays in a child's upbringing. What is deliberately ignored or marginalized defines through omission a set of society's values. Our three scenes articulated the unspoken. They evoked these questions: "What aren't we teaching? Why? And how would we teach these subjects, if we deemed them important?" The role of the scenes was to articulate the issues in order to raise our audience's awareness.

Innocence/Guilt

An explicit curriculum was that of guilt and the loss of innocence. Children acquire values from adults and their peers, and these values vary from parent to parent and locale to locale. The cast discussed how they acquired their own attitudes toward masturbation and how these changed over time. The title "The M-Word" (not saying the whole word) and the third vignette illustrate the taboo surrounding masturbation and the potentially negative consequences of it remaining undiscussed.

Autoerotic Asphyxiation

The final scene, which was, as discussed, a personal testimony, indicated the intensity of the taboo. The label *suicide*, in this case, was preferred over *autoerotic asphyxiation*. While I was supervising student teachers in a junior high school, one of its students, a young boy, strangled himself. Many students were traumatized, wondering why they hadn't picked up the signals, questioning what they could have done. Staff eventually told the students that it was an accident, but no more than that. The "S-word" was alleviated by a vague reference, but the "M-word" remained unspoken.

Anonymity and the Ethics of Personal Disclosure

The ethics of the personal testimony must be discussed, because testimonies usually implicate others—in this case, my father. Norris, Higgins, and Leggo (2004) discuss the problematics of disclosure in research without coming to a definitive conclusion. Even Spradley's (1980) concept of "bracketing out" and Sawyer and Norris's (2004) reframing of the term that they call "bracketing in" provide difficulty. Researchers can make themselves vulnerable by telling their stories. Their identities are known, as are the identities of others who are discussed within the story. All people, including researchers, have the rights to their own stories, but what are the ethical limits of telling stories that implicate others and the risks to the originator? As researchers, we must carefully weigh the pros and cons of what we tell. A cast member in *Mirror Mirror* told a story of being sexually harassed by a cooperating teacher during one of her student teaching placements. We left it ambiguous as to whether it was her story or that of someone else. During the follow-up discussion with the audience, she chose to reveal it as her story; it was a cathartic moment that brought relief. But the decision was hers. In my own vignette about my uncle Leroy [*pseudonym*], I weighed the potential harm to my father (minimal), to my uncle Leroy (none), and the possible benefits to others (major). Because I had already deduced the real story, I did not honor my father's request. Adding him created a story within a story that reinforced the taboo of the "M-word."

Form Analysis

High Energy

The first part of the scene on the playground was high energy and designed to bring the audience in. Actors use an old adage, "Never share the stage with an animal or a baby"—this applies here, since the A/R/Tors portrayed young children at play. Audiences are drawn to the unpredictability of unbridled energy, and animals and babies both have high energy levels. What is important for this opening scene was that the characters appeared to be having fun. The actual games were immaterial; skipping, tag, and mimed swinging would have been equally as effective. This opening had a degree of unpredictability similar to sharing the stage with a baby.

The natural high energy rhythm of the playground scene was vital to set up the undeserved "fall from innocence at the end of the scene." Ooohs and aws were heard from the audience as the tender moments played out. It was an everyday scene played realistically.

Use of Realism

Norris outlines a variety of ways in which scenes can be constructed and discourages the overuse of realistic scenes (1995b). Metaphorical scenes are more open to interpretation, enabling audience members to find a connection to their own particular circumstance. Realistic scenes can be less likely to create such a response. However, the playground section of this scene illustrates an instance in which the use of realism is appropriate.

Lighting

Lighting for the stage is a major literary device. It can direct focus, punctuate, and set the mood. Part one, in which the father scolds his son, ends abruptly with a zero-count blackout after the father's line is delivered. A fade would have lessened the impact of the violence. Audience responses to this technique vary. Often the audience's silence was more impressive than clapping, because the vignette created discomfort. In fact, we sometimes structured the lighting to preclude audience response completely. In this case, during the blackout, the shadow screen was moved forward quickly as a spotlight faded in. This told the audience that the next action was about to begin.

Another technique we employed was speaking in the dark (Chapter 2). Walking into the light while speaking has a different dramatic effect than does beginning in the spotlight. The "Shhh" vignette began the first way. The darkness reinforced the notion of secrecy. The scene ended with me walking out of the light while the light remained on, until a gradual fade. This sent a message to the audience that the scene was not yet over, providing a space for contemplation. Just as thick description and narrative devices are used to frame written research, Playbuilders need to understand and to utilize this art form's techniques and syntaxes, lighting being but one.

Casting

Casting is flexible, and for this show the same actress played both the princess and the rubber, since both were her stories. This, however, is not necessary. (In the first part, her exit gave her ample time to make a prompt entrance in part two.)

Monologues/Personal Disclosure

Monologues are to theater what transcriptions are to traditional qualitative research. They are pieces that elucidate a point in the words of
the character/participant. Short and to the point, they can be powerful.
Long, drawn-out pieces are static and boring, and too much personal
testimony can seem self-indulgent, regardless of the content. In the "rubber" vignette, we broke up the potentially lengthy monologue by inter-
spersing dramatic action. The adage "Show, don't tell" is a useful one
here. Monologues have their place if used discriminately and briefly.

In the scene "Put Downs," in *What's the Fine Line?* (Norris, 1999),
we had both women and men jeered at and receive catcalls. It's a violent
surrealistic scene that represents how people obtain pleasure from making fun of others. It demanded a response, and the scene concluded with
brief monologues directed to the audience. Each cast member (who had
just been portrayed as a bully) stepped into the spotlight and told a real
story about some consequences of bullying. These monologues worked,
because they were a response to the scene but did not constitute the scene
itself.

In *One of These Things Is Not Like the Others*, a few actors wanted
to provide their personal testimonies. These stories were brief and hard-
hitting, but rather than lumping them together, which would have been
theatrically deadly, we scattered them throughout the play. This also
assisted in scene changes. As a monologue was given in a spotlight, set
changes took place quietly in the dark, which facilitated efficient and
timely transitions from scene to scene.

Shadow Screen

A shadow screen is another theatrical device that can use metaphor to
communicate. It was employed for "Cattle Call" in our show *Shadows*
(Chapter 7) and in "Playboy on the Bus," which was also in *Complexities
and Contradictions*. The "M-Word" could easily have been performed
without a screen, having the father enter from the side. However, the
screen was used to heighten the effect of the entrance. The actor stood
next to the screen and backed into the light, which made the shadow
grow larger. He then entered farther upstage. Metaphorically, he became
the shadow of guilt.

In the scene "Playboy on the Bus," we explored the public/private
aspect of sexuality. Individuals got on a bus, each person with different
reading materials. Since the audience couldn't discern what was being
read, we made color overheads of the front covers and projected them
from the back of the screen via an overhead projector. This technique

made the content visible to the audience. A variety of covers was shown; the first was a picture of a plane dropping bombs, and the last was a cover of *Playboy*. The bus driver stopped and kicked the *Playboy*-reading passenger off the bus. The social norm we articulated was that violence was more acceptable that nudity. Without some form of visual projection, the point would have been lost to the audience.

Sequencing of Vignettes

The last note on form is not about the scenes themselves but their sequence. Clearly, there was a progression of intensity with the "M" vignettes; a different order would have lessened their combined effect. Since there were other scenes in the show, these could have also been interspersed, as was the case with the "Dares" in both *What's the Use?* and *Last Call Your Call* (Chapter 10) and the "O" scenes in *Coulda/Shoulda*. The "O" scenes explored sexual putdowns. Hockey players hugging after scoring a goal were called "homos," girlfriends hugging were called "lesbos," and boy/girl huggers, "heteros." We experimented by sometimes performing these scenes together and at other times interspersed throughout the play. Together, they maintained a continuity resulting in clarity. Interspersed, they elongated the effect, heightening ambiguity. Both sequences were effective. The arrangement and the sequence of vignettes, like that of themes in literary works of qualitative research, is an important stylistic decision.

CHAPTER 6

Funky Shirt

Problematizing Clothing Communication through Voices Off and a Dream Sequence

History and Method

Some scenes go through many manifestations before they are refined into a piece that meets our standard. This does not mean that they are never performed until then but that they are presented as works in progress to the audience. Trying to understand the nature of the "perhaps" conflicting messages implied by female attire proved to be difficult. A series of different cast members, over a long period of time, struggled with a variety of vignettes that eventually resulted in the scene shown below. As previously stated, our purpose was not to bring refined understandings to the audience but to enter into dialogue with them so that we could mutually assist each other in better understanding the phenomenon that we were examining. Such was the case of "Funky Shirt."

The scene "Sometimes It's Hard Not to Look," in *Mirror, Mirror*, addressed part of the issue of voyeurism, but not completely. In its development, as was the case of the "Bees and Flowers" scene (Chapter 5), I arranged an improvisation in which chosen cast members did not know the entire plot. Once I had a male and a female volunteer, I explained privately what I wanted the male to do, and I told the female and the remaining cast that the scene was a casual conversation about favorite movies and television shows. While maintaining socially acceptable decorum, the male volunteer was to innocently and progressively adjust his belt and crotch.

The scene's origin was empirically based. I once had a female instructor who wore short skirts and was always adjusting them, tugging on their hems. I found myself looking at her legs, not because I was interested but because her movement drew my attention to them. My visits to her office to discuss my work were uncomfortable, because I lived in dread that she would find me looking at her legs. I wanted to create a reverse situation and see how a female would respond. (Note that actors can choose not to comply with such requests; other volunteers can be sought. I call this "permission to dissent.")

The scene was hilarious, and the reactions of the female were natural, something that would not have been achieved had she had known about the instructions. Our discussions focused on how we can misinterpret actions and looks. More than one male cast member claimed that they found writing on women's T-shirts to be awkward. They wanted to read what was on them but did not want to be accused of staring at breasts. This improvisation evoked such recall, a good example of how an improvisation, like an interview question, can be used to generate real stories and data.

Again an improvisation was employed to assist us in understanding the phenomenon under investigation. This scene related specifically to clothing and how the message received may not be the same as the message sent. The final vignette had three components. Up center stage stood a male and a female in dim lighting. To bring in gender balance, we had one male/female pair down stage right and another down stage left. Lights came up on one pair, and the male adjusted his belt during the conversation. The lights cross-faded to the other couple. This time, the female adjusted her bra strap. Each scene was played three times with the adjustments further exaggerated. Then both pairs froze in half-light. The lights came fully up on the center pair, who, in unison, said "Sometimes it's hard not to look." We performed this a number of times, but during a remount of *What's the Fine Line?* a new female cast member complained. For her, the scene missed the mark in that it did not address *her* deemed inappropriateness of certain male behaviors. More discussions ensued.

We discussed common verbal expressions such as "she asked for it" but rejected them as inappropriate, taking us on a slippery slope. Performing a scene of consequence could be too dark and lead us way from our main focus, which was the male behavior. We wanted to be preventive, not judgmental. We tried a realistic scene with a male approaching an attractively dressed female and found that costuming was a problem. We wanted to have the conversation with the audience but did not want to have it about a specific piece of clothing. An underpinning question was this: "What was the difference between provocative and attractive?"

Eventually, the comment "I am dressing for him, not everybody," stated by a female cast member, provided a key. Rather than having the female justify her clothing, we decided to do a role reversal and have the male first express his like for the article of clothing and then comment on why he thought it was also inappropriate to wear publicly. However, we still believed that the approach was too direct and combative as a realistic scene. To provide distance, we used a drama technique called "voices off," whereby two actors mime the action on stage and another two speak the dialogue from off stage (discussed further in the section "Form Analysis"). Thus the final version of the scene articulated the ambiguity found in both the senders and the receivers of the "messages" in clothing, emphasizing the problematics of attire.

Script

From *What's the Fine Line?*—Commissioned by School Tour

Note that the letters at the beginning of the alphabet denote female roles and those at the end, male characters.

> (*As spotlight comes up, C is sitting center stage, on a couch; Y is standing stage left and begins to approach Y when lights rise.*)

> (*C mimes the actions while A reads the script from stage right.*)
> (*Y mimes the actions while Z reads the script from stage left.*)

Y: (*judging X's appearance*)
z: Is that a new shirt?

c: (*proudly modeling shirt*)
A: Yeah, I just bought it. Kind of funky, hey?

Photo 6.1 • Voices off of character dialogue.

Y: (*puzzled look*)
Z: Yeah, it's great.

B: So are you ready to go?
A: (*reaches for B's hand*)

Y: (*pulling hand away*)
Z: Yeah, sure. Just one thing though. You're going to go change first before we go, right?

A: (*disbelief*)
B: What?

Z: You're going to change, right?

B: Why?

Z: Well, you can't wear that shirt to the party.

B: Oh. So—you're telling me what I'm wearing to the party.

Z: Um, this time I am, yeah.

B: (*laughs*) I don't think so. Come on.

A: (*getting ready to take B's hand*)

Z: No, listen.

Y: (*takes X's hand and pulls her down beside him*)

Z: We're going to walk over to that party, and as soon as we walk in, every guy's eyes are going to be on you. I guarantee it.

(*enter X, who walks around couch, ogling her, and gesturing to audience how "hot" he finds her*)

B: Wade, you're my boyfriend. I'm going to be staying with you all night.

(*X walks across stage, giving her his rapt attention*)

Z: I don't want to fend these guys off all night.

(*the intensity in the voices and gestures of A and Y rise during the rest of the scene, anger and resentment fill the tension*)

B: Oh, get real.

Z: Trust me, I know. I used to do the very same thing.

B: It's just a shirt.

Z: I know that, but—just look at yourself! There's no way I'm going to let you go like that.

(*X does another lustful circuit of the stage*)

B: Look, I'm going to have a sweater, okay?

Z: You're not going to wear your sweater inside.

B: Well, I might!

Z: What if it gets too warm?

B: Oh come on, Wade. You're making a big deal out of this. It's just a shirt!

z: It's more than that!

(*A and Υ turn away from each other as, suddenly, X leans between them and directs himself toward A*)

x: (*seductively*) Hi, there!

blackout

Content Analysis

Public Persona

Humans are social animals, and how our tribe views us is part of our identity. We are aware that others label us and that our actions will have consequences based on the reputation we create. How intelligent and attractive others find us can play a role in how we define ourselves. Labels, such as jock, tramp, nerd, geek, and others, tend to stick. This scene articulates the difference in the degree that these males and females are aware of and to which they adjust to the public gaze.

The female is comfortable with her attire, while her boyfriend is not. They do not share the same belief about the messages that clothing can communicate. In *Complexities and Contradictions,* we performed a scene called "Dresses," in which we heard the female's thoughts as she decided what to wear for the day. The tension between personal preference and public interpretations was made evident.

"Funky Shirt" ends with no resolution. It was designed that way and has sparked many a heated conversation in our postperformance conversations with the audience. Again, in keeping with the constructivist nature of our programs, our aim was to problematize clothing, not to dictate dress codes. Such problematics are discussed in the workshop that follows each performance (Chapter 15).

Who Decides

Throughout the scene, it is the male who objects and then dictates what his girlfriend is to wear. This, too, was a deliberate decision on our part, because it makes evident the power of the male gaze over the female persona. As in Berger's examination of the portrayal of women in art (1972), Culler's (1982) claim that women read themselves through the eyes of men, and Baudrillard's concept of simulacra whereby the map, the fantasy, defines the reality (1983), it is the male who references and defines the female. "Funky Shirt" is steeped in gender politics.

Communication Responsibility

In workshop discussions with the audience, issues of communication responsibility were raised. "What message do you want to send?" was an emerging question, as was "Are you interpreting the message appropriately?" In *What's the Fine Line?* in a scene that was originally named "Tickle" and eventually made the title of the show, a male is playing a video game and his girlfriend enters. He laughs and says "No." He's really into the game, but she persists. Again he firmly says "No." The third time he says "No," he is referring to his loss of the game. They then playfully begin to tickle each other, and each advance is countered by a "No," albeit with a different inflection. Eventually, the scene escalates, with her on the floor, him on top and she screaming "No"! It is a powerful scene and plays metaphorically. It can be, but need not be, about sexual or physical abuse.

In workshopping this and "Funky Shirt," the issue of the responsibility of the receiver was highlighted. In "Tickle," the audience was asked why she didn't stop after the first tickle. The common response was "He laughed when he said it [No]." This led us quickly into how words are more ambiguous than they seem, that much of a word's meaning is in its oral expression (Burniston, 1972). During a tour in a rural community where we were informed by the community's social workers of a possible date rape, "Tickle" became the focus of the high school students. As the discussion progressed, it was evident that it had an impact on male audience members. The issue that emerged was "You need to listen carefully to all the signals being sent, and that isn't easy." It was the audience conversation, not the scene itself, that made the ultimate impact. When designing scenes, we look for ways to raise awareness and provide scenes that can be workshopped, that are "jokerable" (Chapter 2 and Chapter 15). In effect, the scenes must pose a question, not provide an answer. In the case of "Funky Shirt," we problematized clothing.

Form Analysis

Costuming

As shows were remounted with different cast members, there was an ongoing debate about clothing for the female role. Traditionally, cast members wore jeans and black T-shirts, and I, as the MC or joker, reversed with black pants and a denim shirt. On occasions a tie, hat, scarf, or the like was employed to add to the characterization, but for the most part, characters wore neutral costumes. In the case of the funky shirt, some wanted an actual shirt to make it explicit and others did not, wanting the audience to see their own imaginative shirts on the character.

On one tour, we did use a costume, at the request of the actress. In follow-up discussions we got bogged down with the details of the specific piece. From then on we reverted to costume neutral. This generated more comments from the audience, because each had their own shirt and dress code standard.

Voices Off

If the scene was traditionally staged, the two people would speak with each other and act out the scene. We chose to have one couple mime the action and another couple provide their dialogue off stage, employing what Brecht calls the "alienation effect": the invisible fourth wall through which an audience passively peers is disrupted "in such a way that the audience was hindered from simply identifying itself with the characters in the play" (1957, p. 91).

> The audience can no longer have the illusion of being the unseen spectator at an event which is really taking place. The whole elaborate European technique, which helps to conceal the fact that the scenes are so arranged that that he audience can view them easiest that way, is thereby made unnecessary. (Brecht, 1957, p. 92)

By splitting the action and the dialogue, we reminded the audience that they were watching a play. Subtly, we were asking them not to align with either character but to critically examine the situation.

As with the scenes "Pressures" and the "M-Word," there was also a pragmatic reason. Different cast members would play different scenes on different days. By having the script read, we reduced the tensions experienced with line memorization.

Dreamscape

In *The Caucasian Chalk Circle*, through the use of "The Story Teller" (narrator), Brecht creates a play within a play.

> So many words are said, so many left unsaid.
> The soldier has come.
> Where he comes from, he does not say.
> Hear what he thought and did not say: (1961, p. 550)

This technique enables the audience to see what a realistic drama cannot portray. They witness the thoughts of another, and, from that, the issues are enhanced. The dreamscape aspect of "Funky Shirt" provides a similar perspective. The boyfriend's deepest fears are made manifest through the introduction of an imaginary character, heightening the effect. We debated using a strobe light, but owing to the possibility of causing epileptic seizures, we rejected it. Regardless, the dreamscape accomplished our desired effect as the male character was transformed into a pseudonarrator with his nightmare taking place around him.

CHAPTER 7

Cattle Call

Understanding Discrimination through Shadow Screen and Video

History and Method

As was discussed, scenes sometimes went through various iterations. New cast members bring different perspectives (data), and a change of audience may require adaptations. In the case of "Cattle Call," we created two versions. The first was originally prepared for a teen wellness conference sponsored by Edmonton Community Development and the Grey Nuns Hospital. It was then remounted for a live performance at the Western Canadian Association for Student Teaching. The second version was a major rewrite for the Safe and Caring Communities video, *Respecting Diversity and Preventing Prejudice*. Both addressed the same central

theme, but the examples used were different. As usual, our research/
theater projects were driven by community need and request.

A guiding tenet of Mirror Theatre is "don't preach." A didactic
approach can turn off many audience members, so we avoid it. This tenet
was reinforced during an early tour of *What's the Fine Line?*. An eighth-
grade female approached me after the program and stated: "I thought you
were going to come here and tell us not to do drugs. Thanks for trusting us
to work things out on our own" (*paraphrased statement from recall*). Our
pedagogical constructivist orientation enables our audiences to increase
their awareness of the issues without an overt value statement on our part.

One technique used we metaphorically called "the snake swallow-
ing its own tale." As we collected data on examples of prejudice that
we either experienced or witnessed, we asked: "Are there examples of
how we, as A/R/Tors, practice systemic prejudice?" Auditioning, unaf-
fectionately known as a "cattle call" (Wisegeek, 2009), became our focus.
In casting, "the look" of an actor can, at times, be as or more important
that "talent," and although this fact is semi-accepted and understood, we
wanted to bring it into question. In both of the vignettes that follow we
hear the dialogue between two men as they decide how to cast the show.
In presenting this, we communicated to the audience our willingness to
turn the mirror on ourselves.

The two scripts below demonstrate how the medium chosen can
change the presentational style. "Cattle Call" was adapted from a live performance to a video on prejudice. For "Cattle Call" we did not believe
that the shadow screen would translate well into a video performance, so
we rewrote it as a realistic scene. Again we discussed various "criteria" to
determine who would be in the cast. Once the cast was listed, an actor
and I improvised the scene. Near the end of the scene, I added a twist and
asked him if any homosexuals had been cast. His response was classic shock:
"Can we ask for that?" The improvisation enabled us to bring voice to our
collected data and explore its complexities. It eventually ended with our
research questions "What are legitimate selection criteria? What can we ask
for?" Again, the responses would be in the discussions with our audiences.

Script A

From *Shadows*—Commissioned by the Edmonton Community Development and Grey Nuns Hospital—and from *One of These Things Is Not Like the Others*—Commissioned by the Western Canadian Conference on Student Teaching

Note that the letters at the beginning of the alphabet denote female
roles and those at the end, male characters.

An overhead or stage light is turned on with the following definition of "discrimination" projected on a screen:

> Discrimination: The organism's ability to respond
> selectively to stimuli.

(*Voices are heard from behind the audience.*)

Y: So how many people do we need for the show?

Z: Four more. We've got four and need eight. We have six more lined up and ready to go.

Y: Well then, let's get started.

Z: Okay people, you know the drill. Face front, then the side, then front again. On our cue.

Y: Well, let's get started. #1 Please.

A: (*medium-sized, standard posture*)

Z: eeeeyuh . . . Not bad.

Y: 7? She's got cute hair.

A: (*she flips it*)

Z: 7? 6!

Y & Z: Yeah, 6.

Z: Next

        (*A exits downtrodden, and B enters buoyantly*)

B: (*on the heavy side*)

Z: Ohh. (*shock and disgust*)

        (*pause*)

Y: Next.

        (*B exits, gives the finger; C enters*)

C: (*skinny body/bit self-conscious*)

Z: Hmmmm, she has potential.

Y: 7? mmmm . . . 7.5.

Z: But let's see if we can get something better.

Y: Ya, check her off. Next.

D: (*strong sexual energy in a variety of poses*)

Y: Hmmm, pleasurable.

Z: 7.5?

Y: Na, 7. She could lose a few, don't you think?

Z: Yah, I guess.

Y: (*laughs*) Next.

D: (*exits*)

E: (*poor posture, slouches, can't make out body figure*)

       Can you stand up straight?

E: (*no reaction*)

Y: Give us some flair.

E: (*slight reaction*)

Y: Come on baby, let us help you.

E: (*exits without being asked*)

F: (*thin, sexually playful, hair up*)

Z: Nice, 7.5.

Y: Kind of hippy.

F: (*lets hair down*)

Y & Z: (*swoon*) 8.

F: (*starts to leave*)

Z: Thank you.

F: (*she waves*)

Y & Z: (*swoon*) aaaaahhhhhh.

Z: Well guys?

           (*Y and Z walk to the stage while talking*)

           (*A and F resume shadow on curtain during this conversation with a variety of poses*)

Y: Is that it?

Z: Afraid so.

Y: Oh.

Z: Well, there's always tomorrow.

blackout

Script B

From *Respecting Diversity and Preventing Prejudice*—Commissioned by Safe and Caring Communities

Two members of a drama troupe are discussing casting for a new video on "Prejudice." The table is full of files. Large pile is rejections, and a small set is acceptances.

Y is at the table with a coffee cup, and Z is returning with some files from the filing cabinet.

Y: So, how many more résumés do we have to go though?

Z: Only seven more.

Y: Great. Let's make sure these last few make the cast representative. After all, our play is about prejudice.

Z: OK. I've got a suggestion. Rather than just the accept and reject piles, let's make a third for possibilities.

      (*puts the pile between him and* Y)

Y: (*takes the first one and opens it*) Fine. How about Jane?

Z: She's hot! We need at least one attractive person to sell the show.

Y: Too bad she's such a snob.

Z: We can work through it.

Y: We'll put her aside to negotiate.

Z: But she's so pleasing to the eye.

Y: (*putting the file to one side*) Later.

Z: (*picking up the second one and immediately putting it into the accept*) But the Dean's son has to be a must.

Y: It's either him or we can kiss the funding good-bye. (*both nod*)

Z: Neeext.

Y: (*picking up the third*) Next up is Mark.

Z: Is he auditioning again?

Y: Yup. He's a great team player, but he's no actor.

Z: Yeah, but he's such a hard worker, and he's always on time. Not like Steve and Sean. He's a great example.

Y: But he's no actor.

Z: He also comes up with some great scene ideas.

Y: Well, let's put this one with Jane and come back after we've looked at the rest.

Z: (*taking the fourth from the pile*) Okay, next up is Mike.

Y: He's the ugly representative, isn't he?

Z: Don't know. I'll take a look at his picture. (*looking*) No, he's the fat guy.

Y: I think we're talking about the same guy. (*takes file from Z*). Yes, one and the same.

Z: (*takes the file putting it into the accept*) He's a good representation.

Y: Yeh, but don't you think that he's a little tooooo representative?

Z: (*laughs*) Let's look for someone a little less "representative." (*replaces folder in the reject pile*) Who's next?

Y: (*taking the fifth folder*) The East Indian.

Z: What's his name?

Y: It doesn't matter, 'cause the guy can't act.

Z: But he's East Indian. We need some representation.

Y: Is he the only East Indian?

Z: So far.

Y: OK, he's in! (*places file in acceptance pile and looks at the sixth one*) Sue.

Z: If she wants in, That's great!

Y: I knew you were going to say that, but she's never at rehearsals, and she's not a team player.

Z: But she's one of the best actors in the city.

Y: But she often brings the morale of the rest of the cast down.

Z: She will look great on screen. (*Y give Z the stare*) OK, let's put
     her into the maybes, and if we can't find anyone else, we'll put
     her in.

Y: Who's next?

Z: (*taking the seventh folder*) Tom Blades, and we need older
     people for the casting scene.

Y: But do you think he'll fit in with our young cast?

Z: He has the experience and the acting smarts.

Y: That's the problem. Older people can come in believing they
     know it all and get bossy. They don't make good team players.

Z: (*pleading*) Let's try him on probation. Lots of maybes.

Y: Yup, Let's call it a day and finish up tomorrow.

Z: Great by me.

Y: Wait a second. You know, I just realized we don't have any
     homosexuals.

Z: Can we ask for THAT?!!

Content Analysis

Body Image

Shadows was written at the request of Edmonton Community Development to examine body-image issues. Originally it was meant and devised
for a female audience; however, after its design, we found a number of
males in the audience who "tagged along" at the request of their teachers. The dynamic changed with males present. The performance contained a number of relevant scenes from *What's the Fine Line?*, and a few
more were written on the topic. Many dealt with concepts of identity,
with a tension between the internal persona and external expectations,
including the "gaze" of others. Through rehearsals we found that an

awareness of "being watched" is a common phenomenon. We found that Orwell's *1984* (1992) was more real than fictional. The realization that people made decisions based on opinions of others was an insight uncovered by our research.

In the shadow screen version, we articulated the male gaze and how different women perform under that gaze. There were definable physical characteristics that the female A/R/Tors could not readily change but could accentuate with the help of the screen, such as sticking out their chest or behind. There were also personality aspects over which one could have some control. Some shadows showed a sheepish female, and others a flamboyant one. In our discussions about attractiveness, we went beyond the physical to the presence of an individual. Character F had an aura that added to the overall look. We came to understand that body image, in part, is a matter of attitude.

Collectively, the six females represent a wide range of characteristics with overlaps in each. Character A is of average build but has personality. Character C may be considered close to the ideal but lacks confidence. We raise the questions "What is attractiveness?" and "Who decides?"

The Male Gaze

Is beauty in the eye of the beholder? Is it a construction of the mind (Hume, 1987)? Shelton and McDermott (2007) explore the sociological aspects of how they were informally taught their beliefs around beauty. The shadow screen version of "Cattle Call" raises this issue explicitly. In another scene of *Shadows*, a woman decides what to wear. The audience hears her inner dialogue, but the onus is completely on her. In "Cattle Call," the male responsibility is made evident. Although the context is a socially contracted one, owing to the expected nature of auditions, the phenomenon of the impact of clothing on public and personal perception extends well beyond this situation. The male fantasy is made explicit, making males complicit in the construction of the female identity.

Culler's (1982) point that women can read themselves only through the eyes of the male, and Baudrillard's (2001) concept of simulacra, in which the map or concept defines the reality, are made evident in this scene. The male gaze is an act of definition and could be considered a form of systemic violence. The ethical questions "How do men define *woman*?" and "Is it right?" are raised in this scene. In the vignette "Campfire," in *One of These Things . . .* , characters are gathered around a fire and singing songs. Each song is quickly rejected because of its lack of political correctness. A female character stops the singing of "Calendar Girl," (Greenfield and Sedaka, 1961), claiming that it promotes voyeurism, making explicit that the male gaze is apparent in popular culture. The rating of women is also made evident, using the 10-point standard perpetuated by the movie *10* (Edwards, 1979).

Discrimination and Selection Criteria

The video vignette extends the body image issue by asking "How do we define one another?" Here issues of race, talent, size, sexual orientation, and collegiality are added to beauty, addressing the question "In what ways do we judge people?" The definition of discrimination in the first version is benign and value free. The scenes make it evident that discrimination and selection are not as neutral as they appear. Having two characters debate an individual's characteristics demonstrates that the choice and emphasis of certain criteria is a subjective act. If each individual alone chose the cast, the assortment of players would have been different. The scene metaphorically questions all forms of assessment and selection.

Form Analysis

Shadow Screen

Unlike the "M-Word," in which the shadow screen was used metaphorically to portray the shadow of guilt, the screen in "Cattle Call" had very different purposes. Here we wanted to protect the vulnerability of the actresses. In rehearsal, we attempted but failed in articulating the "beauty" of another. Labeling our colleagues was too close to home. In addition, we believed that having each auditioning character completely visible to audience members would be awkward. We wanted to make the judging of others explicit without a direct reference to any person. The shadow screen provided the distance we required.

Also, with the screen, the actors could easily accentuate characteristics through padding and body positioning; the tone of the scene was maintained sans the embarrassment. Later, in *Shadows*, we had a birthing scene that also used the shadow screen. The impression was given without needless nudity or the silliness of playing it with clothes on. A shadow screen can bring focus to necessary detail without the distraction of extraneous detail.

Playing within the Audience

The first version of "Cattle Call" could have been played easily with the male actors on stage. However, we wished to "make the spectator adopt an attitude of inquiry and criticism in his [*sic*] approach to the incident" (Brecht, 1957, p. 136). By breaking the illusion of the invisible fourth wall through which the audience peered, we reminded them that they, like those doing the casting, were watching the scene unfold. This reminder is necessary, because it foreshadows the second part of our program, where the fourth wall is completely dismantled when we invite audience participation through a version of forum theater (Boal, 1979). Here the audience actively engages in rewriting the scenes in search of more ethical stances. Having the actors behind the audience produces an alienation effect (Brecht, 1957) that partially prepares the audience for this experience.

Change of Audience and Form

Although both scenes examine the act of casting and the decisions made, they differ greatly owing to the different audiences and the medium employed—similar to the situation in which a quantitative researcher who designs questions for particular clients and determines whether descriptive, co-relational, or inferential statistics will be used. A sense of audience and medium is present in all research. The juxtaposition of the two scenes described above is provided to demonstrate how the sense of audience and medium to be used influence the research design. Richardson (1990) claims that all research is a form of narrative in which researchers choose a method to construct their stories. In order to best tell its story, Playbuilding configures the data based on its viewers and the medium.

For "Cattle Call" in *Shadows*, we devised a performance/workshop on body image to present to a live female audience. The screen was a dynamic visual occupying a large portion of center stage. When the backlight came on, the images captured the audience's attention. We decided to remount it for the video format, but based on an archival videotape of the WestCAST performance of "Letters to the Editor" in *One of These Things Is Not Like the Others; One of These Things Just Doesn't Belong* (Norris and Mirror Theatre, 1998a), we knew that a direct translation to video would not work. The live-performance version of the scene "Letters to the Editor" used a shadow screen with actors gathered around it reading scripts based on letters to an editor, but the video appeared flat. For the scene's video version in *Respecting Diversity and Preventing Prejudice* (Norris and Mirror Theatre, 1998a), which did employ a shadow screen to portray a nondescript ballerina, we heightened the style and superimposed a number of faces to surround the screen as they commented on a ballet instructor's decision. Such a surrealistic style worked in this case, but the disruption of the fourth wall in the video would be lost in the case of "Cattle Call," because the actors were not behind the audience. The medium dictated another form, and we went with a realistic scene. Film is much more static, with no direct actor/audience contact. Each vignette in the video (Norris and Mirror Theatre, 1999a) is followed by a set of questions left for the viewers to discuss, which moves toward audience participation sans actors.

Although the theme remained intact in the video, the concrete examples shifted as appropriate to our intended viewers. The issues included in each piece were focused for our targeted audience. As with qualitative research, selected representative pieces of data were chosen to support the articulated theme. We used our sense of audience to assist us in our selection.

Photo 7.1 • Shadow screen with quote collage.

CHAPTER 8

I Expect

Understanding the Politics of Student Teaching through Voice Collage

History and Method

After the success of *Mirror Mirror* at the 1994 Faculty of Education's (University of Alberta) Equality and Respect event, Anne Marie Decore, Assistant Dean (Admissions) in the Faculty of Education at the University of Alberta, approached me with a request to focus a performance on the politics of the student teaching experience. Our plan was to create an instructional video in front of a live audience and record both the performance and our discussion with the audience. Faculty would use this video with their student teachers as a catalyst to discuss nonteaching issues relating to student teaching. (I am aware of one instructor who still uses it with his Bachelor of Education students.) It was remounted with a slightly different cast as a keynote at the 1996 conference of the Western Canadian Association for Student Teaching, and we also created a sequel that we wrote with their audience at a closing event.

In the spring of 1994, I invited the cast members of *Mirror Mirror*, former students, and faculty members to join the student-teaching project and asked them to invite others. One member, owing to work commitments, could not attend the video shoot. He was, however, pleased to be part of the writing team. Our overarching question was "What are the relationship issues that are experienced by student teachers, cooperating teachers, and faculty consultants?" In forming an answer, the students represented themselves, and I used my experience both as cooperating teacher and faculty consultant. This was early in Mirror Theatre's formation (prior to our achieving not-for-profit status), and over time we sought the assistance of others within the groups that were being researched.

I was conscious from the beginning that I did not want this project to be a complaint session on the student-teaching experience and made it clear that various perspectives had to be presented. In the scenes "The Visitor" and "Pass the Baby," we portrayed ways in which both student teachers and cooperating teachers misuse their power. We were willing to turn the mirror on ourselves.

In our discussions, two issues merged that led to the creation of the scenes that eventually also became the title of our performance, *Great Expectations.* First, we found that all three groups had expectations about what the student-teaching experience should be like. Second, we discovered that all felt caught in the middle between the other two, often with conflicting messages. We wanted to demonstrate the potential tyranny that expectations can have on others. The following scene, "I Expect" contained three subsections, with a different role in the middle (student teacher, cooperating teacher, and faculty consultant) between the other roles. In this case, rather than scattering the three subsections throughout the play, as was the case with the "O" scenes (Chapter 5), we presented these three subsections sequentially, which communicated that we were looking at the issue from the perspectives of these three major groups.

The script is a series of sound bites about, or voice collage of, expectations that each group has of the others. Like "Pressures" (Chapter 4), one representative character is sculpted while the others speak. Unlike "Pressures," in *What's the Fine Line?* here we use direct address to the audience rather than to the character. In each scene, actors in black carry the character on stage, and a variety of cooperating teachers, student teachers, and faculty consultants sculpt that character. We wanted to portray that even *within* the groups there were differences of opinion. A composite representation would tend to create a meta-narrative, a perspective that we wished to avoid.

To distinguish the three roles, we informed the audience at the beginning of the performance that those dressed in blue sweatshirts were cooperating teachers, those in red, faculty consultants, and those in the metaphorical green, the student teachers. This simple costuming decision cut down on exposition time, enabling the audience to know who was who.

Script

From *Great Expectations*—Commissioned by University of Alberta, Faculty of Education

Note that the letters at the beginning of the alphabet denote female roles and those at the end, male characters.

SCENE 1: THE STUDENT TEACHER   (*Z and Y carry on A as if she were a mannequin and set her up in a standing position. Enter B, who walks around A and inspects her.*)

B: As a cooperating teacher, I expect my student teacher to be professional. (*B raises A's right hand into a pointing position*)

(*enter X*)

X: (*puts one arm around A's shoulders and puts her left arm around his waist*) As a cooperating teacher, I expect my student teacher to be one of the staff.

B: I expect mine to take the first step. (*B moves A's right foot forward*)

X: I'm looking for a wife. (*X kneels beside A and takes her left hand in his*)

B: I'm expecting my student teacher to dress formally. (*B twists A's body and adjusts her clothes*)

X: I expect my student teacher to dress informally, to get along with the class. (*X straightens A's shirt*)

B: I expect student teachers to keep a journal and share their emergent insights about teaching.

X: I don't expect that. I don't have the time for that type of discussion.

B: I expect my student teacher to incorporate lots of material, so I can learn. (*B raises A's left arm, opens right palm up*)

(*enter C*)

C: As a faculty consultant, I expect my student teacher to act as a professional. (*C brings A into aligned position, with arms behind her back*)

(*enter D*)

D: As a faculty consultant, I expect my student teacher to have a binder in which all lessons are organized. (*D puts A's left arms forward, palm facing up*)

B: I expect my student teacher to be enthusiastic. (*B sculpts smile on A's face, hands behind back, leaning forward*)

C: I expect my student teacher to admit her mistakes. (*C straightens A, puts right hand on heart*)

D: As a faculty consultant, I expect a student teacher to be able to discuss his emergent insights into teaching. (*D twists A's body to left and stretches out right arms*)

X: As the cooperating teacher, I expect the student teacher to treat me and the entire class with respect. (*X puts both of A's arms outstretched forward*)

D: As a faculty consultant, I expect my student teacher to treat me as a judge and not as a teacher. (*D twists A's body forward*)

B: I expect mine to party with me. (*B steps into circle of A's left arm*)

C: I expect mine to see me as a teacher and not as a judge. (*C pulls A toward her side*)

(*Throughout the following section, each actor pulls on A as if in a tug of war as they say their lines.*)

D: To be enthusiastic.

B: To be happy.

X: To take everything seriously.

C: To ask questions.

B: To be exceptional.

(*All freeze for a five count, then exit.*)

SCENE 2: THE COOPERATING TEACHER   (*Z and Y carry on E as if she were a mannequin and set her up in a standing position. Enter, F who walks around E and inspects her.*)

F: As a student teacher, I expect my cooperating teacher to like me. (*F puts E's arm around her shoulders*)

W: As a student teacher, I expect my cooperating teacher to act like a professional and know that I am just learning. (*W pulls E's right arm forward*)

F: As a student teacher, I expect my cooperating teacher to take the first step. (*F pulls E's left leg forward*)

W: I expect my cooperating teacher to give me lots of resources to work with. (*W raises both of E's arms*)

F: I want my cooperating teacher to always treat me like a professional and not ever to talk down to me. (*F pulls E's legs together and puts her arms behind her back*)

W: I expect my cooperating teacher to give me a good friendly environment in which to work in. (*W raises E's right arm*)

F: I want my cooperating teacher to give me lots of resources. (*F pulls both of E's arms down to her sides*)

W: I expect my cooperating teacher to provide me with lots of feedback so I can learn. (*W pulls both of E's arms forward.*)

F: I don't want my cooperating teacher to give me any feedback. (*F pulls both of E's arms down to her sides and turns her to face toward F*)

C: As a faculty consultant, I expect a cooperating teacher to treat me as an equal. (*stands facing E*)

D: As a faculty consultant, I expect a cooperating teacher to see me as someone with a legitimate point of view. (*D raises E's right arm*)

F: I want a cooperating teacher who will give me a good report. (*F pulls E's arms down and sculpts smile on her face*)

C: I expect a cooperating teacher to make me feel welcome. (*C turns E toward her and shakes her hand*)

W: I would just like some good feedback, so I can learn. (*W pulls both of E's arms forward*)

F: I don't want any feedback at all. I just want her to give me the chance to learn on my own. (*F pulls E's arms down*)

D: I want the cooperating teacher to take time for me. (*D raises E's left arm*)

ALL: I expect . . . (*they all attempt to twist E into a position*)

SCENE 3: THE FACULTY CONSULTANT (*Z and Y carry on V as if he were a mannequin and set him up in a standing position. Enter B, who walks around A and inspects him.*)

F: As a student teacher, I expect a faculty consultant to treat me as a professional, knowing that I am just learning. (*F puts V's arms behind his back*)

W: As a student teacher, I expect my faculty consultant to have
       been my professor at the university. (*W puts V's left arm over
       his shoulder*)

F: I expect my faculty consultant, NOT to have been my profes-
       sor at the university. (*F puts V's arms behind his back*)

W: Well, as a student teacher, I expect my faculty consultant to
       have a strong background in my teaching major. (*W raises V's
       right arm*)

F: Well, I expect my faculty consultant to have recent experi-
       ence. (*F twists V's body to the left*)

X: I expect the faculty consultant to meet with me regularly to
       discuss the student teacher's progress. (*X shakes V's hand*)

B: No, no, no. As a cooperating teacher, I don't expect this. I'm
       too busy. (*B breaks the handshake*)

W: I expect my faculty consultant to visit me often. (*W shakes V's
       hand*)

F: I expect my faculty consultant to visit me often, but at my
       convenience. (*F takes V's right hand in her left*)

B: I expect the faculty advisor not to judge me. (*B stands on V's
       right side*)

X: Or my classroom. (*X puts V's left hand over his face*)

ALL: I expect . . . (*they all attempt to twist V into a position as they
       repeat some of their lines*)

X: I expect the faculty consultant to back ME up if there are
       problems.

ALL: I expect the faculty consultant to back ME up if there are
       problems.

Content Analysis

Meta-Narrative and Thesis/Antithesis

As mentioned above, we cast each subsection of the scene with multiple
characters. If the focus was on the student teacher expectations, there
would be two cooperating teachers and two faculty consultants, and so
on. Our choice was data driven. In our conversations we found that there
was a wide range of opinions with individuals in all groups. Students
who had more that one student teaching experience reported that each
cooperating teacher had different expectations that positively or negatively affected their relationship. I, as one who visited many schools as a
faculty consultant, affirmed their perception, which could be considered
a form of triangulation (Schwandt, 1997), adding that different faculty
colleagues informally voiced their views on student-teacher supervision.

The multiple voices prevented the establishment of a meta-narrative that would have been established with a single voice. There are many perspectives on what a positive student teaching experience is—much of it is informal and implicit. This scene articulated some of the unspoken issues. It also demonstrated that there are conflicting opinions within each group. Thesis and antithesis on various issues were sought and presented; different opinions on appropriate clothing and the keeping of a journal were but two examples.

Additional Expectations

Expectations can and do extend beyond the formal. Such things as participation in the "library club" (the Friday afternoon social) or looking for a wife/partner can and do occur. During one of my visits to a school, a teacher approached me and requested a student teacher for the next semester. She asked if there were any good-looking eligible men, because she was looking for a husband. In our production, this situation was changed to looking for a wife. Partying, the degree of extracurricular involvement, cigarette and coffee breaks, and partnering were considered to be essential but nonteaching aspects of a positive relationship between teacher and student teacher.

Negotiation of Relationship

I have shown this vignette on student teaching to my student teachers prior to their field experience, encouraging them to initiate a discussion with their other two contacts. While the major emphasis is on success with students, over the years I found that often existing difficulties originate in the relationships among the people in these three capacities. There are differences in styles that can be interpreted as inadequacies, and judgments can easily be formed and perpetuated when expectations are not made clear and negotiated. Creating a space for conversation can contribute to a more positive experience for all.

Rivalries

Although differences in opinion were articulated within each group, the intragroup differences were not explored in the performance. The scene was lengthy as it stood, and although it raised potential areas of miscommunication, such as the tension between theory and practice and the differing degrees of reflection and planning expectations, the variety of philosophies of classroom management data, such as "Forget everything you learned on campus" and "Now you are in the real world," were not represented. Not all data could be performed. The theme of a person in one role feeling caught between the possible rivalries of the other two roles was our major focus.

Evaluation

Although not explicit in this scene, evaluation was an additional theme that was further developed later in the play. It is an ever-present issue that must be addressed. Each party informally assesses the others, but the student teacher has the most to lose. Not meeting the expectations of others can lead to a negative report that can potentially affect career possibilities. Although all are caught in the middle, the student teacher is the most vulnerable.

Form Analysis

Sculpting/Silence

In "Pressures," in *What's the Fine Line?* (Chapter 4), the sculpted characters were eventually given voice. This was not the case in the scene "I Expect," because the character in the middle merely had expectations thrust on him or her, with no opportunity to respond. We decided on this form because many expectations are not articulated, even by those who have them. Usually they are made manifest when a crisis is reached, and this often too late. The silence represents the lack of communication and the potential oppressiveness of the opinions of others.

Voice Collage

"I Expect" is primarily a voice collage set in action. We collected an assortment of expectations, sequenced them, and presented them while sculpting the character. They could have been easily read in a Reader's Theatre format, as in "Pressures" (Chapter 4); however, the sculpting action makes the scene far more dynamic. We layered a voice collage over mime and created a metaphorical scene that did not use standard dialogue. This enabled us to present a great amount of information in a relatively short period of time.

Representative Costumes

Impressionist costumes that convey a message quickly work well in this genre. If we make a slight alteration to a neutral costume (Chapter 6), the audience can quickly know who the character represents. The colored sweatshirts enabled us to easily distinguish the roles that the actors were playing as they entered the stage. With vignettes, economy is essential, because there is no time for long, drawn-out character development. A construction hat, scarf, clipboard, stethoscope, gloves, hammer, or bandage can send an efficient and effective message to the audience.

Sequence

We had a choice to present all three subsections of "I Expect" together or to intersperse them. As mentioned above, we wanted our audience to know that we would be giving voice to multiple points of view. With the scene "Dares" (Chapter 10), the three subsections of the vignette were scattered throughout the play, creating an echo effect that built in intensity. The "O" scene (mentioned above) was performed both ways. The sequencing of similar vignettes and/or their subsections varied based on our theatrical and pedagogical intents. With "I Expect," which was the first scene of *Great Expectations*, our multiple perspective message was vital. This determined our choice of sequence.

Scene Changes

The carrying of the sculpted actors on stage also enhanced the theme: these characters had no control over the expectations that surrounded them. It also facilitated efficient scene changes. Rather than using a blackout and having the actor appear in the light or walk to the spot and freezing, both of which were possible, the carrying of actors, like set pieces, showed their reification in a manner that the other two theatrical devices would not have. Even the type of scene change can have analytical data embedded.

CHAPTER 9

The Party

Understanding Status, Power, and Bullying through Gibberish and Body Language

History and Method

Mirror Theatre had a longstanding relationship with Expecting Respect (ER), a peer education program sponsored by a number of Edmonton's social service agencies, and "The Party" was initially written for our performance/workshop, *Under Construction*. This was the first time that I offered a course on the Playbuilding process, and, after discussions with my students, we agreed to devise a program for ER as part of their course work. It was an opportunity for students to experience the entire process from start to finish within a course setting, and this type of community outreach could be considered a service-learning component. Although *What's the Fine Line?* was a tight show, I resisted a remount, because my students would not have a lived-experience of devising. *Under Construction* was a composite of old and recently devised scenes, and "The Party" was generated in the class.

"The Party" grew from conversations regarding the misuse of power. Often, the extremes of bullying are examined, leaving the audience identifying with the victim. We wanted to change the approach, demonstrating how everyday people can and do mistreat others. Unlike Boal's "Theatre of the Oppressed" (1979), in which participants articulate the oppression in their lives, we asked: "How do we unconsciously oppress others?" Our work was "theatre of the oppressor"; we asked participants to look at themselves in the mirror and determine their uses, misuses, and abuses of power.

Our introduction to *Respecting Diversity and Preventing Prejudice*, a video later produced for a Safe and Caring Communities video (Norris and Mirror Theatre, 1999a), encapsulates our intent:

> Theatre acts like a mirror, reflecting back at us glimpses of our lives. Its purpose is to help us stop, think, and examine our actions. When we look into a mirror we make sight adjustments. We straighten a tie, brush our hair or beard, and generally check out our appearance so that our public image resembles how we would like to be seen. The purpose of this video is to act like a mirror. The vignettes you are about to see depict many examples of prejudice. The easy part is to recognize prejudice in others. The more difficult and challenging is to recognize it in ourselves. When we do, change is possible, as we move from awareness to making adjustments. We invite you to look into the mirror.

We ask a lot from our audiences. We challenge them not to define their oppressors but to examine how they may oppress others. When one identifies with the oppressed, one blames a person who is not present, and thus change is not readily available. When one identifies with the oppressor, one can change one's behaviors. After a performance/workshop in northern Alberta, I was approached by a student who voluntarily stated: "I didn't realize I was bully until I saw your play." She confirmed our approach.

In devising "The Party" we asked ourselves: "In what ways do people misuse their power?" "Status" was one of our responses. We broke this down into a pecking order that included ageism, prestige, friendships, and homophobia. Using this break-down, we created a party scene based on our knowledge of some of the ways that misuse is made manifest. Performance style was another consideration, and we chose to perform the scene in gibberish and mime. One adage of the theater is "You can tell who the king is in the crowd by the way the others behave toward him." We used this concept to assist in the scene's construction.

Script

From Under Construction—Commissioned by Expecting Respect

Unlike in most scripts, there are no lines for this scene; all dialogue takes place in gibberish. It is scripted into essential emotional sections that actors call "beats." Usually actors interpret the character's subtext from the script, but here the interpretation is reversed: the subtext is provided to guide the vocal inflections of the gibberish. The interpretation, however, is never set in stone; different actors can and do improvise their own interpretations around the theme. The general tone of the scene is what is important. All actions given below are meant to function more as tone indicators, rather than as blocking (movement instructions).

The characters enter a few at a time to give the audience time to get to know them. In keeping with Brecht's alienation effect, the lighting person says "Ding Dong" to announce his or her arrival. This reminds the audience that this is a staged event.

Note that the letters at the beginning of the alphabet denote female roles and those at the end, male characters.

Cast
A   Hostess
B   Big Sister/Roommate
C   Friend
D   Uninvited Female (Tramp)
W   Friend's Little Brother
X   Popular Male
Y   Gay

1. A is hosting a party and feels that she is prepared. She haphazardly places imaginary things on a real table and sits down and puts her feet up with a sense of accomplishment. She is upbeat, and we can see her positive energy.
2. B enters, looks around, and is clearly not impressed. In her opinion, the room is not ready. A in gibberish asks her proudly, what do you think? B responds in a disgusted, bossy tone. A tidies up, and B sits relaxed and quite contented. (Both A and B could be considered abusing their power, albeit differently.)
3. (*door bell rings*) A sits there, and B stops what she is doing and answers the door. She gives A a disgusted look.
4. C and W enter, and there is a friendly exchange between B and C. A leaps to her feet and C gives her a hug. (They are obviously close friends.) A pulls C to the side and asks about W, who tries to

talk to B, who ignores him. C instructs W to sit on the sofa, which he does.

5. C goes on at length about why she brought W. A questions, but accepts. They head to the snack table. W tries to join the conversation. A ignores him and continues to chat with C. B also tries to enter the conversation, gives up, and continues the preparations. C instructs W to go back and sit down. Dejected, he follows her suggestion.

6. (*door bell*) B answers, and D enters with confidence. B is confused, reticent but polite. D says hi to A then C. D is ignored and goes for refreshments. She doesn't care about their lack of acceptance of her.

7. B pulls A to the side, asking who invited D. (It is clear that D is a brazen party crasher and perhaps a bit loose.)

8. W approaches D, who gives him the quick brush off. She heads to A, B, and C, interrupts and initiates a conversation. A, B, and C are taken aback but comply. A and C wander off, leaving B trapped.

9. (*door bell*) B, relieved, escapes D and heads to the door. D's reaction is favorably strong, and the entire party freezes and looks at the door. X enters, and from everyone's reaction we know that he is the "Big Man on Campus," and he plays it.

10. A goes to him, obviously interested. X is friendly but continues to greet his subjects. He casually chats with B. W rises to greet X but is ignored. X then chats with C. D waits seductively at the refreshment table, then approaches him, inviting him for a drink, as if it were her party. X follows.

11. A, B, and C huddle and discuss D's behavior. A is angry and ready for a fight. B and C try to calm her down. She is about to proceed when the doorbell rings. B and C convince her to answer it.

12. Y enters (*flamboyant, effeminate, possibly gay*). A is delighted to see him. They kiss and flirt, playfully taunting each other.

13. Y then begins to work the room. He says hello to B and C. Tries to say hello to W, who will have no contact with Y. Not put off, Y goes to D and X, who are deep in conversation. D gives a friendly hello, while X, too, has nothing to do with him.

14. Now fuming and ready to feud, A storms to D. She starts to stare D down.

Lights: blackout.

Content Analysis

Audience Participation

This scene was sometimes immediately followed by an audience participation session before we proceeded with the rest of the scenes. Breaking the vignette sequence enabled us to remind the audience that we wanted them to be critically involved. First we asked them "Who's who?" based on body language, tone of voice, the way the characters were treated, and how others treated them. We then asked the audience to create a status line based on their observations. Total agreement was not achieved, because different audience members focused on different aspects of the characters' behaviors to determine status. Illustrating the ability to "read" status was our pedagogical intent. At times, we also invited the audience to enter into forum theatre (Boal, 1979) and make suggestions about how the characters could improve their behavior toward one another. Audience input was integral to the content of this scene.

Alienation

The alienation of others can take many overt and covert forms, and they were articulated both in rehearsals and presented in the scene. When a person is ignored, she often feels excluded and alienated. Ignoring a person may be intentional, as in the case of the big sister, or unintentional, as in the case of the Big Man on Campus. We would define the intentional case as an abuse of power and the unintentional one as a misuse. Still, the effect was the same. The little brother felt alone in a crowd. The implicit question was "How can our acts of exclusion be considered a form of abuse of power?" The vignette "Birthday Party" in *Fair Play Rulz* problematizes exclusion through a discussion of whom to invite to a party. Being left out can hurt. "The Party" and "Birthday Party" make alienation explicit.

Being Talked About

Twice in "The Party" we witness how individuals are bullied even though they are not immediately present. The little brother is discussed by A and C. He is aware that the conversation may be about him and is hurt. A, B, and C discuss D, the party crasher, but she seems not to care; although in their mind her status is lower than theirs, in her mind, she has higher status. Their opinions don't matter. The two examples deliberately show contrast: the concept of "being talked about" can have different effects based on the senders' intentions and the receivers' receptions.

What's the Fine Line? ends with the scene "Rumors." Actors are in a straight line across the stage, and the character on stage right whispers to the next person in line, who reacts and passes it on, and so forth. The audience does not hear the conversation, but each character makes large gestures and sounds loud enough for the audience to hear but soft enough that the words cannot be distinguished. The second-to-last person in line turns to the last person and says, "Hey, you should hear the rumor that's going around about you," making it clear that the last person is the one being talked about. These scenes make explicit that a person can be bullied while absent.

Homophobia

Although society's attitudes regarding sexual orientation are changing, homophobia still exists; some people put lesbian, bisexual, gay, or transgendered individuals low on their status list. Because the scene is short, we chose to use overt gestures to convey sexual orientation with the recognition that such behavior is not representative of everyone. We exposed the stereotype and discussed it in the follow-up conversation. We also made the character's signals ambiguous. Flamboyance may not always be a sign of sexual orientation. The issue is why flamboyance or sexual orientation should matter. Implicitly, we ask the audience members to examine their own status lists and the criteria used to form them, sexual orientation being one criterion.

Ageism

During our many visits to schools, the issue of ageism was brought up by students and discussed in our rehearsals. A major pecking order in schools is systemic. The senior grade has the highest status, and the lower grades have sequentially lower status. Audience members easily pick up that the male is younger than his female sibling. Age can be an inappropriate exclusionary criterion, especially in the early years. It may even trump gender, as made explicit in this scene.

Power in Relationships

The vignette opens with a power struggle. Each roommate has her own criteria, and they are in conflict. There is no negotiation, only a battle of insistence and resistance in their attempt to define the space. It is a metaphor for many conflicts. Owing to interruptions, the friction doesn't escalate, but we are certain that it will continue. Implicitly, we ask: "What would be a healthier and happier roommate relationship?"—and this question has been discussed with audiences. In their responses they, not the actors, are defining what they consider appropriate and inappropriate.

Jokerability

The rationale for the selection of scenes for inclusion is not solely about content. Although we wish to raise our audiences' awareness about the issues/themes, we also want to be able to engage them in meaning-ful discussions. This scene is one that we can say is easily "jokerable" (Chapter 15), in that there is enough dysfunction, conflict, and misuses/abuses of power that could be rescripted with help from the audience. The status line is an easy structure to joker, because it initiates low-level engagement. As the conversation develops, opportunities emerge to move to forum theater, wherein audience members either redirect the scene or go on stage and try to enact it themselves. Content is sought that not only raises awareness but that also can be shaped into scenes that invite audience engagement.

Form Analysis

Gibberish

Obviously, this scene could be scripted with real dialogue. Many could use the preceding outline to generate words to be spoken. Although gibber-ish does cut down on memorization time, especially when casts continu-ally change, time saving was a byproduct, not our intent. Dialogue would readily tell who the metaphorical king was. We wanted to *show* it instead and trusted in our audiences' abilities to discern it. In addition, the high energy of gibberish and the challenge to understand it usually increases audience attention. It is good to employ after a hard-hitting scene, because it brings levity to the ethos. (We used music, another nonverbal tool, for changing the mood after powerful testimonials in *What's the Fine Line?*) The sequencing of scenes is important to the overall structure, and a scene with gibberish can be used to dramatically change the tone.

Deprivation of one sensory input forces one to rely more on other senses, attending to their details. By taking away language, we invite the audience to focus on other elements. In depicting status, we believed the interaction to be more important than what could be said, so we removed the extraneous pieces to create a pithy scene. This approach is similar to that of a qualitative researcher who judiciously edits a transcript, selecting only that which is necessary.

Exposition/Entrances

As characters make their entrances for the first time, it is important for the audience to get a general idea of who they are. This exposition, as it is referred to in the theater, could be done through a costume, a prop that accompanies a pre-established character (police hat or stethoscope), a formal introduction by another character ("This is my older brother, Tom"), or through a number of other theatrical devices. With traditional theater, audiences can get to know the characters over time. However, this is not possible with vignettes, because most scenes run three to five minutes in their entirety. Clear exposition is vital in order for the audience to understand each scene.

For this scene, the entrance at the door must be clear. To assist the audience, all other action stops, and all characters look at the door. This tells the spectators where to focus. Once entered, the characters must define themselves quickly. In *Great Expectations* (Chapter 8) the actors begin with "As a student teacher, I . . . ," making his/her role clear. Since no words are used in "The Party," clarity must be provided through body actions and the way in which characters in the room respond to those entering. Careful timing is a must so that the audience can pick up people's attitudes toward one another. Once these are known, the scene can progress. In traditional qualitative research, participants' backgrounds are often given before data on the topic is provided. Exposition focuses in the same manner.

Doorbell/Alienation Effect

Mirror Theatre's drama style lives between realistic and impressionistic. Too much realism can prevent the alienation effect (Brecht, 1957). A real doorbell sound provided through sound effect would present a different message than one made with the voice. We chose the voice, not out of expedience but to reinforce that the scene is manufactured, similar to having signs drop from the ceiling in *The Threepenny Opera* (Brecht, 2005) to indicate themes. Audience laughter at the sound was an indication that the "ding dong" was effective.

CHAPTER 10

Dares

Understanding Risk Taking through Variations of a Theme

History and Method

In Mirror Theatre's early history, we avoided the topic of substance abuse, because it was overexposed. Schools were inundated with guest speakers and performances addressing this topic, so instead we focused on the then less-covered topic of bullying. Using a formal assessment of the Expecting Respect (ER) peer education program, we determined that the students wanted more emphasis on drugs and alcohol. I brought the information to that year's Theory and Practice of Drama/Theatre in Education class, and we agreed that this would be our topic. *What's the Use?* was the title of this collection of vignettes.

An earlier program, sponsored by the Alberta Alcohol and Drug Abuse Commission in the Drayton Valley area, focused extensively on risk taking. The community requesting that program asked us to explore this topic because of increased teen deaths involving snowmobiles. Using the concept of edgeworks (Lyng, 1990), whereby individuals enjoy the rush of risky behaviors, we developed scenes that focused on risks and consequences. I brought this concept up with the cast of *What's the Use?*, and "Dares" was created. Since consequences can vary, three scenes were devised, progressively, with escalation of the consequence. Our question was "When does the consequence outweigh the fun?"

Later, the Alberta Alcohol and Drug Abuse Commission and the Canadian Brewer's Association commissioned us to devise a show on under-age drinking. We created a number of new scenes in the tour of *Last Call, Your Call* and included "Dares," because we concluded that a combined set of reasons for early alcohol consumption was peer pressure coupled with the element of the risk from breaking a taboo.

Script

From *What's the Use?*—Commissioned by Expecting Respect—and From *Last Call, Your Call*—Commissioned by Alberta Alcohol and Drug Abuse Commission and the Canadian Brewer's Association

DARE #1   Note: Gender is not important, although a mixed cast is preferred.

(As lights fade in, all are in slouched positions in a straight line facing the audience.)

ALL: We're bored. There's nothing to do in (*name the location performing in*).

A: I have an idea. I've got a game to play.

ALL: What's the game . . . It better be good . . .

A: It's good. It's called "dare." I have five flavored jellybeans in my hand. They're gourmet jellybeans!!! Each one is a different flavor. They are cherry, strawberry, popcorn, watermelon, and vomit!!!

ALL: (*group reacts with groans to vomit*)

A: So, who wants to play? (*waits for group reaction*) Come on guys, it's only jellybeans.

ALL: Okay. (*agree to play except E; all look at E*)

E: (*hesitantly*) Okay, but I'll throw up if I get vomit.

A: (*to B*) Okay, you start. (*holds out hand with jellybeans; B takes one and puts in mouth*)

B: MMMMMM, it's watermelon.

ALL: (*everyone reacts; A moves down the line to C*)

A: Your turn. (*holds out hand with jellybeans; B takes one and puts in mouth*)

C: MMMMMMMMMM, it's cherry.

ALL: (*everyone reacts; A moves down the line to D; D is hesitant to take a jellybean*)

A: Come on . . . there's still three left. It's only jellybeans. (*D takes a jellybean*)

D: (*relieved*) Popcorn!

A: (*group reacts*) Told you! (*moves down the line to E*) Your turn.

ALL: (*look and laugh at E*)

C: (*chuckles*) Only two left, strawberry and vomit.

A: Odds are fifty-fifty.

D: Ask yourself, "Do you feel lucky?"

E: (*E is hesitant to take a jellybean; finally takes one, and it is the vomit jellybean; rushes off stage as if to puke*)

Lights: blackout.

DARE #2

(*As lights fade in, all are in slouched positions in a straight line facing the audience.*)

ALL: We're still bored.

A: I have another idea. I've got a better game to play.

ALL: (*sit up immediately with rapt attention*)

B: Another game?

C: Is it better than the last one?

E: I hope so.

A: It's even better. I have three 20-dollar bills in my pocket that I'll share with most of you. So here's the game, I have a number in my head between 1 and 5, if you don't guess it, I'll give you get $20. If you do guess the number, I get to slap you across the face.

ALL: (*group reacts*)

A: So who wants to play? (*waits for group reaction*) Come on guys; it's free money.

ALL: (*agree to play except E*)

E: Do I have to?

A: No.

B: Chicken.

ALL: Cluck, Cluck.

E: Alright, It's only a slap.

A: (*to B*) Okay you start. (*poised to slap*)

B: 5?

A: No (*hands B a 20-dollar bill*)

ALL: (*everyone reacts; A moves down the line to C*)
A: (*looks at C*)
C: 1?
A: No. (*hands C a twenty-dollar bill*)
A: (*looks at D*) Ready?
D: 6?
ALL: (*laugh*)
A: (*seriously*) I said, "1 to 5!"
D: I know, just kidding! 3?
A: No. (*hands D a 20-dollar bill*)
ALL: (*everyone reacts; A moves down the line to C*)
A: (*looks at E*) Two numbers left.
E: Why do I have to be last?
D: Fifty-fifty chance for $20.
C: Or a slap in the face.
E: (*hesitates*)
ALL: (*all other players urge/tease E on*) Go E. Go E. Cluck, cluck.
E: (trying to convince self) It's only a slap in the face. It's not that bad.
A: 2 or 4?
E: 4?
A: (*slaps E across the face; this is done as stage fighting with a slapstick*)

Lights: blackout.

DARE #3

ALL: We're bored again.
A: I have another idea. This is the best game ever!
E: Not another one! I don't like you're games.
ALL: (*laugh and give E a hard time*)
C: Don't be a sore loser.
D: It can't be that bad.
A: Alright; here's the game. I have five shooters. Four are Baja Rosa, and one is poison.
B: You've got to be kidding right?
C: You wouldn't do that to your friends?
A: Come on guys, it's free booze! Baja Rosa.
E: I'm not playing. (*exits; everyone reacts to E leaving the game*)
A: (*takes a shooter away*)
ALL: (*agree to play*)
D: (*to B*) Okay, you start.

B: (*B is a little hesitant but takes the shooter, feigns poison, then smiles*) Baja Rosa.

A: (*to X*) Three shooters left.

C: I don't know if I like this game.

B: It's okay. I bet they're all Baja Rosa.

C: (*C takes a shooter*) Baja Rosa!

A: (*to D*) You're the last one, and only two shooters left. Now you get the fifty-fifty chance.

D: It's not fair, because E left!

ALL: (*mixed reactions, some urge, some caution*)

C: (*reaches for a shooter*)

Lights: fade to black.

Content Analysis

Degree of Risk

In keeping with our belief that thesis and antithesis should be presented, we did not want to present a scene in which risk taking was critiqued. As the scene suggests, without a sense of adventure, life can be boring. Risk is a natural part of life. We play games, participate in sports, and make financial and business decisions that involve a degree of risk, and it is sometimes the risk than makes the decision exciting. What the scene brings into focus is the consequences. In cast discussions we have asked "Where is decision making taught? How do we teach our young to weigh out the potential harm before taking action?" Such actions could include drug and alcohol use, gambling, and speeding in a snowmobile or a car. We concluded that there are few venues wherein our youth can discuss risky behaviors. Flinders and colleagues (1986) examine curriculum bias based on what isn't taught, the null curriculum. This scene addressed the null curriculum by role-playing situations in which risk is involved.

Edgework

Lyng's (1990) pioneering work on "edgework" examines the incongruence between a society that strives to reduce risk while many of its members seek out high-risk activities. He claims that the consequence is secondary to the experience: "some people place a higher value on the experience of risk than they do on achieving the final end" (p. 852). He claims that the need for arousal and the reduction of tension are two factors than may contribute to voluntary risk taking and that personality predispositions and intrinsic motivation can create a proclivity to situations in which risk is involved. Involvement in extreme sports, gambling, and crime are three areas where risk taking is manifested. Ignoring the motivating factors could produce a plausible scene, whether it is performed metaphorically or realistically. Edgework provides insights into what appears to be destructive behaviors. We ask "Why do people take risks?" And "Can they meet these needs in safe ways?"

Boredom

Related to edgework is boredom. The scene's opening line, "We're bored. There's nothing to do . . ." is an empirical one. Students, especially in rural communities, have told us repeatedly that they would welcome productive outlets for their energies rather than turning to some less "savory" activities. Lack of access to recreation was a factor that they claimed led them elsewhere, and they publicly requested that their community provide them with some structured play. A.S. Neill's criticism of schooling is that it starts at the neck and works up (Miller, 1966). He is an advocate of holistic education, whereby the heart (emotions) and the body are connected with the head. Our youth seem to be saying the same thing. Many are asking for opportunities in which they can feel fully alive.

Photo 10.1 • I'm bored. There's nothing to do in . . .

Localize

By saying "We're bored. There's nothing to do in (*name the commu-nity*)," we make the play personal. It breaks the fourth wall and tells the audience that the actors are very much aware of where they are. Our aim is to connect with our audiences, and every time we performed the scene, its opening line generated laughter. The audience is told that we believe the play is about them and their quest to create some excitement. Whenever a particular, such as a street, store, or school name, can be used, we localize it, with the belief that it helps the audience to identify with the characters and the issues in the scene.

Popular Culture

Bringing in popular culture is similar to naming the community as we let our audiences know that we have some understanding of who they are. In the dance scene in *What's the Fine Line?*, each year we replaced the music with an up-to-date piece. A way to quickly alienate an audience (but not in the Brechtian sense!) is to have them perceive that you are not in tune to their situation. Relevance is a factor. In the first dare, we referenced a variety of flavors that were available at the time, including vomit. This informed the audience that we were aware of their popular culture, which also assisted us in connecting with the audience.

The content of the three subscenes has tangential research imbedded in them with the wider lived-experience of our audiences is imbedded into them. Expressions of the day, sports events, currently playing movies, and so on all help to create scenes that are detailed to the year and to geography.

Form Analysis

SEQUENCE (THROUGH-STORY) AND REPETITION   Unlike in *Great Expectations* (Chapter 8), in which three variations were performed in direct sequence, the preferred method for this variation of three scenes was to scatter them throughout the play, *What's the Use?*. They became a through-story. Although the play mostly remained a collage of vignettes, this sequence provided some stability of character, allowing us to play variations of a theme. The repetition factor also played a role. Having all the A/R/Tors slouched in a similar position at the opening of each scene provided a quick exposition (Chapter 9) for the second and third variations of the scene. The audience knew immediately what was up, reducing their work.

Although the concept of dares was repetitive, they differed in the degree of risk. By having three variations, we were able to demonstrate a variety of perspectives. In the video, *Respecting Diversity and Preventing Prejudice* (Norris and Mirror Theatre, 1999a), we had a scene in a cafeteria entered by a young woman. One time, all the people sitting at three tables reject her; another time, two tables fight over her; yet another time, she is defiant and makes her own space; and in still another, she scans the room and exits, giving up. By performing many variations, we break the metanarrative of one perspective; we see many possibilities that place some responsibility on both those at the tables and the young woman. With "Dares," audiences at first witness compliance to peer pressure and later defiance due to the consequence. This provides a balance of thesis and antithesis that a single scene could not.

In "Dares," our question as researchers and pedagogues is "What degree of risk are you willing to take?" Three scenes, interspersed throughout the play, *What's the Use?*, ask this question. Repetition and variation of a scene can provide fuller, more diverse perspectives on the topic.

Stage Fighting/Slapstick

Stage fighting (Hobbs, 1995; Suddeth, 1996) is a precision art. It takes a long while to rehearse, with safety at its core. In the second vignette, a slap was used as the consequence, and the actors practiced the slap to make it realistic. The "victim" would turn his/her head as the perpetrator's hand passed by. To heighten the effect, we employed a slapstick to create a loud sound. First used in commedia dell'arte (Rudlin and Crick, 2001), a slapstick is two slats of wood fastened by a spring. As it is swung back, the slats separate; as it is brought forward, they connect with a loud snap. Actors would feign hitting each other with these on stage, hence the root of slapstick comedy.

In our scene, an A/R/Tor stood off stage or at the back of the audience watching the action, timing the sound with the associated action. With practice, the sound matched the movement, as the A/R/Tor on the stage held the back swing momentarily to signal the sound effect. The vignette dramatically ended with sound and a blackout.

CHAPTER 11

Are You Really Listening?

Understanding Prejudice through Inner Dialogue

History and Method

Around the time of Mirror Theatre's creation, Alberta Education and the Alberta Teachers' Association collaborated on a program called Safe and Caring Schools. *What's the Fine Line?* was a keynote at their initial conference, and we performed vignettes at some of their subsequent workshops and conferences. Later, they produced a series of five videos on Safe and Caring Communities. Their intent was to make a number of issues known to adults who worked with school-age children. The adage "It takes a village to raise a child" was part of their rationale to expand their work, and they wanted material that could be used with bus drivers, lunch supervisors, coaches outside the school system, youth workers, law enforcement personnel, tutors, outdoor program directors, and others who had direct relationships with children and youth. We were awarded the contracts to create the last three parts of the series, *Respecting Diversity and Preventing Prejudice* (Norris and Mirror Theatre, 1999a), *Dealing with Bullying* (Norris and Mirror Theatre, 2000a), and *Resolving Conflict Peacefully* (Norris and Mirror Theatre, 2001a). The videos were to be used as a catalyst for discussion with adults who worked with children.

We listened to the needs of Safe and Caring Schools, adapted scenes from *What's the Fine Line?* and *Coulda/Shoulda,* and researched and wrote new scenes for each of the videos. "Are You Really Listening?" is one of the vignettes that was written especially for this program and the medium. Devising scenes for a video production was initially a challenge, because film has its own syntaxes, different from those of the theater. However, as rehearsals progressed, we found that some ideas could be more easily presented in the video format. McLuhan (1967) claims that there is an intricate relationship between content and the medium that is used to convey it. The written word accompanied by photos is different from text without pictures. Video is very different from theater: the use of close-ups, panning, and zooming, for example, replaces what the human eye may do with a live performance. We found that, over time, we needed to adjust our thinking to write for video. The new form also enabled us to think about the content differently.

Rehearsals began with the cast members brainstorming the types of prejudice of which they were aware. We asked: "What are examples of prejudice that we have either experienced or witnessed?" The list grew throughout the process as the cast members became more sensitized to the topic, permitting us to generate data from both internal and external sources. During one rehearsal, a former student of mine who had participated in an earlier Safe and Caring Communities video heard of our production and brought a friend to a rehearsal. Her friend told us a story in which her white friend shoplifted, but she, a Cree, was the one arrested. We often found that data came to us, rather than via the systematic approach of traditional research. We were given permission to adapt this story for the video, and it became the scene "Who's the Shoplifter?"

In our discussions, we found that many prejudices, because of political correctness or other reasons, remained implicit, unspoken. In confidence, we examined some of our own personal ones, asking "In what ways do we harbor prejudicial thoughts?" Looking at the jokes we told and or laughed at was a useful data source. Our "quickies" list grew, and we devised the scene "Are You Really Listening?" and the scene "The Party of Bigots" as composites of inner prejudices. A parent/teacher meeting was chosen as the context for "Are You Really Listening?" because it could include adults from a community. A seemingly benign topic, fundraising for a school trip, was chosen, and the conversation was interrupted with voice-overs in which the characters revealed their thoughts about one another. Such thoughts articulated both positive and negative class, gender, nationality, and ability biases. Close-ups of the characters were presented while their thoughts about the other people were heard with echoes. The video medium enabled us to make explicit the implicit prejudices that surround us and are imbedded in us.

Script

From Respecting Diversity and Preventing Prejudice—Commissioned by The Society for Safe and Caring Communities (Alberta)

Cast:

- A   Female Parent (President of PTA)
- B   Female Parent (stutters)
- X   Black Man, immigrant from Africa, speaks with a thick accent
- Y   Black man (lawyer)
- Z   Stay-at-home dad or gay male with children

(*Close up of blackboard. Written in chalk: "PTA meeting tonight. 7:00 p.m."*)

(*Slow zoom out. As A speaks, we see X seated on the left, then B sitting, then Y and Z sitting as A walks to center of the screen.*)

A: Hi everybody. I see that we are all on time, great. I came in earlier and set everything up, and I put pens on the table so we could all write things down. (*sits and passes pens around*)

A: I thought I had enough for everybody?
(*Y holds a pen up*)

A: Oh, you already got one. Great. (*close up of A*)

A: Today we have a lot to talk about. Let's see. Okay, first thing we have is the grade nine band trip. We have to raise money. Okay, so we need some fund-raising ideas. (*close up of B*)

B: (*stuttering*) Wha, wha, wha, what are . . .

A: (*interrupting*) The dates? May 17, 18, and 19, and they are going to Vancouver. Okay, so we need some ideas. Anybody have any?
(*short pause*)

A: Okay, I well have one. I was thinking that we could sell whipped cream pies for a dollar and then throw them in teachers' faces. My little Suzie . . .
(*close up of Y; we hear his thoughts with a slight echo*)

Y: Oh, course she has to go first. (*sarcastically*) She's the happy homemaker. This is her big outing for the month. She couldn't make it in the real world, so she gets her thrills from running this group. Why doesn't she just go back to the kitchen and let us come up with the good ideas.
(*close-up of A*)

A: So, anyway, that was my little idea, and I definitely think that we can make tons and tons of money.
(*close-up of B; we hear her thoughts with a slight echo*)

B: Thank god we have an articulate woman on board. She's nicely grounded in the reality of the kids, not like these jerks from the business community. I can trust her and her ideas.

A: So, anyways, I think that that would be a fabulous idea, a dollar a plate. That would sell tons. So number one (*writing down*), whipped cream pies. Any other ideas?
(*a hand crosses the camera, and it turns and zooms in on Z for a close-up*)

Y: We'll I have an idea.

A: Sean.

Z: Last year's bake sale, my carrot cake sold out in twenty minutes flat. (*proudly*) And if I remember correctly, we made a ton of money.
(*close-up of A; we hear her thoughts with a slight echo*)

A: I am sure his ids are all mixed up and his ideas are so gay (*realizes what she has thought, laughs, and repeats*), gay.
(*close-up of X; we hear his thoughts with a slight echo*)

X: Sure, we made money from it, but what a wussy plan. No way would you find me baking. He might like acting like a woman, but not me.
(*close-up of Z*)

Z: And that's why I think a bake sale's a definite must.
(*close-up of A*)

A: Okay, noted. Any other ideas?

X: Oh yeah. (*close-up of X*)

X: I have an excellent idea. I once did a walk-a-thon, and I'll tell you for every ten minutes that we walked our sponsors . . .
(*close-up of B; we hear her thoughts with a slight echo*)

B: Get to the point already. He always goes on and on searching for the right ideas. If he wants to be a Canadian citizen, he should speak like a Canadian.
(*close-up of Z; we hear his thoughts with a slight echo*)

Z: Here he goes again, smile and nod, smile and nod.

X: So a walk-a-thon would be great.
(*close-up of A*)

A: A walk-a-thon, great. (*writes it down*) Okay. How about you Diane, any ideas?
(*close-up of B*)

B: I, I, I was th, th think . . .
(*close-up of Y; we hear his thoughts with a slight echo*)

Y: No wonder she's on welfare. (*disgusted laugh*)
(*close-up of X; we hear his thoughts with a slight echo*)

X: Why doesn't she speak more eloquently? Doesn't she know how much she is inconveniencing us? She certainly doesn't deserve to be on this committee.
(*close-up of B*)

B: C, C, Carwash.
(*close-up of A*)

A: Carwash, great. Okay, anything else? Steve?

Y: Okay, a partner at my firm headed a casino for his son and raised a ton of cash.
(*close-up of A; we hear her thoughts with a slight echo*)

A: Thank god for the lawyers, they always have such wonderful ideas.
(*close-up of Z; we hear his thoughts with a slight echo*)

Z: Lawyers are the workhorses of society. They get on the highway of life and crap all over it.
(*close-up of X; we hear his thoughts with a slight echo*)

Z: He's so smart. We should accept his idea.
(*close-up of B; we hear her thoughts with a slight echo*)

B: He's so bossy and a snob. He thinks he owns the world.
(*close-up of A; we hear her thoughts with a slight echo*)

A: Thank god for the lawyers, they always have . . .
(*two-second close-ups of Y, Z, B, Y, Z, B, X, and A as we hear overlaps of everyone's thoughts*)

Content Analysis

Although racial prejudice was still a major issue, we chose to look at the subtler forms of prejudice that may go undetected. In the vignette "The Party of Bigots," we connected a large number of "quickies" into a collage of phrases that demonstrated prejudicial attitudes. These included "time of the month," "Nazi" (when talking about a German sports team), "gay" (as a put-down), and "gyp" and "Jew" when referring to the small amount of potato chips in a bag. They were provided to raise awareness about prejudicial comments. The collage-of-phrases format is effective in quickly portraying the range of a phenomenon. We used the collage technique in our production *Mirror Mirror*, and one audience member approached me a few days later claiming that her family had a major dinner table discussion about many of the prejudicial comments, recognizing certain phrases that they had used and made a commitment to stop them. *Are You Really Listening?* uses such a format for witnessing how people judge one another based on class, gender, and other factors.

Class/Socioeconomic Status/Employment

Lawyers, teachers, unemployed people, immigrants, and those on welfare are the groups represented by the characters. Although additional characters could have been used, and genders could have been reversed, these choices represent some of the more widely recognized classes in North American society and the varying attitudes toward them. One female character aligns with business and gives extra credence to a comment from a successful lawyer, while others disregard the lawyer's opinion owing to his profession and personality. The scene portrays both positive and negative opinions as one person's thesis is rebutted, albeit internally. As in the vignette "The Party" (Chapter 9), there is a status line that each person holds. We ask: "How can a group effectively function when undercurrents of class prejudice remain unspoken and unchallenged?"

Stuttering/Bullying/(Dis)Ability

Having a stuttering character was deliberate. Langevin, Bortnick, Hammer, and Wiebe (1998) discuss the negative attitudes toward those who stutter, and this example of prejudice was included to demonstrate the wide range of examples of its occurrence. We also included accents as another aspect of speech and how we form opinions based on how another person talks. To demonstrate these problems, we have two individuals who are alienated by each other's speech reject each other. In our discussions, we found that victims of prejudice are not exempt from their own prejudicial behavior, and we made this explicit through these two individuals. In this case, after a performance an audience member commented on her work with the problems of stuttering and bullying, leading us to further research. Our readings of research and conversations with audiences were important data sources.

Wait Time

Tannen (1990) claims that people from different regions have different wait times when it comes to conversational dialogue. Those with longer wait times may perceive those with shorter ones as interrupters, and those with shorter ones may believe that those with longer ones are not engaged.

Having the president of the PTA not waiting before giving her own idea had Tannen's research as its empirical source. We can form negative opinions about others owing to our regional and/or cultural differences.

Bashing Others

Imagine if the name of a particular ethnic group were substituted for "teachers'" when a person suggested "throwing pies into teachers' faces." There would be a public outrage. Yet teacher bashing is acceptable. Their stereotypical portrayals can be found in popular culture, from literature to television and movies. "Lawyers are the work horses of society" was adapted from *Megatrends* (Naisbitt, 1982), in which lawyers were negatively compared to beavers. We discussed how groups and occupations are portrayed and asked why some forms of bashing were more acceptable than others.

Speaking for Others

Although it was not prejudicial, we also included another example of bullying. Speaking for and volunteering others can be an act of bullying. The one who volunteers a person takes away the voice of that person, placing him/her in an awkward situation not of her/his choosing. The suggestion of pies in teachers' faces has a bullying element to it as well as a person outside of their representative group volunteered them. As is evident within "Are You Really Listening?" many of Mirror Theatre's scenes have numerous layers of issues imbedded.

Form Analysis

Inner Dialogue/Echo

In the movie *Yentl* (Streisand, 1983), Barbra Streisand's character sings her thoughts. This convention quickly enables the audience to distinguish articulated thoughts and unspoken thoughts. We employed the echo to achieve the same result. After its first use, our audience would know the convention and its purpose. While filming, we had close-ups of each character with a range of facial expressions while his/her "thoughts" were read to him/her. All the characters then audio recorded their lines, and the soundtrack was a linked to their visuals. In this way, we were able to communicate who was thinking what.

Adaptation to the Stage

As discussed in Chapters 4 and 7, inner dialogue provides insights into the character that may be missed if only spoken words are used. The echo in the video simplified this. On stage,, we would employ different devices. We would have a second actor, dressed in black, stand behind each of the characters. When a character's thoughts were to be presented, we would have the character freeze and the actor behind place his/her hand on the counterpart's shoulder and speak. Then the action would resume. Although many variations are possible, inner dialogue need not be thought of solely as a film device. With different techniques, it can be staged.

Metaphor

Are You Really Listening? transcends the content that it portrays. It acts as a metaphor for all occasions when one person judges another. We invite our audiences to ask: "How do I read extraneous data into what a person says or does?" The ending is "hyper real," showing the noise that goes on unheard but that is present at meetings. Although the scene's ending is an exaggeration of the phenomenon, a comment from my brother-in-law after watching the vignette supports the use of the metaphor, or caricature, in our representation of data. He claimed that this scene was the "most real" of the scenes in the video. For him, the embellishment through the echoes of many voices simultaneously, did not detract from the truth of the lived-experience but instead made it explicit by drawing focus to the noise of inner dialogues.

Photo 11.1 • Inner dialogue of a meeting.

CHAPTER 12

Who's with Whom?

Understanding Prejudice through Mime

History and Method

"Who's with Whom?" was another vignette written for *Respecting Diversity and Preventing Prejudice* (Norris and Mirror Theatre, 1999a) (Chapter 11). We explored our own direct and indirect experiences with prejudice by telling stories of events that we had encountered or witnessed. We discussed the issues imbedded in our stories and explored how they suggested potential scenes, as was typical with our process. Once we had generated a critical mass of ideas that were written on recipe cards and sorted (Chapter 2), we broke into small groups to devise a few scenes. "Who's with Whom?" came from a story of mine.

The vignette's empirical root was a comment from my daughter's junior high school Asian friend, who told my daughter that they couldn't hang out in high school, because she would be expected to be present in the Asian corridor of the school. This was a high school that publicly boasted that there was no prejudice within its walls. In our discussions, we problematized the concept of community, comparing it with cliques and gangs. In an earlier tour, one cast member mentioned that whenever we form a circle, we have our backs to others, articulating how nonmembers might perceive a tight community.

What's the Fine Line? (Norris, 1999) has a scene, "The New Kid at School," that demonstrates how a stranger may be treated or mistreated. The story is a compilation of examples of bullying that happen when a student moves from a rural to an urban school and was partially based on a story told to us by a junior high school student. We reviewed the issues presented in this scene; however, we concluded that the new-kid story didn't provide a broad enough perspective, because the new kid was portrayed only as a victim. To round out our new scene, which takes place in a cafeteria, we asked "What are the responsibilities of the community?" and added "What are the responsibilities of the individual?" We created and performed four different endings to our new scene that addressed both of these questions.

As with "The Party" (Chapter 9), words were not necessary to tell the story. New people can size up a group quickly and determine who may or may not be accessible. Since the data was more visual than verbal we chose mime as our form of presentation. We had a diverse cast for this production and could easily have shown differences among people based on race and gender, but we chose to make them more universal. The differently colored sweatshirts, used years earlier in *Great Expectations* (Chapter 8), would readily portray the similarities and the differences of the characters who are making exclusionary/inclusionary practices explicit. By using these, we optimized the scene's generalizability through metaphor of color. In this way, audience members could read their own specific examples into the story without resorting to the ethnic or gender-specific variables of individual cast members. The costume brought focus to the metaphor.

Script

From *Respecting Diversity and Preventing Prejudice*—Commissioned by The Society for Safe and Caring Schools and Communities (Alberta)

Cast (by colored sweatshirt, A, B, C are female; T, U, V, W, X, Y, Z are males)

There is a door at up stage right and three circular tables arranged in the room in front of the door. One is center; one is down left; and one is down right. The scene is a lunch room/cafeteria.

Red	Green	Blue	Assorted
T	W	A	C
V	Z	U	
B		X	
Y			

1. **T** enters wearing a red sweatshirt and sits at the down right table and opens lunch bag.
2. **U** enters wearing a blue sweatshirt. He scans the room and sits at the down left table and unscrews bottle cap.
3. **V** enters wearing a red sweatshirt, nods to T, who nods back. V taps T on the shoulder and sits. V opens lunch bag and begins to chat with T.
4. **W** enters wearing a green sweatshirt and carrying notepaper; assesses the room and chooses the vacant center table. He begins to write.
5. **X** enters wearing a blue sweatshirt, sees U, and quickly heads to him. It is obvious that he knows his place. They chat as he sits.
6. **A** enters wearing a blue sweatshirt, assesses the room, and crosses to V (in red). He acknowledges her, but X and U call her over. (The actors playing both A and V are of East Indian descent. Although as characters they affirm their identity, the convention of another identity, that is, the colored sweatshirts, takes precedent.) A joins U and X but exhibits tension over leaving V. She then falls into a natural conversation with U and X.
7. **Y** enters wearing a red sweatshirt and sits at the closest table, center. He begins to open his lunch bag, taking out an apple, but he eventually notices that everyone is staring at him. He slowly realizes his error and gets up and moves to the table with T and V.
8. **B**, wearing a red sweatshirt, and **Z**, wearing a green sweatshirt, enter together chatting. They scan the room, each realizing her/his place, say goodbye and join their colors.
9. **C** enters wearing a blue/green sweatshirt. (This is a composite sweatshirt stitched from one-half of a blue and one-half of a green sweatshirt cut diagonally.)

Ending Option A: They don't see her. She scans the room, sees no place for her, and exits.

Ending Option B: She goes to her half-color green and is ignored; then to her half-color blue, and they push their trays in her way, communicating rejection. She goes to reds. Y shakes his head rejecting her. She sits on the floor making her own space.

Ending Option C: She stands between the green and the blue tables. A tug of war follows, each table pulling at their color side of the sweatshirt.

Ending Option D: She enters wearing a pink sweatshirt, scans the room, and exits.

Content Analysis

Friends/Communities/Cliques/Gangs

Communities are problematic in that they celebrate both inclusion and exclusion. People typically identify with some but not others. Staff rooms can have the jock table and the bridge groups, and school corridors can be divided by race or other interests. Some communities are passively exclusive and could be considered cliques, whereas the more overt groups may be called gangs. To a large extent, identity is referenced in relation to others—to those who are similar and to those who are different—and we often associate with those with whom we have things in common. This is natural and could be considered healthy; however, there are implicit rules at play that could be forms of systemic violence. Articulating them may assist in more inclusive decision making.

Through the vignette we ask "What are appropriate/inappropriate reasons to include/exclude others? What implicit rules dictate who can associate with whom? How do we (should we) treat an outlier? What can an outlier do to be included?" Prejudice and bullying are both underpinned by a sense of indifference to those who don't belong. The vignette challenges the rigidity of a community's boundaries, in search of more permeable boarders that may accommodate those on its margins.

Group cohesiveness can also be negative for its members. Norris (1989) discusses how a grade-eleven class working on a Collective Creation (Berry and Reinbold, 1984) or a Playbuilding project (Bray, 1991; Weigler, 2002) was stalled owing to an unwritten rule of "working only with friends." The teacher/director brought this situation to the students' attention, and the class negotiated an explicit rule of not working solely with their friends. The explicit rule freed them from the implicit one, and they were happy to be more inclusive.

External Influences/Internal Responses

As mentioned above, an earlier scene, "The New Kid at School," placed the character in the role of a victim. For this scene, in keeping with our intent to explore both thesis and antithesis, we chose to focus on both external factors and internal responses, since both contribute to the situation. Early in the scene, a male in a red shirt unknowingly sits at the wrong table. Everyone in the room, including the person at the table, indicates disapproval by stares. He gives in and moves to the "appropriate" table. Had the person at the table been friendly, he may have stayed, but given the existing circumstances, he chose not to. His choice, however, rested between external pressure and internal need. A natural group did exist, and he changed tables.

The East Indian female had two apparent affiliations, race and the color of her shirt. Since she was the first female to enter, joining her gender group was not an option. She acknowledged her other possible community, but because of peer pressure, she eventually chose to go elsewhere.

For the female in the blue-green sweatshirt, a natural affiliation does not readily exist. She can partially identify with the green and tries, then with the blues. Feeling excluded, she tries the less obvious reds. In defiance she sits on the floor. Unlike the first entrance by this actor, when she assessed the room and left, the second time she creates a space of her own. After the four variations have been presented, it is clear that external influences are mediated by internal responses.

The Exotic

In the third variation, the half-and-half blue-green character is fought over by two groups. In our rehearsals, we discussed how difference can be made exotic and sought. Although the outcome of this situation may be partially positive, we concluded that the making of a difference into something exotic could be a reification of an individual and consequently prejudicial. The acceptance of a person's superficial difference does not empower that person to be a full community member. And fighting over the newcomer's appearance does not indicate acceptance of her as a sentient being.

Rules of the Game

Sometimes the implicit rules that community members fail to articulate, even to themselves, provide the greatest difficulty. An exercise in *The Gamesters' Handbook* (Brandes and Phillips, 1980) has a member of the group leave while those remaining create a rule for the person to guess using yes/no questions upon his/her return. It is a good activity for learning to make deductive and inductive reasoning explicit, as well showing how an implicit rule, while obvious to those in the culture, can exclude newcomers who are not aware of the rule. For the red-shirted Y, it takes awhile before he realizes that he has done something wrong. Gaining entrance into a new community can be a minefield that requires astute navigation. A student, during a tour of *What's the Fine Line?*, suggested a "welcome wagon" run by students. The question is whether or not fitting in should be the sole responsibility of the newcomer.

Form Analysis

Mime

In a general sense, mime is a form of communication through movement without the support of words. It can be classical, like the work of Marcel Marceau, or informal, whereby actors use movements alone to tell a story. In our case, we used informal mime to present examples of discrimination in a lunchroom. When devising a vignette, we looked at the essential content element and explored what dramatic forms might be best used to convey it. As discussed above, the spoken word not only was not needed but could also unnecessarily have cluttered the scene. Mime, by bringing focus to the action, made the judging of an individual by visual appearance explicit. The medium chosen was appropriate to the message (McLuhan, 1967).

Costume

Costuming was essential for the success of this scene. The sweatshirts quickly met our exposition needs by letting the audience know an important detail about those entering. The half-and-half blue-green shirt quickly conveyed a difference that would not have been as easily and quickly conveyed by other means. (As a side note, I have asked acquaintances who are color-blind whether this medium excludes them. Their feedback has informed me that they can pick up the subtle differences in hues; one individual claimed that he "could see colors better," because he perceived more nuance for each color, albeit in shades of grey.) Other costuming choices, for example, using differently shaped hats, could alleviate difficulties with color perception.

Casting

Over the years, Mirror Theatre has had a range of cast members from diverse cultural and racial backgrounds. When appropriate, we bring issues of race into our programs, but this is not always possible, owing to cast composition and availability. Although the colored shirts provided flexibility, we found it ironic that even though we had a multicultural cast with a male and a female of East Indian descent, a black man from Kenya, a black man with roots in the Caribbean, and a Cree woman, we chose not to use this diversity in this scene. The sweatshirt metaphor, with its characteristic of universality, was preferred. We did, however, have the East Indian female approach the East Indian male before being called to her blue table. We deliberately acknowledged their difference, something we could not have done with an all-white cast. Representation from a diverse set of groups can strengthen the effectiveness of the performance as well as the data generated from them.

The castings of the final four options could have gone two ways. We could have had four individuals enter, each with her/his own response or portray four responses from the same individual. Each approach would have brought a different focus to the scene. Four different actors would show how different people react. Having the same actor would show some of the options that one individual would have. We chose the latter approach, partially because of expediency; we ran out of cast members. Although others could have been contacted and used in the scene, using the same individual raised the question "What choices could one make?" Practical issues dictated an appropriate philosophical ending.

Background Music

Although not completely necessary for the scene, music did fill the empty sound space, informing the audience that there wasn't a problem with their ears or the soundtrack. A neutral piece was chosen so that the music wouldn't provide an unintended point of view.

CHAPTER 13

Whose Pencil Is It Anyway?

Understanding Conflict through Standard Dramatization and Scene Reconstruction

History and Method

Initially our shows and tours were devised for secondary-student and adult audiences, but as word spread, we were asked to create a program for elementary students. In early rehearsals, we discussed how students learn cultural mores, or "rules of the game." Such rules were not always appropriate, although they often underpinned beliefs and actions. We recalled what rules we grew up with, and these served as both a list of issues from which to build scenes and a resource for a quote collage to end the program. Our purpose was to articulate and question ingrained codes of behavior. This is the list.

Explicit	Implicit	Adult Imposed
Finders keepers, loser's weepers.	If you're picked last, you're a looser.	If you can't play together nicely, your friend will have to go home.
First come, first serve	If you read at lunch, you're a nerd.	Can't you play quietly?
Can't tag the tagger.	Healthy lunches are for losers.	That one's not safe.
Whoever smelt it dealt it.	If you're not good at gym, you're less of a man.	It's all fun and games until someone loses an eye.
Last one in is a dirty rotten egg.	Majority rules.	
Boy's fleas, girl's fleas.		
Cry baby.		
Bigger (*etc.*) is better.		

"The Birthday Pencil" took its root from the generated statements "finders keepers, loser's weepers" and "majority rules" and was originally scripted as a series of beats, allowing the actors to improvise the dialogue. Both the beat version and the text version are provided below. Again, the scene had an empirical source, but its actual content was a plausible generation. However, audience members did confirm that they had found themselves in similar situations.

Beat versions have the advantage of focusing on the essential elements, permitting the actors to take ownership of the scenes by using their own words. As they improvise their impressions of the situation based on their own personal histories, new ideas emerge and are added. The scenes change as they are made personal. With scripted versions, A/R/Tors still add their own interpretations through vocal inflections and body language. The scripted advantage is that specific generated details are not lost. For the video, shooting the scene was semiscripted, and the closing line, "majority rules," was forgotten by the A/R/Tor. The explicit statement, "majority rules," gives as an explanation to why the lunch lady gave the pencil to a particular student. After listening to the opinions of many, she deduced the "truth." This was a dimension of the scene that we wanted to include. Both scripted and improvisational scenes bring their own sets of advantages and disadvantages, the forgetting of key elements being one.

Literature on conflict resolution and bullying also informed our discussions, scene composition, and audience participation. Falikowski (1996) discusses four types of possible resolutions: win/lose, lose/lose, win/win, and lose/win (the opposite outcome of the first). We decided to play the scene as a win/lose and have the audience look for alternative possibilities. Smith and colleagues (1999) report that there exists a lot of female-to-female bullying. Using this data, we cast this scene with a female antagonist and a female protagonist.

Script A: Beat Version

From *Fair Play Rulz*—Commissioned by School Tour, Safe and Caring Schools Video, and Edmonton Fringe Festival

Cast:
> D—adult (teacher or playground/lunch supervisor)
> C—female student who lost pencil
> B—female student who found pencil
> X, Y, and A—friends of B (Gender distinction is not important.)

Beats:

B is walking behind C when pencil falls out of C's pocket.

B picks it up and puts it in her pocket.

C confronts B about the pencil and wants it back. B says no and defends herself with "finders keepers, losers weepers."

B's friends (A,Y, and X) come along to see what's going on. B says that C isn't playing by the rules and that it's not fair. They argue.

D comes to see what's going on here. C says B took her pencil. B says it's her pencil. They argue a little. D stops the arguing.

D takes the pencil and asks each one of the kids (A, B, C, X, and Y) whom the pencil belongs to.

A, B, X, and Y say it belongs to B. C says it's hers.

D hands the pencil to B.

(end)

Script: Text Version (Revised)

Cast:

    D—adult (teacher or playground/lunch supervisor)
    C—student who lost pencil
    B—student who found pencil
    X and Y—friends of B

C: (*walks by and drops pencil*)

B: (*sees pencil and picks it up*)

C: Oh, hey, B, thanks; that's my pencil. Can I have it back?

B: I just found it. You know the rules, C, finders keepers, losers weepers.

C: That's so unfair; it fell out of my pocket, like 1 second ago, and you pick it up now and think it's yours?

B: Hey, you know the rules. That's your problem.

C: Oh, come on, give it back. That's my birthday pencil.

B: I don't think so, it's mine.

(*enter X and Y*)

Y: Hi, B, what's wrong?

B: C isn't playing by the rules.

Y: What rules are those?

B: So I found the pencil, so it's mine.

C: Yeah, right, like it's yours. It fell out of my pocket, and one second later, she picks it up and now she thinks it's hers.

X: Can you prove it's yours?

C: Yeah, we can go see my friend A (*person not in scene*); she just gave it to me today for my birthday.

Y: Yeah, but you lost it (*pointing to* C), and you found it (*touching* B), so it's hers now.

X: Come on, let's go.

(*They begin to turn, and C grabs on to the pencil still in B's hand; the following three lines are said over one another, and a tug of war ensues.*)

C: It's mine.

B: No, it's mine.

X: It's not your pencil. It's B's pencil.

D: (*enters*) What's going on here?

Y: C, give it to B.

B: Let go!

(*C regains control of the pencil*)

D: What's going on here?

B: Oh, yay, now you got us in trouble with the lunch lady.

D: Okay, what's the problem?

C: She's a liar, and she stole my pencil.

X: That's not true.

B: It's my pencil.

Y: And she's not a liar or a thief.

C: They are totally ganging up on me, because they're her friends.

D: (*takes pencil*) All right, whose pencil is it?

(*following four lines are said over one another*)

C: It's my pencil.

B: No, it's mine.

Y: Give it back.

X: It's hers.

D: One at a time. C?

C: It is my special birthday pencil. I just got it today. It's not even sharpened.

D: X?

X: It's B's pencil.

D: Y?

Y: It's B's pencil.

D: B?

B: It's my pencil, and my birthday was yesterday.

C: And they are totally lying.

D: (*looks from person to person*) B (*giving the pencil to B*), Majority rules.

B: Thank you. (*exits stage right with X and Y; D exits stage left*)

C: (*looks at D exiting*) Miss D?!

Content Analysis

Conflict Resolution

Conflict resolution is no easy task, and the scene was designed to have two competing rules, ownership versus finders keepers, losers weepers. The girl who found the pencil knew that it belonged to someone else but was convinced that her rule of "finders keepers" was a superior one. Here is where the first impasse occurred. The scene highlights that two different value systems underpin the justification for ownership of the pencil;

consequently, neither she nor the girl who lost the pencil could resolve the conflict. Later, when the scene is workshopped with the audience, the underpinning value system is examined.

Mediation of conflict is also explored through the scene with the introduction of an outside party, in this case, an adult. The adult has her own value system and makes her decision based on "majority rules." From her perspective, the conflict has been resolved by the decision. In the video workshop, a distinction is made regarding solving the "situation" and solving the "conflict." If either party leaves feeling slighted, the conflict has not been resolved. Lingering resentments will keep the conflict alive, festering to erupt at some later time. Reconciliation is the ultimate goal.

Changing from Win/Lose to Win/Win

There are four possible outcomes in the conflict. If the pencil was broken during the conflict or kept by the adult, the result would be lose/lose. If character A received the pencil and B did not, there is a possible win/lose result. If the reverse happened, we would have a lose/win. The goal is to have a win/win situation. This means all parties, including the mediator, need to adopt a spirit of mutuality, be willing to take the other people's needs into consideration. The scene presents

Photo 13.1 • Ownership tug of war.

the conflict; however, the teaching occurs during the workshop, where winner/loser variations are introduced, sometimes by the audience members. With audience participation, data does not remain static but evolves as all participants create meanings from the performance. With Playbuilding, the narratives are not the definitive word but aim to evoke conversations (Barone, 1990). The audience members rewrite the scene in search for the win/win result. In so doing, they teach themselves how to find it.

Types of Conflicts

This scene articulated a peer-to-peer conflict, one of many types of conflicts discussed during rehearsals. Others examined, but not performed, were superior/subordinate conflicts, wherein there is an official imbalance of power, such as registering a telephone complaint, and potential conflict with strangers in which a long-term relationship is not expected—for example, waiting in traffic, which can lead to road rage, and impatiently waiting in a check-out line. Underlying assumptions, preconceptions, and issues of status were also discussed.

Conflict-Resolution Strategies

The performed scene demonstrated an adult intervention as a strategy. In this case, a mediator was imposed rather than requested. However, the scene does convey one possible route to resolution, via a neutral outside party. Taking turns, a willingness to compromise, and letting go are other paths to resolution. In the performance of the scene *What's the Fine Line?* in the play with the same name, a conflict escalated during a workshop. The scene was reworked a number of times with audience members on stage. Eventually, the male volunteer walked off stage. He approached me as we were striking the set and told me: "Sometimes the best thing is to walk away." He communicated his awareness that sometimes winning is not worth it. A conflict can be resolved if one party abandons his/her concern about the situation. Thus the alternative of "letting go" emerged from a workshop. Audience members used the scene to create their own insights.

Types of Personalities

In designing this and other scenes, we found that short descriptors of the characters helped. Actors sometimes use animal motifs as sources of motivation, and we found a parallel in the conflict-resolution literature. Falikowski (1996) uses animals to describe five types of personalities and how they approach conflict (Competing Shark, Avoiding Turtle, Accommodating Teddy Bear, Compromising Fox, Collaborating Owl).

We have used these types in discussions and as sources for character development with actors, applying them in order to guide the approach and tone of characters' behaviors within the improvisations. The literature on bullying had informed our acting. Here, the literature guided the improvisation.

Democracy

A fundamental principle of democracy is that the majority rules. At times, elections are won and lost by narrow margins, with the voices of a large number of people being ignored. In rehearsals we asked: "Can the majority act like a gang, bullying the minority with their sense of entitlement? With victory, can the wishes of the minority be ignored?" Coloroso (2002) claims that bullies have the power to exclude, and Tardif challenges the exclusionary power of the majority: "Honourable senators, the strength of a democracy is reflected in the way it treats its minorities" (2006, p. 856). The scene grew from our brainstorming of "majority rules," with the lunch lady making her decision based on the majority. Thus the scene imbeds questions of assumed democratic practices.

Photo 13.2 • Majority rules.

Loyalty

In the scene, B's friends quickly align with her. They believe her and support her without question. The very act of forming a community is an exclusive one. Even informal memberships of circles of friends exclude many parties, and the group's membership has its privileges. B has the strength of her group and through it can indirectly exert her power. In this instance, it works. The scene questions the misuse of power that may come from a circle of friends.

Form Analysis

Realistic Scene

Unlike many of the other scenes provided, this scene is an example of the most common type, a realistic drama. It plays as a sound bite with a beginning, middle, and end, using no additional theatrical conventions. The style is a useful one but can be overused in a vignette style of performance. A variety of presentational styles is encouraged for this type of format—a repetitive style can become monotonous.

Exposition

As with all short scenes, an economic exposition is vital so that the audience members can quickly know who is who. Calling the adult "the lunch lady" rather than by name immediately tells the audience "what's up." Also, when the group of three enters, they enter from the side of the stage closest to B, gather around her and address her. It is clear where their loyalties rest. Small theatrical details convey a lot of information, and their use keep the drama flowing. Entrances, exits, and proximity, along with the spoken word, create the total effect.

Problem Plays

For all of our productions, we created vignettes with problems. Although each scene was underpinned by research, all scenes were constructed in such a way that they invited conversation. They avoided being didactic and did not preach our answers; rather, they moved toward the dialectic, inviting our audiences into the conversation. Using principles of problem-based learning (Duch, Groh, and Allen, 2001), we invited our audiences into the discussion, asking them about ways to improve the situations. Such scenes, therefore, have to be written with specific conflicts and possible directions in mind that can be taken during audience participation. An underlying question is "Can it be jokerable?" (Berezan, 2004), meaning "Are there elements that can be taken further?" These are a few questions that could extend the conflict scene with audience involvement:

- Who and where are the peacekeepers in this scene?
- What is give and take? What could A and B do to bring about peace?
- What values (rules) do the characters hold? How do these help/hinder the situation?
- What changes would you recommend for character A or B?
- What suggestions do you have for the lunch lady?
- Who won? Who lost? How could we make this a win/win situation?
- How do external forces affect conflict?

Additional scene ideas could also be planned during rehearsal to extend the exploration. A meeting with A and B with a mediator, revealing the inner thoughts of A and B, hot-seating a bystander, and presenting a future scene with A and B if the situation is not resolved are other possibilities. Usually, once the workshop gets going, audience members suggest ideas of their own. In keeping with our aim to encourage student voice, our ideas are only back-up plans, to be drawn on if and when needed/helpful.

CHAPTER 14

Distillation

Understanding Qualitative Research through Metaphorical Machines

History and Method

Although a number of Mirror Theatre's performances were commissioned for conferences, *ReSearch RePlay* was primarily written at a conference, about the conference, in order to be presented as its closing keynote. Similar to a Three Day Novel Contest, whereby authors gather to write an entire novel over a short period of time, this collective playwriting challenge took place between a Thursday night opening keynote and the Saturday afternoon closing performance. It was a risk for the organizers of the 6th annual Qualitative Health Research conference in Banff, but they were familiar enough with our work and were open to a new form of conference "assessment." We were to reflect the conference back on itself through scenes generated from the conference sessions.

Unlike most Mirror Theatre programs in which participation is open to all those interested and available, casting, in this case, was invitational. Under typical circumstances, casts had eight to ten weeks to devise a show with two to three rehearsals a week. With the shortened timeline I wanted a cast with strong creative, analytical, performance, and interpersonal skills. The abilities to collaborate and work well under pressure were paramount; the lack of these can be the "Achilles heel" of any performance. I wanted a cast that I could trust to get along, and so I invited accordingly. While not everyone had worked together, all had a positive working relationship with me, and I knew that the group dynamic would be productive.

We met a couple of times in Edmonton, Alberta, before our trip to the conference in Banff, Alberta. These meetings had a two-fold purpose. First, I wanted the cast to become acquainted with one another before our road trip. We discussed previous projects in which we were involved and our thoughts on the process. Second, I wanted them to warm up to the topic. I distributed a list of the titles of sessions, and from these we began to surmise what we might encounter. We tried generating scenes but with the lack of detail, they didn't fully develop.

Props and costume pieces had to be anticipated, so I assembled what I believed to be the essentials from my performance "tickle trunk." Assorted hats, a stethoscope, a ball of yarn, a variety of percussion and Orff instruments (1977), and other sundry items were packed in cardboard boxes. We left our portable stage lighting system behind, because the stage crew of the Eric Harvie Theatre would assist us on the Saturday. The rest we would improvise on site.

Upon arrival in Banff, I handed notebooks to the cast in which to record their thoughts and scene ideas during the conference sessions. The Edmonton rehearsals reminded us that the stories relied on details. Usually we devise a script using personal stories that are rich with "thick description" (Geertz, 1973b). In this case, we had no such experiential bank. The notes were foundational to our scenes. We went through the conference program, and cast members in groups of one or two chose sessions that were of interest. The Friday sessions were our "data-gathering" stage, and we met over lunch and supper to share our findings and bring a communal understanding of the possibilities. Quotes, buzz words, strong stories, and research issues were our foci. During the opening of the conference, delegates were informed of our process, and since the context of a conference is meant to disseminate research for others to use, no ethical permissions were required. Like researchers who integrate some of the substance of a conference presentation into their own works, we also did, albeit, theatrically. The delegates were not participants being studied. It was their research content that was incorporated into our performance.

After the sessions on Friday morning we met at lunch to share our notes. Potential scenes were noted, and emerging themes were discussed. We did the same on Friday evening, with a growing list of scene ideas and a short rehearsal of some potential ideas. These would incubate as we slept and provide the foundation for the next day's devising.

We met at the theater and rehearsed on stage as the stage crew listened in on our work. Instinctively, they began to build the set and design the lighting around us. We provided them with notes, and they obtained a scrim to act as a shadow scene for two of our scenes. A general wash of lighting was standard, with spotlights focused on certain areas. For example, the first scene opened with an off-stage narrator commenting on the devising process while the actors on stage were in groups of two spread across the stage area. Each group was in light, but darkness separated them. As they mirrored one another's actions, the narration continued. The narration alone would have been boring, but, coupled with the action, the scene metaphorically spoke of reflection, maintaining interest. After we gave the crew the tone for this scene, they aimed the lights as we rehearsed other scenes. A spiral of scene construction, notes, and simultaneous creation and then back to scene construction took place from 9 A.M. to 4 P.M., culminating with a run-through to sequence lighting cues with the scenes. The audience arrived before we were finished.

After the performance, per Mirror Theatre's style, we moved into audience participation and discussion. Audience members commented on the scenes, and we replayed a few, seeking different variations and insights. In this way, we were able to include their voices of reflection about the performance and the conference. The conference assessment then was an "envaluative" one (Kieren, 1995) that was more dialogic than top down.

Script

From *ReSearch RePlay*—Commissioned by 2000 Qualitative Health Research Conference (International Institute for Qualitative Methodology)

Note that the letters at the beginning of the alphabet denote female roles and those at the end, male characters.

    U: (*voice over microphone with blackout*) What is qualitative health research?

V: Well it's (*hesitates*) it's ahh (*pause*), hmm... Let me show you. (*lights up*)

(*Cast members are in the same positions as the blackout. They reassemble making a machine with interconnected movements. Machine sounds of blurp, woosh, and clink are heard.*)

V: (*adjusts the machine as he sings*)

> They call it the good old mountain dew.
> And them that refuse it are few.
> You may go round the bend
> But come back again
> For that good old mountain dew.
>
> My uncle Nort is sawed off and short.
> And he stands about four-foot-two.
> But he thinks he's a giant
> When he drinks him a pint
> Of that good old mountain dew.

V: (*sipping from mimed glass*) Pure essence.

W: (*stands and crosses to V*)

V: Here grandpa.

W: (*clears throat and takes a sip and spits it out*) Impurities.

E: How do you define that? (*exits*)

X: There's no truth in that. (*exits*)

D: (*crosses to V, takes glass, and sips*) Tastes fine to me.

Y: Let me try. (*takes glass*) Lacks depth.

C: (*glugs it down*) But it has texture.

V: (*beckons B, who tastes*)

B: Too raw, I like it refined.

A: (*crosses and sips*) I like it this way.

V: Me too. (*hands it back to grandpa*)

z: It's your bias. You made it.

v: I give up.

Lights: blackout.

Content Analysis

A Collage of Qualitative Research Issues

From our session notes we amassed a number of research issues that were taken from the conference sessions. In past performances we used voice collages (Chapters 4 and 8) to create an overview of issues to portray the complexity of phenomena. In this case our research question was "What is qualitative research?" and the term *distillation* provided us with a metaphorical vehicle on which to build our response. Alcohol is another product of a distillation process, and we paired that with our research. Using other qualitative research terms, we metaphorically evaluated the alcohol. In so doing, the concepts themselves (truth, point of view, texture, refined versus raw, and the bias of the researcher) were brought into question. Through metaphor, the terms were made problematic.

Essence

Some qualitative research genres seek the essence of a phenomenon or construct (Giorgi, 1997; Koch, 1995). Through saturated data they analyze or distill the information into universals with the belief that everyone has these in common. *Essence* is also a term that can be used to describe the quality of perfume of alcohol. The scene challenges the belief of commonalities and through the characters, demonstrates that it can be a matter of style. As with the arts, the concept of quality is ephemeral, and the scene metaphorically questions the very underpinnings of research in general. Grandpa represents traditional practice and rejects the novel. Others have varying opinions that lessen the power of tradition. The scene asks "Is there an essence or is it a matter of taste?"

Distillation Metaphor

Closely connected with the concept of essence is the act of distillation. The distiller or researcher makes many adjustments until the product emerges. Although much research outlines the general treatment of the data from generation through interpretation to dissemination, the specific details of the method are often vague, giving a sense that all researchers act in a similar fashion in all stages of their research. The particulars are sacrificed for economy. This scene makes explicit the artistry or bias of the researcher. As Spradley (1979) suggests, the researcher is the instrument, and the research product is influenced by the instrument used. What is distilled or edited is in the hands of the researcher. Distillation does not eliminate the impurities. In fact, alcohol is a poison and can be considered *the* impurity. What is distilled is the substance. Metaphorically, the scene makes explicit that the research act is highly influential on the product. Distillation or analysis does not produce an essence or truth. It is framed (Goffman, 1974) by the entire process.

Form Analysis

Machines

Making machines (Spolin, 1963) has been a longstanding improvisational activity in drama classrooms. Student actors create abstract or realistic ones using both gestures and sounds. The intent is to teach unison by having each part connected to the rhythm of the whole. Usually one actor begins, and the machine is added to, one part at a time. However, the process need not be linear, with the last addition being in the last place. Actors can choose where they see fit to add.

Machines act as visual and auditory metaphors, evoking and inviting interpretations of those in attendance. In a past production on student teaching (Norris and Student Company, 1991), we created dramatic teaching machines of realistic machines such as a merry-go-round, a pop machine, and an assembly line. Without giving the names, we asked our audience to observe the machines to determine how teaching was similar to the machine represented. This sparked many insightful comments for the teacher educators and the preservice students, expanding our understanding of the pedagogical dimensions in our actions.

The concept of "distilling research data" led us to the alcohol still as a machine. As distillers we fine tune by adjusting knobs and levers to achieve our product. Through the metaphor, we ask "As researchers, what adjustments do we make?" Again, we pose the question rather than providing an answer. In so doing, we aim to invite conversation rather than shut it down (Smith and Heshusius, 1986).

Casting

In keeping with the improvisational tradition, the actors did not plan how the machine would be built. Their roles were not cast; rather, during each rehearsal, an A/R/Tor began with a movement and a sound. From that the machine would grow. The only stipulation was that it would be linear, reaching across the stage to make each part visible to the audience. The role of the grandfather was predetermined as that of the A/R/Tor who retrieved a chair and sat on stage left of the emerging machine. The A/R/Tors did have their lines predetermined as they separated from the machine and tasted the "research."

Transition

A performance can lose its audience when there are long pauses between vignettes, so devising attention needs to be given to minimize the time between scenes. The opening of the play began with five groups of two students facing each other. One person from each group would move slowly, and the other followed, creating a mirror image of each other. Each group was in its own spotlight. Rather than having a narrator introduce the play, which we thought necessary, we added these mirrors to create a visual collage. Having the narrator alone would have opened the performance with a short lecture, which we did not want. The question "What is research?" was our segue. The machine was formed with each actor leaving her/his spotlighted position. The machine scene flowed naturally from the first scene, making a smooth transition.

Exposition

Because scenes are short, it is important for the audience to know quickly who each character is. Although the machine was abstract, we did want the audience to know that it was a moonshiner's still. A conversation with grandpa could quickly achieve this, but we wanted to keep him as the judge at the end of the scene. The folk song, "The Good Ole Mountain Dew," sung by the distiller hinted at what the machine might be. As the product was tasted, the machine's purpose was clarified. The simple phrase "Here grandpa" immediately told the audience that the person singing was the grandson of the man sitting at the end.

PART III

The Performance Workshop

> We need to be attentive and vigilant if we are to open texts and spaces, if we are to provoke the young to be free. (Greene, 1995, p. 121)

Denzin (2003) acknowledges the pedagogical nature of qualitative research. That given, most forms of qualitative research are didactic, with a solo narrator providing his or her story of the research, complete with the insights that the researcher has gained. Even most forms of participatory research are presented as printed text using distillations of the data that are conducted by the research team. However, researching the ways in which research can be disseminated interactively and dialogically may be the next major frontier of qualitative research.

In Part II we witnessed how the research teams collaboratively devised dramatic stories. Part III is a report of how those stories are presented to live audiences who don't merely passively receive them but become involved in co-creating new meanings for themselves and all those assembled, including the A/R/Tors. Although just one chapter in this book, it could be expanded into an entire book. It builds on the constructivist theory (Phillips, 1995), which acknowledges that the known cannot be separated from the knower (Norris, 2008c), and the curriculum theory, which encourages democratic forms of instruction/engagement (Henderson and Kesson, 2003); audience participation philosophy and practices are presented and discussed.

Working publicly with large groups of people to collaboratively and theatrically examine an issue is a little-used dissemination approach. This section discusses the philosophical approach of the group facilitator, a recommended tone, and potential techniques that assist in rigorous exploration and provide emotional and physical safety. The discussion includes personal anecdotes that demonstrate how these techniques are employed in real-life situations. But the chapter is not prescriptive; it recognizes the problematics of participatory dissemination. Although the new frontier requires much more study, not to go there will keep the field of qualitative research entrenched in didactic forms that distance researchers from their audiences.

CHAPTER 15

Participatory Dissemination

Working "with" an Audience

Prologue

On stage, a group of six A/R/Tors are standing in a straight line across the stage facing the audience. The A/R/Tor on stage right turns to the one next to him or her and says "Did you hear about X?" (X being the person at the end of the line) and whispers in the person's ear. Over a minute passes, with each listener responding differently to the story he or she hears. One giggles, another expresses outrage, one turns back to confirm. This is done in mime with minimum improvised dialogue, such as "What?" "Really!" "No!" "Can't be." The substance of the rumor is kept from the audience; they are not privy to the content and hear only each character's reaction to the whispered story. In fact, the A/R/Tors have no story; they feign whispering. The secrecy heightens audience curiosity, maintaining their interest. The scene acts as a metaphor for all rumors, and the lack of substance prevents the audience from becoming bogged down in the details of a particular one. We want to discuss the various dimensions of rumor telling in general.

When the whispered story reaches the second-to-last person, there is a hesitation, but the character eventually decides to tell the last person that there is a rumor about him/her. This last person looks despondent and says "Not again" and exits.

From off stage a voice yells "Cut."

The play *What's the Fine Line?* ends with the Joker walking on stage saying "That's one way that the scene can end, but we've rehearsed many. Let's look at another. Rewind to the beginning." The A/R/Tors mime backward movements, voicing electronic tape sounds. The audience usually laughs, responding to the humor of the rewind style.

The Joker now says "Run through the scene in fast-forward." The cast complies, and when the scene quickly returns to the second-to-last person, the Joker says "Pause" by miming the pressing of a button on an imaginary remote control. Everyone freezes. Again, laughter usually ensues.

The Joker now presses and says "Play," and normal speed resumes, with the last character changing the ending to "Who told you?" The Joker again yells "Cut" and asks the character telling the story to come to center stage.

The Joker asks the character whether he/she should or shouldn't tell. The character shrugs. The Joker turns to the audience and asks "What do you think he/she should do?"

Silence.

"If you knew there was a rumor about a person who you knew, what would you do?"

Silence.

The Joker searches the audience for the slightest twitch as an indication of a willingness to speak and finds little.

An A/R/Tor speaks up, just as one audience member raises her/his hand.

The Joker audibly sighs with relief and says "Yes. Thank you."

(*Laughter at the humorous sigh.*)

The responses vary: "Don't tell, that's snitching."

"Don't tell, but confront the person who told you, on your own."

"Tell; he/she deserves it."

The audience quickly becomes engaged with responses to both the scene and each other's comments. The Joker thanks the audience members for their ideas and asks for two volunteers to help the character in making a decision. By this time there is usually no problem in having two audience members who have committed to the importance of the task to come on stage. The Joker, however, is quick to point out that the volunteers should be sincere, not pressured by a friend.

The two volunteers come on stage, one standing on each side of the character. They are to be "voices in the head," one being the voice "for" and another the voice "against," telling the person who told him/her the rumor. Other audience members make suggestions from their seats, and we collect a number of good reasons to tell or not to tell. The process ends with a tug of war, with each voice taking turns giving reasons. The volunteers are thanked and return to their seats; the character returns to the scene, and the play resumes with his/her decision.

The "game is afoot," as Sherlock Holmes would say, and over the next 10 to 15 minutes the A/R/Tors and audience members discuss issues that the ending scene and other scenes in the play have evoked. They rework and rework scenes in order to explore possible, appropriate ways to deal with the situations presented. They then divide into small discussion groups (usually 10 or less) led by an A/R/Tor.

Dissemination of Participatory Research

The preceding text is an example of how Mirror Theatre, a Theatre in Education (TIE) (Jackson, 1993) company, disseminates its research in a pedagogical manner. Mirror Theatre's four–part participatory research dissemination stage begins with a series of vignettes that highlight the complexity of the issues chosen for examination. The performance is designed to encourage our audiences to examine the issues rather than align with any single character (Brecht, 1957). Such a format aims to create the type of open text that Greene (1995) promotes. Scenes of thesis and antithesis that avoid synthesis invite audience members to find their own synthesis. Since the dissemination is live, the A/R/Tors have the opportunity to work with the audience members in processing and reprocessing the material, making the research dissemination phase highly participatory.

After watching the performance, audience members are then invited to redirect the characters, making suggestions on how to change what the characters say and do, pointing out misuses and abuses of power. In so doing, they indirectly articulate to themselves and their peers what they believe to be appropriate or inappropriate behavior. This second phase acts as a mirror as the participants rethink situations in their own lives and rework the drama on stage.

This form of dissemination moves from a didactic portrayal to a dialectic conversation in which the audience and cast reexamine the issues through a series of popular theater techniques (Boal, 1979). The Joker employs "simultaneous dramaturgy," in which the audience members redirect the characters on stage, and "forum theater," in which the audience members replace the A/R/Tors on stage, giving the characters their own take on the situation. The process is designed to be a constructivist learning experience (Phillips, 1995; Schunk, 1991), in which the participants co-create meaning. Like constructivist teaching, working with a live audience is full of uncertainty, with a high degree of contextual uniqueness. It is the ability to read a situation, draw from previous knowledge and experience, and make choices from all these variables that separates the professional pedagogue from the technician.

> If the model of Technical Rationality is incomplete, in that it fails to account for practical competence in "divergent" situations, so much the worse for the model. Let us search, instead, for an epistemology of practice implicit in the artistic, intuitive processes that some practitioners do bring to situations of uncertainty, instability, uniqueness and value conflict. (Schön, 1983, p. 49)

In the third phase, the audience breaks into small discussion groups with the A/R/Tors in order to discuss how the scenes apply to their own contexts. The back of the program (Appendix G), acting as a prompt, has provided the audience with some framing questions before the start of the performance. The A/R/Tors, using the program as a guide, lead the participants through a minirehearsal, similar to the Playbuilding process described in Chapter 2. Each group discusses scenes that resonated with them and/or shares stories on the topic that have not been addressed.

In the fourth phase, the groups report back to the large group with a verbal report on their work. They summarize their discussion, tell a story, and/or present a scene of their own, highlighting other issues and possible solutions. This final phase is also workshopped, similar to the second phase. In total, both the audience and A/R/Tors go through a series of hermeneutic circles (Gadamer, 1975) as they visit and revisit the issues by listening to the stories of others. This process is unique for research dissemination as the final product is co-created by the original researchers (A/R/Tors) and their audience. Data and insights no longer remain fixed. Rather, they co-emerge (Kieren, 1995; Varela, Thompson, and Rosch, 1992) through dialogue.

By far, the majority of audience members were fully engaged in the process, appreciating its participatory style. Responses from students cited in previous research include: "Thanks for not preaching at us. We had other theater groups come telling us not to do drugs and other things. That doesn't work. Thanks for trusting us to work things through ourselves" (Norris, 1999, p. 287); "You were in that play. You know the grade seven boys aren't half as bad since you came" (Norris and Mirror Theatre, 2001d, pp. 127, 128).

The pedagogical dissemination phase that Denzin (2003) encourages has been informed by the works of Boal (1979, 1992, 1995), Rohd (1998), Sternberg (1998), and others. Although they provide techniques for workshopping (Jokering) social issues through theater, their approaches usually assume that the small group of assembled participants have agreed to attend. Their payment of admission or workshop fees are evidence of their interest. School tours and conference presentations cannot assume a high degree of prior knowledge of the process before the event, and although a general consent form to attend is given (Appendix A), the full extent of the program emerges from performance through the workshopping.

Joker as Participatory Researcher

The Joker (Berezan, 2004; Boal, 1979; Bowman, 1997; Hewson, 2007; Smith, 1996) takes a central role in this spiral dissemination phase of the research by brokering the prepared scenes with new emerging interpretations. Such a role is complex, because it involves responding to many unanticipated variables as the A/R/Tors and audience members enter into dialogue. The Joker walks a fine line between accepting the audience's ideas and challenging them to think beyond them. It requires quick thinking and decision-making skills. The Joker accepts offers from an audience and suggests ways to examine them, creating pedagogical moments by asking in-depth questions and using audience comments to create new scenes for the A/R/Tors to try out on stage. Dissemination in Mirror Theatre's version of Playbuilding is not merely the performance. The conversation, not the prepared piece, is the essential element.

This section is a detailed reflection of my lived-experiences as a Joker of over two hundred audience participatory workshops. Its goal is to provide insights for others who wish to disseminate research through live participatory theatre. My intent is not to close down the conversation (Smith and Heshusius, 1986) with definitive statements and conclusions about the role of the Joker. Rather, I recognize that there are many appropriate responses to situations, and each has its own set of advantages and disadvantages. I use what Henderson considers "unbounded questions" (1992, p. 50) that are not meant to shut down inquiry but to guide practice through their open-ended approach. I enter into what I call enlightened decision making (Norris, 1989a) whereby I act with the understanding that my actions are problematic. By reporting these, I trust that others will find points of resonance and "conspire" (Barone, 1990) with me in creating pedagogically informed participatory research environments.

My reflective questions search for meanings rather than truths, since I recognize that my acts are unique to the manner in which I interpret my lived-experience. I ask: "What decisions do I make? What choices do I debate prior to the decision? What rationale do I provide myself for the making of those decisions? What philosophy underpins those decisions? What internal and external tensions do I experience when making those decisions? How does my practice change through reflection on my practice?" Such questions avoid the positivist orientation of technique and move us "into modes of collaboration very different from the forms of exchange envisioned under the model of applied science" (Schön, 1983, p. 323). Employing a reflective practitioner approach, I recognize that (1) each context is unique, (2) the researcher tries to understand the situation as found, and (3) each situation is problematic (p. 129).

The Tone of the Joker

Initiating a conversation with an audience can be a daunting task, because it is not the traditional mode of theatrical interaction. Boal claims that with Aristotelian theater "the spectacle begins. The tragic hero appears. The public establishes a kind of empathy with him" (1979, p. 36). Brecht (1957) desires a distance from the character, so that audiences can avoid emotional attachment. He "wants the theatrical spectacle to be the beginning of action: the equilibrium should be sought by transforming society" (Boal, 1979, p. 106). But although Brecht moves from a didactic approach to one in which audiences are encouraged to question, this questioning is done privately. In Aristotelian and Brechtian theater, audience members remain in their seats. Boal's forum theater challenges the passive role of spectators by encouraging them to take on the new role of "spect-actors" (Boal, 1992) by coming on stage and taking the role of the protagonist, breaking the hegemony of audience silence (other than laughter and applause).

ESTABLISHING AN INVITATIONAL TONE   Mirror Theatre's program begins with a Brechtian style of theater, with the performance then moving to forum theater with the workshop, inviting audiences from their seats and placing them under the metaphorical and literal spotlight. This part of the program relies on volunteers who must be made to feel safe if they are to publicly explore the text with the Joker and A/C/Tors, since the research will be processed in vivo, in front of others.

Neelands (1984) discusses the importance of negotiation and contracting with students and participants in educational drama situations. Usually in these contexts, those gathered know one another, plan to spend some time together, and expect some degree of participation. Since this is not the case with Mirror Theatre's programs, the spirit of invitation has to be strong. The audience needs to be warmed up to both the topic (through the performance) and the process (through emergent modeling).

As is the case with the example opening this chapter, a natural flow from the end of the play to the beginning of the workshop immediately following the last scene creates an easy transition to forum theatre. Audience members can remain in their seats as they provide comments. We employ what Boal calls "simultaneous dramaturgy" (1979, p. 126). For this technique they are seated, making suggestions to the characters (A/R/Tors) through the Joker, who orchestrates these suggestions on stage. Beginning with simultaneous dramaturgy, the Joker invites all present to participate within their natural comfort ranges.

I remember well when I was first introduced to Boal's work, albeit an adaptation by another company. We were greeted at the door and told that it was participatory, and if we did not intend to participate, we should not enter. While the contract was made explicit, I found it exclusionary, because some who might benefit from the experience and/ or have a valuable contribution to make were excluded, owing to the participatory expectation. Had they attended, they may have eventually become comfortable with the style. Still, I entered. After viewing a scene, I mustered enough courage to raise my hand to make a comment. The Joker quickly silenced me, claiming that I could not speak from the safety of my seat but must come down on stage to try it out. The audience applauded with encouragement, and I entered the arena, not with enthusiasm but more out of embarrassment if I had sat down after the supportive applause. I felt systemically bullied by the Joker, with the audience becoming his unknowing accomplices. Once I tried my perspective on the scene, I became aware that the Joker and the A/R/Tor had already predetermined the right and wrong of the scene, and I was forced to acquiesce to their perspective. Not knowing many people in the room, I went along with the Joker's wishes with a heavy knot in my stomach. I felt voiceless, manipulated, ashamed, and oppressed. The theater that was meant to liberate had rules that excluded and alienated. It was exclusive, not invitational or dialogical.

In this instance, participation on stage was the norm, and Boal's simultaneous dramaturgy was not even considered. In Mirror Theatre's workshops, the participants are invited to participate at their own comfort level of participation, being a spectator, an arm-chair director, or a spect-actor. Many audience members may have ideas that are worthwhile to explore, but owing to their fear of the stage they may not feel comfortable articulating their ideas in a spotlight. Over the years, I found that some Jokers believed that all must be prepared to participate on stage. In these cases, I witnessed people leaving. It seems to me that a theater that is meant to liberate should not be exclusive. There need to be a few avenues for people to give voice, if they choose to give it.

Learning-style theory (Myers and McCaulley, 1985) informs us that extroverts think best with their mouths open, and introverts think best with their mouths shut. The silent can participate by working through things, albeit privately, learn from the experience, and change accordingly. This theory suggests that all audience members be invited to participate but that coming on stage should be optional. If not, we either make our programs exclusive or run the potential of bullying the participants. A tone that accepts participants according to their degrees of comfort and accepts all ideas as possibilities to explore is what we desire. It is in keeping with both a constructivist pedagogy and grounded theory research (Strauss and Corbin, 1990).

To safeguard such a tone, one must make certain that those who volunteer do so willingly and in safety. I have found, at times, that friends volunteer one another. This places a possible unwelcomed spotlight on an audience member. As Joker, I slow down and ask the person if he/she would like to come up or not. I state that I would not want to force volunteers, because my doing so would make me a bully. On some occasions, participants choose not to participate, and I thank them, informing them they have every right not to. On other occasions, a person is eager. In both instances, I thank her/him with applause.

Through this approach, I let the audience know that we are all accountable for our actions and that those actions come from a willingness to participate, not by some demanding set of procedures that force compliance. They know that the invitation is there but that they do not have to accept it.

However, all invitations are problematic, because they expect a decision from a person who may not want to be burdened with the decision in the first place. Invitations can be impositions to those who did not want the invitation thrust on them. The affects of an invitation are complex, and a Joker needs to be aware of this complexity as she/he invites an audience member to engage in any degree of participation. I continually ask the unbounded question "Is there systemic coercion in the invitations I make?"

In addition to blending the rumor scene, the last scene into the workshop, we have also used prologues at the beginnings of our plays as a means of inviting our audiences to view the performance with a critical eye. The following two examples are direct invitational addresses to the audience, one by the Joker and another by a group of A/R/Tors.

Joker: The play you are about to see is one we don't like. We wrote it, and we are proud of it, but we still don't like it. It is based on actual events that show people receiving needless pain. What we would like you to do is to watch the scenes, noticing when certain characters are abusing and misusing their power. Abusing is when people are aware that they are hurting others, and misusing is when they hurt others but are not aware of it. Take a close look, and think how you could rewrite the scene in order to eliminate the pain. After the play is over, you will be given the opportunity to rewrite the scenes by directing the characters on stage or by actually coming on stage yourself and trying out the situation.

In this case, the audience immediately knows the Joker as one who appreciates their ideas. In addition, they are prepared for the ultimate dissolution of the fourth wall.

A variety of methods have been used to inform the audience of their potentially upcoming role, and in the play *Coulda/Shoulda*, a rewrite of the play *What's the Fine Line?*, the A/R/Tors performed the prologue:

(*lights up*)

A/B/C/D/X:	(*circle Y upper stage right*)
Y:	(*breaks free and crosses to down stage left; looks back to the group*) I coulda…
A/B/C/D/X:	You shoulda…(*cross and circle Y, mumbling "You shoulda" lines*)
B:	(*breaks free and crosses to center stage*) I coulda…
A/C/D/X/Y:	You shoulda…(*cross and circle B, mumbling "You shoulda" lines*)
X:	(*breaks free and crosses to down stage right*) I coulda…
A/B/C/D/Y:	You shoulda…(*cross and circle X, mumbling "You shoulda" lines*)
C:	(*breaks free and crosses to upper stage left*) I coulda…
A/B/D/X/Y:	You shoulda…(*cross and circle C, mumbling "You shoulda" lines*)
A:	(*A breaks free and crosses to down stage center*) (*to audience*) Our play is about choices.
D:	(*crosses to the right of A*) It shows people in difficult places.
X:	(*crosses to the left of A*) Places where they don't always make the best decision.
B:	(*crosses to the right of D*) So take a close look.

.

Y:	(*crosses to the left of X*) Asking what you might have done.
C:	(*crosses to the right of B*) To make the scene better.
A:	What coulda the characters have done?
B/C/D/X/Y:	Shoulda done
A:	Coulda done
A/B/C/D/X/Y:	Shoulda
Y:	(*breaks free*) Coulda (*crosses and sits on sofa*)
A/B/C/D/X:	Shoulda (*exits*)
B:	(*crosses to upper left*) Coulda
A/C/D/X:	Shoulda (*exits*)

(*lights dim*)

This scene was a successful attempt to embed the invitation within the play. In this performance, the Joker appeared at the end of the play using the "cut" technique and reminded the audience of the prologue. In these two examples, the scenes were defined as problems, inviting the audience to provide insights.

Creating an Adventurous Tone through Uncertainty

A second tone that is set up early in the process is a sense of uncertainty and adventure. I, as Joker, inform the audience that after the performance segment, I do not know what is going to happen—and I don't. The old adage of never sharing the stage with a baby or an animal applies here, because unpredictability draws an audience in. The audience, in negotiation/conversation with the A/R/Tors and Joker, will determine the shape of the workshop. I work hard not to have some preset solution worked out in advance and truly try to listen to them. During the Jokering, audience members are very attentive as they witness the cast and their peers try to address social issues through the drama. The sense of uncertainty keeps us all intrigued with the emerging story.

This route provides a venue for the audience members to work things through. It does not impose our own solutions, which is bad pedagogy and research. My guiding unbounded questions are "How is my brokering of scenes over-framing the work?" and "Is my guidance fostering or inhibiting voice?" Trying to keep a sense of openness to the participants and uncertainty that Greene (1995) and Schön (1983) suggest is not an easy one. There exists a tension between participant input and the goal of creating meaningful explorations. Not all suggestions are productive ones, and on rare occasions, I consider a suggestion inappropriate. My heart beats as I try to find a way to accept any offer and direct it toward a fruitful exploration. Unpredictability comes with no guarantees. I recognize the problematics of a Joker framing an audience member's suggestion, trying to both accept and stretch it.

Early in my work as Joker, I tried for the happy and positive ending, but after awhile, I gave up on this approach as I realized that I forced the drama too much into my own image. Later on, I became more comfortable in allowing the drama to unfold. Sometimes a suggested outcome seemed undesirable: that the new kid at school decided to take a cigarette to fit in; an under-aged person took the drink in spite of the discussion; and sometimes the bully does not stop his/her behavior. In the workshop, as in life, we are presented with tough choices, and not all decisions end on a positive, uplifting note. I am as uncertain as the audience members are of how the improvised scenes will conclude, and such uncertainty not only keeps my Jokering an open process but also indicates my appreciation of audience input and commitment to the dialogic process.

As Joker I also feel an increased tension when teachers and parents are present during primarily student audiences, because some adults have expressed a desire that the workshop quickly generate appropriate solutions. Such is not our process, and, as Joker, I feel trapped in competing expectations. "Just tell them how to behave, and they'll do it" seems to be the perspective of some, and, of course, that has limited results. One teacher approached me with the comment "I know what you are doing, and I agree with your approach, but it is too hard to watch." Creating open spaces (Greene, 1995) for the participants to process the research means to go into a realm of uncertainty. But it is also this uncertainty that keeps them engaged.

I have found two approaches that seem to please all parties. At times, in a performance workshop I suggest that the ending is but one way that the scene could conclude, and I ask the audience for other possibilities. We redo the scene, looking for a different outcome, and conclude with a comment something like "There are many possibilities. The choice is yours when you have to face it in your life." Usually we don't have time for a second version, nor do we necessarily want one. We want our audiences to leave haunted, thinking about the issues and how they might apply the gleaned insights to their own lives. I sometimes conclude with "This is one ending that can happen, but there are others. The challenge facing you is to decide what ending you would to see like when you face this situation." The tone of adventure keeps the audience's attention and is true to the philosophy of working through a situation rather than imposing a preset conclusion. It does, however, place an enormous pressure on the Joker to facilitate meaningful explorations regardless of the outcome.

Creating a Playful Tone through Humor

Although humor is a matter of personal style, I have found that my use of humor and willingness to laugh at myself helps to loosen up an audience and create a playful tone. I am known for my puns and groaners and, over time, have felt comfortable bringing them to the stage. I can guarantee a laugh when I make reference to my bald head, and I search for opportunities to make other humorous comments. Early in my work as Joker, I avoided this side of self, because I wanted to keep the work serious, falsely equating humor with the lack of seriousness. Gradually, my humor slipped out, and I found it to be effective. The following example illustrates my evolving use of humor.

A technique using inner voice (to be discussed later) has three audience members come on stage. One takes center stage, and the other two take on roles as inner voices, one "for" and the other "against" an action. I'd take out a coin and flip it, giving one of the voice volunteers the call. The winner would choose to be the voice for or against. On one occasion, I had forgotten a coin and asked an audience member for one. I jokingly showed it to someone else saying "See, it is only a nickel, I don't want the person asking for a quarter back." The audience laughed. I kept the strategy even when I had a coin in my pocket. Such humorous moments were avoided early in my work but slowly emerged as a way to keep the audience comfortable when examining difficult situations. Comic relief has become an important part of my personal style as Joker.

Creating a Rigorous Tone through Questions and the Mantle of the Expert

While playful, the work still maintains a rigorous tone. I have found that the use of questions (Morgan and Saxton, 2006) and using the "Mantle of the Expert" (Wagner, 1976) keeps us on task. The act of asking an audience to comment on the scenes immediately puts them in the role of the expert, because the Joker implicitly tells them that they have insights that are worth hearing. However, in many cases, this is not enough. Many volunteers need assistance in processing the material while under the spotlight. The Joker guides, supports, and protects the volunteers by using questions to provide indefinite possibilities around which they can build a scenario. To get them started, I use questions such as "What do you hope will happen? What do you think the character should say or do? Are there other alternatives?" Then I build on their responses by asking follow-up questions to the specifics they provide. This approach becomes playful as volunteers and audience members witness the fleshing out of a character. At times, members of the audience join the process, providing their own questions and ideas. The process could be considered brainstorming, as congruent and conflicting ideas are provided from which the volunteers and A/R/Tors choose to incorporate into their next reenactment.

Questions, however, can be controlling, and I try to be cautious about leading questions. Some males have suggested a "fist fight" to confront a bully. While I may not personally wish to explore this option, I do not want to ignore it either. A question such as "Do you think that this would work?" takes me nowhere. It communicates to the volunteer that the Joker doesn't like the direction, making the conversation a difference of opinion between the Joker and the audience member. At the same time, it is my duty to encourage significant exploration. I am also suspicious that some audience members may make such a suggestion to see a fight on stage, not really believing that it is an appropriate response; rather they want to test both my resolve and my sincerity. During the first few times this occurred, I stumbled for an appropriate direction. Over time, I deduced that the rigor came not from examining the fight itself but from its consequences. I now fast-forward the scene to the end of the fight, asking what they believe the consequences might be.

Still, I debate my decisions. Questions shape the direction of the session and dwell between the poles of freedom and control. I believe that I must continually recognize that a Joker's stance is problematic. In so doing, I can act as a Joker who facilitates thought more than he dictates directions. When on the spot, one cannot always easily find the question that evokes thought yet does not censor or overly prescribe. I believe that the stronger ideas emerge when the audience processes the issues themselves. I try to be vigilant in determining the questions I give, always searching for ways to place the audience in the role of the expert. I guide my practice through the unbounded question "How do I provide possibilities for rigorous exploration without rejecting possibilities?" Over-framing can inhibit dialogue if the Joker has pre-established the desired outcome.

Tones are amorphous at best, but I have found that trying to establish them creates an atmosphere that keeps the audience comfortable, thoughtful, and engaged. The preceding examples emerged over time in my own practice, and now that they have become explicit, they are ones that I can call on at will. I have developed my own stock pieces to assist me, some of which may be of use to others. But the technique alone is not enough. I believe that a Joker must be continually aware of the huge responsibility of assisting others in processing sensitive material. One's actions are always problematic, and keeping this in mind helps one to better achieve balance in those countless on-the-spot, decision-making situations.

The Amoral Stance of Mirror Theatre's Joker

The basic philosophical stance of the Joker in Mirror Theatre's work is underpinned by the belief that the Joker must remain amoral. That is, a Joker resists making a value judgment on any decision. Rather, she/he attempts to facilitate values clarification in others. Freire (1986) believes that education needs to be an instrument of liberation, and Fullan (1982) claims that change that comes from above is dictatorial and so encourages a grassroots bottom-up approach. Performances that preach appropriate behavior take a top-down approach, and, although well intentioned, they employ the method of the oppressor. As Joker, I underpin my work with the beliefs of Freire, Fullan, and others who take a democratic approach in facilitating meaning. Consequently, I, too, am transformed through the process, because I am open to learn from the Other. I try to take an amoral stance, so that the audience members have voice rather than having morals imposed on them by the script, the A/R/Tors, and/or the Joker.

Audience members have indicated their support of such a stance through unsolicited comments. After our program entitled *Last Call, Your Call,* which dealt with underage drinking, I was approached by a member of the school's Students Against Drunk Driving (SADD) program, who provided this unsolicited comment (paraphrased): "I think you got it right. You don't tell them what you think they should do, but you ask them for their opinion. This makes them really think about the issue. Great show."

What makes such comments powerful is that they were not obtained through leading questions in questionnaires or interviews, but were unsolicited, volunteered on site. In another program, called *Friends, Family, and Foreigners,* which dealt with daily conflicts in adolescents' lives, an audience member recognized a cast member who worked at the same NHL arena as she. The young woman approached the A/R/Tor with the paraphrased comment "I liked that you didn't talk down at us but valued our opinions." In these and other instances, the philosophical stance of the Joker has been reinforced. Participants appreciate the constructivist style as opposed to a didactic presentation. With an amoral Joker, the program can better examine moral issues.

However, maintaining such a stance while responding to audience input is not easy. In a scene called "What's the Fine Line?" (also the title of the play in which it first occurred), a male character is playing a video game, ignoring his female companion, who is sitting next to him on a sofa. During the workshopping of this scene in the *Friends, Family, and*

Foreigners program, one junior high female student stated that the character should spend less time trying to score with the game and more time to score with her.

I was taken back with the explicitness of the suggestion and did not want to pursue the "scoring" line, but not to do so could have moved the Joker into a potentially argumentative situation. At the same time, the student did have a point. My tension was how to accept her idea without positively reinforcing the scoring issue (a recognized value judgment on my part). This time, paraphrasing was my way out. I responded: "So you believe that he should spend more time developing relationships with people and less time with machines?" She nodded. I then asked "How can we approach the character to help him see that?"

Had she persisted with the sexual focus, I would have followed her lead and related it to another scene in the program that dealt with parents arguing over when it was the right time to have "The Sex Talk" with their son. This could elicit a discussion on the scoring comment. Thus slight redirection, through paraphrasing to examine the complexity of a comment, is another technique that can be employed. It enables the conversation to continue in a negotiated direction without over-moralizing.

However, as Joker, I do find redirection and all of my actions problematic. Every comment I make is based on my own bias and comfort level. At the same time, I don't want to be overly controlling. I trust student participants and appreciate their struggles, so I listen to them, trying to assist them in working issues through. But since we all are involved in the process of self-discovery, using the drama and the thoughts of others to refine our thinking and behaviors, many ideas are roughly formed and articulated. We need to accept one another as works in progress. I read the audience, including the teachers and students, trying to determine the community's level of comfort. On one occasion, a parent informed me during an earlier telephone conversation before the program that dealing with bullying was permissible, but no sexual reference would be tolerated. The sexual harassment scene was eliminated for that performance. Perhaps this previous situation influenced my redirection of the "score with her" comment. A Joker makes many decisions that "try" to keep the conversation open and moving forward, recognizing the political complexity of the work. I ask "How do I challenge presently held beliefs without alienating the person who made the suggestion?" *What's the Fine Line?* could also be an appropriate title/question for all of Mirror Theatre's work.

But an amoral stance does not mean that the Joker remains passive. Rather, the Joker is like a muse, ever beckoning to reconceptualizations, playfully challenging all positions. She/He tries to keep the metaphorical "balloon in the air," not allowing it to settle. Once a possibility is found, a redirection is sought to look at the issue/situation from another perspective. The Joker's role then is to "stage" the drama, so to speak, not to direct it. She/He must tread softly, so as not to disrupt the trust established between self and the audience but to act firmly enough to create a rigorous engagement. As in the preceding story about scoring, a Joker experiences a tension between one's own values and values inherent in the situation. Living such a tension defines some of the lived-world of a Joker.

In the case of "score with her," I redirected the volunteer's position with a paraphrase, emphasizing a different aspect of her comment. From my reading, she agreed with the direction; however, I cannot be certain. Perhaps she felt vulnerable and complied to the power of the Joker. As is discussed later, I continually ask myself the unbounded question "How do I misuse and abuse my power?" Most often, however, the issue is processed within the drama, and the outcome unfolds from the improvisation.

Yet there have been a few occasions when I have taken a stand on homophobia. When working with preservice teachers, I ask them to clarify for themselves their negotiable and nonnegotiable rules. The same applies to a Joker. For me homophobia is a nonnegotiable. Here, I do enter the drama, asking whether people believe that homosexuals should receive the death penalty? Most, regardless of their positions, are shocked by such a question. I then report the statistics that indicate that approximately one third of all teen suicides are homophobia related. I claim that negative treatment of this group can lead to death. I say that people may hold a position on either side of the issue, but our negative behavior toward these individuals needs to be questioned.

Silence is usually the first result of such a comment, but slowly a conversation emerges. Females seem to be the most open to homosexuality, but they are often silenced by the bravado of male put-downs. My strong voice can clear the space for their voices. I hesitate before speaking, but most often, on this issue, I speak.

Students have questioned me during and after these sessions, and usually a typical question is about my sexual orientation. I am tempted to say that I am married with two kids (which may not necessarily mean that I am straight). In some ways, I believe that such a comment strengthens my position, because I am not a self-identified member of a group, promoting my own agenda. I respond, however, with the question "Does it, should it matter?"

The tensions experienced during and after such occasions are not to be avoided, but they are an indication that participant thinking is occurring. Although I believe that I acted authentically, I recognize the problematics of my voice. The major tension is finding an appropriate balance between a Joker's facilitating voice and the voice of the audience members.

Safety

While I try to create a safe environment for audiences, audience members are not always as generous to one another. A Joker must be vigilant to protect those within. There have been times when I have been concerned with the physical and emotional safety of certain individuals even when they were not.

EMOTIONAL SAFETY   While most who volunteer are willing and able, there are a few who become the deer caught in the headlights and freeze on stage. Others are inaudible, and the audience becomes restless. The Joker has the responsibility to keep those who volunteer safe from embarrassment.

Peer Pressure to Volunteer   The use of volunteers raises a number of emotional safety issues and, as mentioned earlier, people volunteering other people is a common occurrence. In fact, I can remember doing the same thing when I was in grade 10. As Joker, when I ask for volunteers, I try to preface my request with a comment that it is up to an individual to volunteer. We don't want people to come on stage because of peer pressure.

Inability of a Volunteer   At times, even an enthusiastic volunteer has difficulty on stage. Some freeze, some don't have the improvisational agility, and some can't project their voices. I try to deflect their discomfort by asking the audience and cast for suggestions before the improvisation begins, or have the volunteer be the inner voice of a cast member, or ask him/her to become a director on stage, and I repeat to the audience what this person says. These are some of the staple techniques that I employ to provide safer spaces for volunteers. In some ways, a volunteer's lack of stage presence creates the greatest tension for me, as Joker, because I try to keep the drama moving for the audience while simultaneously saving face for those who are floundering. However, at times, when I intuitively believe that the ability is there, I direct the volunteer, asking her/him to stand up or move elsewhere, and so on. Such is the nature of audience participation. We want to have audience input but not at the sake of our volunteers' dignity. As Joker, I am vigilant, always looking for ways to celebrate voice, and I am torn between giving a person an opportunity to shine and addressing an audience's understandable impatience. Most times, however, the volunteer is capable of holding his/her own. Whoever enters the arena is sincerely thanked for the input.

Unknown Factors   Sometimes we have become aware of pertinent background information after the event, and had we known, we might have taken a different tact. Teachers and peers are privy to background that is unknown to the Joker. During one tour of *Coulda/ Shoulda,* a female volunteered a male student sitting near her to play the bully. When questioned, he enthusiastically agreed. In developing a character and making choices, he was bombarded with questions from this female and others. He comfortably responded to the questions. Later, I was made aware that in this school, he was considered the bully, and the female used the opportunity to confront him. The teachers considered this encounter a valuable way to address the issue, but had I known, I might not have followed this path, perhaps employing a role-reversal. I voiced my concern about his safety as well. I would not like any scene to bully the bully. The staff informed me that he seemed to weather it well and perhaps learned something. There are elements to the dramas taking place on stage of which Jokers and A/R/Tors may not be aware. We need to be vigilant, determining the comfort level of our audience, so that we do not end up violating them in the name of liberation.

PHYSICAL SAFETY

The physical safety of volunteers often is at risk when fights are suggested to resolve the bullying and the conflict scenes. Although I sometimes question the sincerity of some suggestions, I do feel some obligation to pursue the suggestion. When there is time, I give a short lesson on stage-fighting and discuss the importance of physical safety with the adage "Don't try this at home." This helps release some of the evident adrenaline. Then I fast-forward the scene to the end and explore the consequences and later rewind the scene and reexamine it, looking for a win/win scenario. This approach usually provides the "kicks" for those who want a fight, yet moves the drama to a rigorous exploration. When I don't have time, I skip the stage-fighting lesson/ demonstration.

COORDINATION OF VOLUNTEERS

There are many coordination issues that arise with the use of volunteers—although not as major as safety issues, decisions around these do make up the landscape of the Joker.

Too Many Volunteers   Although the lack of volunteers can be a problem early in the Jokering process, this is seldom the case once the process gets moving. Many want their say over the situation and/ or comment on another's comments. The fires of great discussion rage on, and time is quickly shortened. I have found myself saying "only two more comments," correcting myself when a third and then a fourth hand are raised enthusiastically by participants who have not yet had input. Some A/R/Tors have commented that I go on too long, whereas others claim that it's just right. Pace is an individual thing, and there is seldom agreement among all participants. So the clock in my head debates the issue, deciding when enough time has been allotted to a certain topic and when another comment or two are necessary. Including all voices can be as problematic as excluding some. The decision to move on with another hand or two raised is not an easy one, and I continually wrestle with it. I am never confident about such decisions.

Time to Move On   Imbedded in the preceding section is the aspect of being the time-keeper. Usually the performance runs about 40 minutes in the two-hour program, and in the remaining 80 minutes there will be time for Jokering, time for small discussion groups, and time for reporting back. Casts are made aware that I will be reading the audience in order to determine the duration of the Jokering. My inner dialogue races to determine the level of interest and productivity of the Jokering. If strong, I continue; if not, I divide the audience into small discussion groups. The decision has an effect on what is to follow. Some A/R/Tors who lead the small groups claim that they wish that they had more time to work in small groups, but others desired less. Although I try to accommodate, I cannot predict the future, and so I ask the A/R/Tors for their trust and patience.

Dominating Person   A problem similar to that of "too many volunteers" is "addressing the dominating volunteer." Some people have yet to learn to take turns, and I succumb to the forlorn face of one who has spoken more that the rest but seems disappointed when not called on yet again. One wants to reinforce enthusiasm, but not at the expense of others. I usually ask "Who hasn't spoken?" or "Who hasn't had a turn?" to indicate my reasons for exclusion. The decision to ignore or to exclude is not one I make lightly.

The Jocular Volunteers   In a program during the fall of 2001, two males volunteered to come on stage to explore the issue of buying liquor for an under-aged person. Intuitively, I could see that they were determined to undermine the work. Such a belief was confirmed by the cast and adults in the audience, one of whom claimed that he thought that we were going to "lose it."

As the two young men came on stage, I began asking them character development questions with the comment that we needed to understand the person's background in order to understand how he/she behaved in this situation. Each of their answers provided me with another question, and in effect the characters they were about to play were hot-seated. By slowing down the drama and looking to the past, I was able to apply my desired degree of rigor. The volunteers had input but of the accountable kind. At the same time, they, too, saved face. There was never a direct confrontation between them and the Joker. As Joker, I became their muse, helping them to flesh out and give depth to what I anticipated would be a superficial and silly rendition. Slowing down the drama with probing questions is one way to encourage rigor without embarrassing less-than-serious volunteers.

RIGOR   Rigor is the bottom line in all the work that we do. We want the casts and the audience to be rigorously engaged in examining the substance of our research, making connections to their own lives. situations, and issues. Without rigor, our work has less meaning. Although most audiences and volunteers rise to the occasion, I have experienced difficulties with some volunteers, who seem to view the event as an opportunity to "showboat" or to generally fool around. I am convinced that the desire to see a fight on stage comes more from a sense of fooling around than from a rigorous engagement. Fast-forwarding to the consequences and hot-seating for character development can bring rigor back into the session.

USE OF LANGUAGE   One question we are sometimes asked before visits to schools is about the language content, and, on occasion, a volunteer, when she/he comes on stage, asks "Can I swear?" To some extent, the comfort level of the audience determines my response. I ask "Is it necessary to the scene?" and "What is the school policy?" In one school, one teacher claimed that the language usage was appropriate and realistic, whereas another teacher was offended. Any issues-based drama is guaranteed to raise some eyebrows. As Joker, I don't intend to offend, but I realize that the drama may. For me, language in a play in context is appropriate, but the context of the school must also be taken into consideration. As in the school mentioned above, there will be differences of opinion. I accept that this type of difficulty will not be readily solved.

Techniques

Boal (1979), Neelands and Goode (2000), and others have provided a number of techniques that can be used in Theater in Education (TIE) and

Drama in Education (DIE). Following are a few that I have found useful in my work as Joker. Although most have been referred to in previous discussions, they are highlighted here with a bit more explanation.

THE REMOTE CONTROL

Our technological age has made our audiences familiar with some of our theatrical techniques. In rehearsals, we do scenes out of chronological order, repeat some, and create out-scenes to better understand the issue. Many of these never find their way to the script. The "remote control" enables us to explore ideas out of sequence, and I employ these as Joker.

The first technique that I teach the audience is pause. When the cast is to redo a scene, I ask audience members to raise their hands when they perceive a misuse or an abuse of power. When a hand is raised, I yell "pause." The A/R/Tors instantly freeze in a tableau, and I ask the person who raised his or her hand to speak. Depending on the amount of time it takes, I keep the A/R/Tors frozen, or ask them to relax. This is a tool that I use, and it is also comfortable for the audience to use. They get my attention, and I vocalize the pause.

Sometimes the pause leads to rewinding the scene to an earlier moment, when the seeds of a decision started to germinate. I go back to this point and ask the character what she/he was thinking and what he/she wanted to happen. The audience and I hot-seat the character and then let the scene continue with the new-found thoughts that may change the outcome.

When working on our elementary program, *Fair Play Rulz*, I brought a real remote along and asked audience members to actually press the buttons and yell the directions "play," "pause," "rewind," and "fast-forward." This gave the Joker an opportunity to reinforce the portal through the fourth wall and warm up the audience for additional participation. On some occasions, I asked them to yell in unison, which this age group seemed to enjoy.

The remote control enables a Joker to have control over time, and I determine/decide where we might better explore the issue. The A/R/Tors and audience are also invited to make suggestions to rewind or fast-forward a scene. The fast-forward and rewind actions and sounds always got laughs from our audiences.

OUT SCENES

Most of the scenes to which we rewound and fast-forwarded were, of course, improvised on the spot. They were, in effect, scenes not in the play, or rehearsed scenes. As Joker, my mind continuously races, searching for scenarios for further investigation, basing them on details that audience members have provided. As Joker, I generate problems for audience members to solve. I give brief suggestions and let them go. Often I don't have an end result in mind, and when I do, I try to ignore it and listen to the emerging scene that is often better than I hoped for. In addition to using past and future scenes, I sometimes explore side-scenes with characters who may not be in the existing scene. A conversation with the guidance counselor is one that I often use. It changes the energy to a more reflective sort. Although out-scenes have a purpose of their own, I sometimes employ them as a rescue device. When I deduce that a particular scene is going badly, I search for an out-scene that can change its direction.

In the scene "To the Movies" (Norris and Mirror Theatre, 2001a), an out-scene in which the mother asked the older sister to take her younger sister along was preplanned. It was not presented as part of the performance but held in reserve as a possible workshop scene.

HOT SEATING   I often layer the guidance counselor out-scene with hot-seating. The person who will be playing the guidance counselor (sometimes a teacher) takes center stage, and in addition to questioning him/her, the student audience instructs the guidance counselor how to behave. I am amazed at their insights on what makes an effective counselor/teacher. When the scene commences, there is an added richness concerning how to mediate a situation. Pauses are frequent, with the emphasis on the guidance counselor's behavior. The audience processes the situation from a different point of view. Hot-seating, as mentioned earlier, can bring depth and belief to a future scene.

INNER DIALOGUE   Inner dialogue is another technique to slow the drama down for depth and belief. As in the example from *The Caucasian Chalk Circle*, mentioned in Chapter 6, the characters and the audience become privy to what was thought and not said. This technique became highly effective in exploring gangs in which peer pressure emerged as a stronger motivator for aggressive behavior than a desire to hurt. Many informed us, "I don't want to be the next victim, so I will participate as an accomplice." Inner dialogue can bring another layer to the situation, in addition to what appears on the surface. This provides not a "subtext," as it is usually labeled, but the dominant text, which is obscured through the action. These inner dialogues can suggest many possible out-scenes for future exploration.

VOICES FOR/AGAINST   In my early work, I used the strong visual image of devil and angel on each side of the decision-making character, who debated the course of action to take. Each took an outstretched arm and tugged on it whenever a suggestion was made. This technique helped the audience look at the pros and cons of the decision being made. During one production with adults, a client approached me, claiming that a few audience members took offense to my use of the devil/angel metaphor. They reacted negatively to "summoning the devil."

My knee-jerk reaction was to dismiss the comment, as I do with many "politically correct" attitudes that reduce use to the lowest common denominator. The tug-of-war metaphor with the devil and the angel works, with the audience visualizing the tensions within the character, and I was reluctant to abandon it. Still, their concern haunted me and was cause for reflection. During my next few experiences as Joker, I focused on this metaphor and found another flaw in the process that disturbed me even more. By defining one act as supported by the devil and the other by the angel, I was overtly articulating my predisposition to the situation. I immediately changed these two inner-dialogue characters to "voices for" and "voices against," thereby removing my biased position. Although I mourn the loss of the striking visual images, I do believe that the new approach is more in keeping with my philosophy. Still, on occasion, an audience member will revert to the culturally known metaphor of devil/angel.

Tips

Many of the things that I do now emerged unexpectedly from my practice. Once I had made them explicit to myself, they were added to my repertoire of possible choices. I have shared them with colleagues and students who have found them useful. The techniques discussed below are based on my reflective practice research. They are things that I had found myself doing that led to reflection.

JOKER MOBILITY   As mentioned, a major role of a Joker is to bridge conversations among A/R/Tors and audience members by creating a portal through the fourth wall. One day a cast member commented on how she liked the manner in which I moved around the stage and back and forth into the audience. She considered such an act a reinforcement of audience voice. Using this observation, I began to make note of my movements. When obtaining input from students, I found that I moved close to them, bringing the focus of all to the speaker. I became a metaphorical spotlight. When making suggestions to A/R/Tors or questioning their characters, I was on stage. When scenes were being improvised, at times I would stand in the audience watching. Other times, I would be half on stage with my focus directed to the emerging scene. Such mobility can foster audience input, because it reminds audience members that there can be movement between the spaces, and my focus on a scene can let the audience know where to place their foci.

Although useful, this technique, too, is problematic. By taking a stronger on-stage presence, the Joker is able to direct a hard-to-focus audience. However, another cast member commented that the position was upstaging. This led to a brief discussion on theatrical conventions and assessment criteria. Swortzell (1993) questions the value of TIE using a particular set of theatrical criteria. These may not be as absolute as he claims. Different genres have different practices and values. In the case of participatory theater, a different set of rules may apply. The dissolution of the fourth wall is one such break, and such an act influences a larger set of acts. Joker mobility is a technique that I employ to keep reminding the audience that the fourth wall is permeable. The position of the Joker can produce Brecht's alienation effect—however, it can also be somewhat problematic.

ASKING FOR PARTICIPANTS' NAMES

Because Mirror Theatre uses multiple casts, the A/R/Tors' real names are substituted for the letters, because an A/R/Tor may play a different character on a different day. When audience members come on stage, we follow the same practice. They play a character using their own names. Early in our work, a cast member requested that we make certain that the audience understood that, although the A/R/Tors were using their real names, we weren't playing ourselves. Consequently, I got into the habit of saying "the character that "Georgina" is playing" rather than "Georgina." This practice carries through when working with audience members. The phrase is a standard that I often use. It serves as a distancing device to protect those who try on difficult characters in front of their peers.

Names are also requested from those speaking from their seats. Individuals need to be given credit and take responsibility for their thoughts. I have found that when I am discussing a particular idea, referring to the person who offered it by name usually brings a smile to his/her face. It can build trust as those who provide input are recognized for their efforts. While naming may seem obvious to some, it is a device that can assist in building positive connections.

LIGHTING

A shift in stage lighting can also communicate a change in direction to an audience. As in the opening example, when the Joker cuts to the last scene, the stage lights are on and the house lights are off. The conversation begins this way, with the audience in the safety that the darkness can provide. I would never use a spotlight, but I do enter the audience to close the gap between me and the person talking. This provides the other audience members with a focal point. After a couple of such encounters, I ask a cast member to bring up the house lights but keep the stage lights on. The gradual shift of lights onto the audience warms them up to speaking before I move to the situation in which they can be seen sitting, let alone being seen on stage.

When small groups present their own scenes, I ask if they would like to use stage lights without house lights, and most often this is their choice. While I do not know for certain, I believe that their choice is partly based on the thrill of experiencing theater and partly because they can avoid being able to see their audience. During the Jokering, however, I prefer both sets of lights to be on.

On a more pragmatic note: Lately I have found that looking directly into the audience with stage lights on produces headaches. The dissolving of the fourth wall has had a negative physiological effect. I plan to Joker more in the threshold between the spaces to minimize this effect.

PARAPHRASING   A Joker must always be cognizant that the audience does not usually have the skills of the cast, and although many do a good job of improvisation, few are good at voice projection either on stage or making comments from the audience. Paraphrasing is the technique I employ when working with the audience. Employing it achieves three results: (1) It lets the person speaking know that I heard; (2) it allows the rest to hear; (3) although some audience members can be heard, if I do it only for the softer voices, I bring attention to the quieter ones' inabilities.

BUZZ WORDS AND PHRASES   Throughout my practice I found myself using words and phrases that I knew I could use in the future. I usually record these during our debriefing sessions to help me remember them. After a while, they emerge naturally in my speech. I call these "buzz words" and highlight a few of the central ones here.

Use/Misuse and Abuse of Power   "Misuse and abuse of power" is common in my repertoire; it emerged during my early work and has become a favorite phrase. I ask the audience to examine scenes looking for uses, abuses, and misuses of power. As mentioned earlier, I define *misuse* as doing things that hurt others unintentionally, causing pain without the sender's awareness. *Abuse* is deliberate, and often the abuser takes pleasure in the act. I claim that many times we hurt one another without knowing it and that this would be a misuse, rather than an abuse, of power. Discussing the misuse of power while a scene is paused assists the audience to understand that many so-called transgressions are not meant to be so, that most of us do indeed try to be good to one another. We look at the scenes to become aware of our misuses. As indicated earlier, one student directly informed me that she didn't realize that she was a bully until she saw our play.

Don't Try This at Home   I use "don't try this at home" as a comic way of reinforcing the importance of a situation. Although it is often used with stage-fighting, I also use it when it is obvious that an outcome was less than desirable, leaving a character in needless pain.

Resolving Situation or Conflict?   Many times a scene has a resolution, but the conflict remains. For example, a student loses her pencil (Chapter 13) and another finds it. The teacher gives the fancy eraser to one and the pencil to another. I ask "Have we resolved the conflict or just the situation?" Receiving part of the pencil may appear to be a win/win situation (see next heading), but resentment can be harbored by one or more of the parties, with the conflict festering and being manifested in other situations. As Joker, I encourage conflict, not situation, resolutions.

Win/Win and Easier Said Than Done   Another way I approach a situation in which one character is left in physical or emotion pain is by asking "Who was the winner, and who was the loser?" I explain the concepts of lose/lose, win/lose, and win/win and ask the audience and the characters to see how we can find a scene that ends with win/win. Although the resulting scene seldom gets there, the exploration has assisted us in processing the situation. I end with the phrase "Easier said than done."

Homework, and I'm Not There Yet Either   Sometimes the phrase "easier said than done" is followed up with: "That is your homework; we haven't been able to work it through here, but it is a situation that you will probably face many times in your life. Good luck with your homework." In tandem, these statements reinforce that dealing with these situations is tough work and will take more than a lifetime to master. I also add: "I'm not there yet either, and teachers and other adults tell me that they, too, are struggling with this issue." This lets our student audiences know that life will be full of such challenges and that we adults also have similar interpersonal struggles.

Refinements

Much of the preceding material has gone through many refinements, based on my reflective practice and input from others. Some previously held beliefs and practices were changed or deleted, and others were added based on emergent needs. For me, refinement through reflective practice is a sometimes painful yet always rewarding aspect of self-study research.

Small Group Workshops

As mentioned earlier, a portion of our program is small group work in which each actor takes approximately 10 participants to further discuss the research findings (the performance). During this 30-minute to 40-minute period, they go through a minirehearsal with the participants. Using the questions on the back of the program (Appendix G), they ask the group members to discuss the scenes with which they identified and to relate them to their own personal experiences. Many times, the group generated a new scene based on the stories they told and the insights they gleaned. Often, such scenes would be performed for the entire audience in our plenary gathering.

As Joker, I would circulate from group to group, listening, sometimes adding a comment or two, but mostly coordinating for the plenary, asking how much time the groups needed before regathering. There was never a common pattern. Some groups would finish early, while other groups could go for hours. Consequently, I would have a short plenary if all the groups wanted more discussion time. On other occasions, I would cut the group work short to give those who prepared scenes more time to perform.

The Jokering after the performance and after the small group discussions could never give all participants a chance to speak. We found that the small groups enabled many more participants to publicly process the research and, through their stories and scenes, to provide additional data and insights.

Working with A/R/Tors

The majority of this chapter has focused on my work as Joker, but the major role of the A/R/Tors should not be underestimated. The A/R/Tors spent hours in rehearsals, focused on our collective understanding of the phenomena, and this theatrical research genre provided the foundation on which improvisations with our audiences could be built. Many a time, an A/R/Tor will set up a scene as an audience member speaks and interject with her/his own perspective, when needed. Still, A/R/Tors also know when to hold back, because it is the audience member's thoughts that we want to stimulate. The relationship between the Joker and A/R/Tors could be considered a division of labor. The A/R/Tors carry the play, the Joker carries this part of the workshop. On a number of occasions, A/R/Tors have informed me that they were grateful for the break. An A/R/Tor was able to catch his/her breath before leading the small group discussions.

During our many rehearsals, a high degree of trust is established. We come to know one another well and enjoy the significance we have found. In spite of this, I found that some A/R/Tors were uncomfortable with me, as Joker. Although our devising was collaborative, my Jokering was far more directorial. Out of expediency, I would create the scenes for them to improvise, based on audience input. Some felt vulnerable, because they had to create anew on stage; some felt that I had not given them enough background information; and others were quite comfortable with the shift, because they did not regard me as director in this situation but as Joker and muse.

Based on this feedback, I changed part of my rehearsal process. In addition to articulating the Jokering role to the cast, I often Jokered scenes with the other A/R/Tors after small groups had presented their scenes. This approach better prepared us for the difficult work we would face in front of a live audience. I also encouraged the A/R/Tors to take over, if and when they got an idea, since we all could be Jokers and muses to one another.

After each performance/workshop, we met to debrief. Discussions focused on all phases of our participatory dissemination process. Difficulties found in the Jokering and small group work were major items, as was fine-tuning the performance. I took notes, especially of data that could expand our understanding of the phenomenon under investigation and of insights that could improve our dissemination. Our debriefings could be considered to have been informal, mini-action research cycles (Kemmis and McTaggart, 1988).

Epilogue

In conclusion, disseminating research with a pedagogical intent through participatory theater is complex work that has been researched by but a few (Berezan, 2004; Hewson, 2007; and Smith, 1996). This chapter has been written as a reflective-practice study to articulate to colleagues, students, and myself some of my lived-experiences and the meanings and insights that can guide the practices of a Joker. They are written/given to inform, not dictate practice. There are few definitive techniques that a Joker, and all who subscribe to a constructivist and emancipatory pedagogy, can apply. Each individual and each context is varied, and thus each decision is unique to that individual and context. As professionals, we use our reflected-on-experiences and the narratives of others to assist us in refining our emergent practices, knowing that many of our actions are problematic. The role of the Joker is not only to provide possibilities but also to continue to playfully ask "What if…" As Joker, I often close our programs with this comment:

> One of our earlier plays was called *No Easy Answers.* Many of the decisions that we make are difficult ones. We hope what we have presented to you will assist you in the tough decisions that you will have to make through your lives. You have our best wishes.

The cast applauds the audience and thanks them for their thoughts and input.

I conclude this chapter and book with a verbal collage of some of my experiences as a Joker using a parody of Jacques' speech in *As You Like It* (*As You Like It*, Shakespeare, 1972d). Such arts-based approaches are becoming more prevalent in the research literature (Leavy, 2009). Dunlop (2002) turned her qualitative research into a novel, and Conrad (2001) used a script format to present some of her data on using drama to address media and advertising issues. I choose to conclude with "found poetry" (Butler-Kisber, 2002). Those who employ it condense transcripts into often poignant poems. The following poem summarizes my role as Joker in facilitating the processing of a research-based play through participatory theater.

All the world's a stage,

And the Joker bridges the two.

In that space he/she plays many parts,

Primarily the master, or mistress, of ceremonies

Who hosts the event as coordinator of A/R/Tors and their audiences.

Dissolving the convention of the fourth wall

The Joker allows safe passage of thoughts and bodies

Between these all too often separate worlds.

Deciding when to open or shut the portal makes the Joker a time-keeper,

Who reads the substance of the scene and the interest of the audience,

Internally debating when to probe deeper and when to move on.

But always a playwright who gathers the thoughts of others

To construct scenes, ideas, and conversations

That permit a playful yet rigorous interrogation

Of the follies of daily living.

Hence, the Joker is a muse

Who always invites but never fully accepts another's thoughts.

Through probing questions and improvised scenes

The Joker weaves a myriad of dilemmas

For learning and a(muse)ment.

While central, the Joker, however, does not want center stage.

"The play's the thing" remains his/her adage

And the Joker moves from the stage to the audience,

Watching what her/his meddling has evoked.

The passer of the torch is vital for the play to continue

As A/R/Tors and audiences rework and reconceptualize

The issues laid before them.

Still the Joker interferes

With a gentle suggestion to assist the stumbling mind,

With a paraphrased comment to magnify those slight of voice,

With a challenge for those who think they got it right;

But always with love and care,

Knowing that such work floats fragilely,

On a delicate layer of trust.

The final role of the Joker is that of curtain,

Who thanks the players,

Haunting them with the challenges and wisdom

Played within this interlude.

So while the curtain falls, the play remains

Through lives yet lived.

The Joker then becomes merely a player, sans lights, sans A/R/ Tors, sans audience;

But the issues remain.

Appendix A

Permission Slip

I hereby give my permission/do not give my permission for my son/daughter
(please circle) (please circle)
_____ to attend the *What's the Fine Line?* performance/workshop for the purposes of their education and for research into disruptive youth. I understand that the play deals with the abuse of power that takes place in our society and asks the audience to examine how power is abused in their immediate lives. Issues concerning sexual harassment, peer pressure, and decision making will be dealt with in the play, the discussion/workshop, and the research data collection. I recognize that these problems need to be articulated and discussed in order to be resolved. I am aware that these emotional issues are sometimes difficult to face and that the school will provide trained staff to assist students, should the need arise. (**Please note:** During approximately 40 performance/workshops conducted at another school, no such need arose. Students were engaged in healthy productive discussions.)

I further understand that the play and the workshops will be both audio and video taped **solely** for research purposes, and no others will have access to the tapes (legal purposes withstanding). I am aware that the data will be coded and disseminated in written form with anonymity guaranteed. (NOTE: The research project has been approved by the University's Ethics Committee. Tapes will be destroyed after the project is completed.)

Student's name:_____   Signature_____

Parent's name:_____   Signature_____

This permission slip must be returned to the school by **Date** _____

Appendix B

Membership Agreement

3.1   The objects of the Society (Mirror Theatre) are:

3.1.1   To use theatre and educational drama as tools to foster the emotional, intellectual, physical, social and spiritual well being of all people.

3.1.2   To use theatre and educational drama as tools for reconceptualization and social change.

3.1.3   To undertake or commission the writing and/or performing of plays which fulfill the objects of the society.

3.1.4   To undertake or commission the writing and/or delivery of drama workshops which fulfill the objects of the society.

3.1.5   To promote research in the use of theatre and educational drama as tools for social change and personal development.

3.1.6   To promote education on the use of theatre and educational drama as tools for social change and personal development.

3.1.7   To hire qualified personnel who may assist the Society in achieving its objects.

3.1.8   To solicit volunteers who may assist the Society in achieving its objects.

3.1.9   To enter into contract with institutions, agencies, organizations, and individuals whose programs can assist both them and the Society in fulfilling the objects of the Society.

3.1.10 To establish programs which assist the Society in fulfilling its objects.

3.1.11 To provide support to the projects of individuals and groups when their objects parallel the Society's objects.

3.1.12 To lease, purchase, or acquire the facilities, equipment, and materials necessary for the Society to achieve its objects.

3.1.13 To raise funds in any way to achieve the objects of the Society. This includes accepting gifts, donations, grants, legacies, bequests, and inheritances, as well as reserving the right to decline unsolicited donations.

3.1.14   To borrow funds and lease, mortgage, sell, and dispose of property of
          the Society and establish a line of credit to achieve the objects of the
          Society.

3.1.15   To use funds of the Society only according to and in pursuit of these
          objects or other charitable objects which meet the objects of the
          Society.

Consequently, Mirror Theatre is a collective of individuals who desire to use drama as a means of social change. Over its history it has compiled a large number of scenes to meet this goal. Its members share their work with each other through the Mirror Theatre Society in order to fulfill these goals. All scenes and materials generated through Mirror Theatre's work remain the property of Mirror Theatre, as they have been paid for through honoraria and contracts. All members in good standing have access to scenes if (a) permission is granted by the Board, (b) acknowledgment of Mirror Theatre is provided in each and every presentation, and (c) a royalty may be requested if money is received as a result of using Mirror Theatre scenes.

I agree with these rights and responsibilities of being a member of Mirror Theatre and will adhere to them.

_____   _____

        Print and Sign Name   Date

Appendix C

Program Front Cover

Balance

Idiocyncracies   Scared Stiff

Point
of
View

Personal
Life?   *Decisions*

Bursting *Bubbles*

**AM
I
READY?**

Relationships

The First
Frontier

Can Teaching   *QUEST*ioning
be Taught?

Teacher
MASK

Identity

We are ALL
STUDENT
TEACHERS

Pass the Baby   Recipes

Appendix D

Actor's Contract

Devising/Performance/Workshop Contract

As a member of Mirror Theatre, I agree to write programs and perform with the understanding that the works that are generated and performed through the collective remain the property of Mirror Theatre. I also understand that, as a member of Mirror Theatre, I may seek permission from the Board to perform vignettes in programs of my own and/or propose programs to the Board for approval.

In this instance, I agree to assist in the devising of the touring show _____ for a coauthored devising and performance fee of _____. This includes the _____ performance/workshops.

By signing this, I indicate that I am a member of Mirror Theatre in good standing and agree to the rights and responsibilities as outlined in the bylaws and policies of Mirror Theatre.

_____	_____
Actor	Date
_____	_____
Artistic Director, Mirror Theatre	Date

Appendix E

Course Outline

EDSE 424—Theory and Practice of Drama/Theatre in Education

Times: 1:00 to 2:20 and 2:30 to 3:50
ROOM: Ed N 4-104
INSTRUCTOR: Joe Norris
OFFICE:
OFFICE PHONE:
e-mail:

General Orientation

This course employs a new pedagogical orientation that is based on the theories of constructivist knowledge and cooperative learning. According to such theory, we are all responsible for our own and one another's learning. It is my hope that we can generate a "team" spirit that is essential to collaborative learning and drama projects.

1. This is "our" course. Although we may have different roles, each of us is responsible for her/his own learning and the learning of others.

2. Structures can assist us but can also inhibit us. Although the scheduled time is from 1:00 to 3:50 on Tuesdays and Thursdays, this may not be the best arrangement for learning experiences of this nature. After a while, some of these class times will change. They may start earlier or be moved to evenings or weekends.

3. Since we will be working in schools throughout the greater Edmonton Area, some travel time will be required before and after each school visit.

4. Since we are responsible for one another and are working as a team, grading individuals is antithetical to the process. Consequently, I have obtained permission for this course to be graded as credit/no credit. While no grade will be given for the following, unsatisfactory attendance, participation, and assignments can mean no credit will be given for this course.

5. The instructor will provide ample and continual formative evaluation throughout the course.

6. Changes in the traditional ways of doing things bring new tensions. A collaborative process in which many have some say in decision making is far more messy than a process that is predetermined from the top down. The messiness, in this case, is a good and natural thing.

Aims

The general aims of this course are

1. to better understand a collaborative process through reflection and discussion;

2. to understand the theory and practice of Drama/Theatre in Education troupes through the examination of exemplars and through participation in an Action Research project;

3. to use process drama techniques for self and others to uncover significance.

Assignments

1. *Focused Journal / Recursive Writing / Readback:*

The learning experiences in this course should be cumulative, and the reflective assignments build on one another. They consist of three separate features: journal entries, recursive writings, and a readback. You will be expected to keep a journal that will contain approximately 12 one-page entries. These will feed 2 recursive writings that are three to six page entries that examine a particular issue in more depth. The read-back is a 8 to 12 page take home final exam that summarizes your learning throughout the semester.

Journal

Action Research has as its underlying premise, reflective practice. Through a spiral of plan, act, observe, and reflect phases, Action Research enables participants to learn through an integration of theory and practice. Journal reflections are similar to the current educational drama belief that we learn by doing and by reflecting on that doing. You will be asked to keep a daily journal that focuses on the process of collaborative work, the role of TIE in schools, and your insights into the topics chosen for our TIE project. A journal can be a powerful learning tool. It is your responsibility to find significance.

All assignments are **designed to be learning experiences** that will expand your understanding of your personally held beliefs and the beliefs of others in the field. Constructivist theory would claim that we talk, write, work, and play our way into understanding. Each assignment should (a) expand your awareness of issues in drama education and (b) provide you with some possible directions for action.

The course is developmental, working in a spiral rather than a linear fashion. We will follow an action research cycle in which we plan, act, observe the action, reflect on its implications and formulate a new plan. This organic structure increases relevance, student co-ownership, flexibility, and uncertainty.

READBACK

Using constructivist principles, you should be creating your own ideas on the theory and practice of Drama/Theatre in Education. For this assignment, you will reread all journal entries and recursive writings, asking "What am I trying to tell myself?" Your responses will highlight for you some of the issues you consider important in TIE/DIE. This approach will make the focus of your essay on TIE/DIE. Since this class is a collaborative one, the assignment will be electronically submitted and will be compiled into a book that will be distributed to each class member. This is due last class.

Due Dates:

Each Thursday	*Journal Entry*
October 16	First Recursive
November 15	Second Recursive
December 4	Readback

2. Participation

Using the participation checklist you will assess your own participation in class. You are expected to attend all classes, contributing to the projects undertaken and to participate in the tours to the chosen schools.

Required Texts

Jackson, T (1993). *Learning through theatre*. New York: Routledge.

Nachmanovitch, S. (1990). *Free play: The power of improvisation in life and the arts*. Los Angeles: Jeremy P. Tarcher, Inc.

There will be a $15.00 handout fee to cover handouts that are in addition to the texts.

Please Note

1. The Faculty of Education is committed to providing an environment of equality and respect for all people within the university community and to educating faculty, staff, and students in developing teaching and learning contexts that are welcoming to all.

    The Faculty recommends that students and staff use "**inclusive language** to create a classroom atmosphere in which students' experiences and views are treated with equal respect and value in relation to their gender, racial background, sexual orientation, and ethnic backgrounds."

    We are encouraged to use gender-neutral or gender-inclusive language when appropriate and to become more sensitive to the effects of devaluing language in order to create a thoughtful and respectful community.

2. Your attention is drawn to the University Regulations and Information to Students found on pages 64 to 97 of the 2001/02 Calendar. In particular, note Section 23 on **Academic Regulations** and Section 27 covering the **Code of Student Behavior**.

Appendix F

Expecting Respect Questionnaire Summary

(The comments were written on the real forms.)

March 1ˢᵗ, 2000

Do you believe that the drama was worthwhile? In what ways? Or why not?

There was an overwhelming positive response to the drama. Many comments were made on its realism, how it was informative due to its concrete examples, and how the audience obtained ideas of how to present material. Below are emergent themes and numbers of responses following under each theme.

Value of program

Fourteen respondents made comments such as "cool," "interesting," "entertaining," "excellent," "informative," "fun," "creative," and "learned lots."

Realism

Many liked the concrete nature of the performances and believed that they accurately represented the world in which they live. Comments made were "realistic," "made it real," "showed us how we act in schools," "relates to everyday life," and "believable/ happens in life."

Presentation

It was suggested by six respondents that a new way of dealing and presenting new ideas was shown to them. They felt that the drama enabled them to deal with new situations. Specific comments about drama included: it "suggested how to deal with new issues," "showed how to get message through," "gave a new way to present information."

Immediacy

The fact that the drama was enacted before the participants made a number of respondents appreciate the importance of seeing it themselves. Seven respondents expressed their appreciation by stressing how seeing the performance aspect of drama had made participation eventful. Comments articulated were "seeing it was worthwhile," "it is easier to see and situate," "issues were seen instead of heard," "different situations could be seen."

Engagement

Drama was also seen as an engaging activity. Five respondents felt that it made them get interested and involved. For them, concentration was greatly maintained owing to the drama. Consequently, a lot was learned in this respect. Comments made were "made you want to get involved," "helped one to delve deeper," "made one learn a lot," kept our attention," "kept audience awake," "everyone was involved."

Interaction

A respondent felt that made ideas were synthesized and integrated owing to the interactive mode of the drama. Much of the discussion that led to new ideas was due to this quality. Specific comments made were "it integrated ideas," "made taking part in discussion worthwhile," "generated discussion," "generated new ideas."

Future Direction

A sizable number of respondents want further directions in presenting their ideas before peers. The five who responded made it clear that program facilitators take cognizance of the fact that acting is not for everyone. Instead, it should be made optional. Comments made here included: "acting is not for everyone," "participation should be optional," "not everyone is comfortable," "further direction needed for students."

Attitude

There were two respondents who expressed their liking for the drama leader as well as acting. They felt that the need for more drama had been planted and that there was an opportunity for developing it more in length. Comments made include: "I liked the leader," "love acting," "need a bigger drama next time."

Appendix G

Program Back Cover

For Discussion Groups

The Play

1. This scene reminded me of _____ event.
2. This scene disturbed me because . . .
3. I was pleased by this scene because . . .
4. I didn't understand this scene because . . .
5. This scene accurately describes _____ issue/experience.
6. This scene made me remember/rethink _____ behavior of mine.
7. This scene made me remember/rethink _____ relationship.
8. I saw myself as a "victim/villain" in this scene.

Extensions

1. What issues of yours didn't the play touch on?
2. When I return to my setting I plan to do _____ differently.
3. I would like to discuss/prepare/present this scene at the plenary session.

Concept

1. How is (this topic) defined and translated in life?
2. How is (this aspect of the topic) defined and translated in life?

Use these as discussion starters. A member of the cast will make notes during the discussion and use them in the plenary session, which may also take a dramatic format.

References

Ackroyd, J. 2000. Applied theatre: Problems and possibilities, *The Applied Theatre Researcher*, http://griffith.edu.au/centre/cpci/atr/journal/article1_number1.htm.

——. 2007. Applied theatre: An exclusionary discourse? *The IDEA Journal/ Applied Theatre Researcher*, www.griffith.edu.au/_data/assets/pdf_file/0005/52889/01-ackroyd-final.pdf.

Anderson, C. 1989. *Literary Nonfiction*. Carbondale: Southern Illinois University Press.

Applegate, E. 1996. *Literary Journalism: A Biographical Dictionary of Writers and Editors*. Santa Barbara: Greenwood Press.

Bagley, C. 2008. Educational ethnography as performance art: Towards a sensuous feeling and knowing, *Qualitative Research* 8(1), 53–72.

Bagley, C., and Cancienne, M. B. 2002. Educational research and intertextual forms of (re)presentation: The case for dancing the data, in C. Bagley and M. B. Cancienne (Eds.), *Dancing the Data*. New York: Peter Lang Publishing, Inc.

Bakhtin, N. 1981. *The Dialogic Imagination*. Austin: The University of Texas Press.

Banks, A., and Banks, S. 1998. *Fiction and Social Research: By Ice or Fire*. Walnut Creek, CA: AltaMira Press.

Barber, M. 1989. Alma Gonsalvez: Otherness as attending to the Other, in A. B. Dallery and C. E. Scott (Eds.), *The Question of the Other*. New York: State University of New York Press.

Barone, T. 1990. Using the narrative text as an occasion for conspiracy, in E. W. Eisner and A. Peshkin (Eds.), *Qualitative Inquiry in Education*. New York: Teachers College Press, pp. 305–326.

Barone, T. 1995. The purposes of arts-based educational research, *International Journal of Educational Research* 23(2), 169–180.

———. 2007. A return to the gold standard? Questioning the future of narrative construction as educational research, *Qualitative Inquiry* 13(4), 454–470.

Baudrillard, J. 1983. *Simulations.* New York: Semiotext(e).

———. 2001. Simulacra and simulations, in M. Poster (Ed.), *Jean Baudrillard: Selected Readings.* Stanford: Stanford University Press.

Benjamin, J. 1990. An outline of intersubjectivity: The development of recognition. *Psychoanalytic Psychology,* 7, 33–46.

Berezan, D. 2004. A joker in the classroom: A qualitative inquiry into the essences of the joker role in Mirror Theatre and their correlation to reflective teaching practice. Unpublished masters thesis, University of Alberta, Edmonton.

Berger, J. 1972. *Ways of Seeing.* Markham: Penguin Books.

Berger, P., and Luckman, T. 1966. *The Social Construction of Reality.* New York: Doubleday.

Berry, G., and Reinbold, J. 1985. *Collective Creation.* Edmonton: Alberta Alcohol and Drug Addiction Commission.

Bloom, L. Z. 2003. Living to tell the tale: The complicated ethics of creative nonfiction, *College English* 65(3), 276–289.

Blumenfeld-Jones, D. 1995. Dance as a mode of research representation, *Qualitative Inquiry* 1(4), 391–401.

———. 2002. If I could have said it, I would have, in C. Bagley and M. B. Cancienne (Eds.), *Dancing the Data.* New York: Peter Lang Publishing, Inc.

Boal, A. 1979. *Theatre of the Oppressed.* London: Pluto Press.

———. 1992. *Games for Actors and Non-Actors.* New York: Routledge.

———. 1995. *The Rainbow of Desire: The Boal Method of Theatre and Therapy,* Adrian Jackson (Trans.). New York: Routledge.

Bowman, R. L. 1997. "Joking" with the classics: Using Boal's joker system in the performance classroom, *Theatre Topics* 7(2), 139–151.

Brandes, D., and Phillips, H. 1980. *The Gamesters' Handbook.* London: Hutchinson.

Bray, E. 1991. *Playbuilding: A Guide for Group Creation of Plays with Young People.* Sydney: Currency Press.

Brecht, B. 1957. *Brecht on Theatre: The Development of an Aesthetic.* New York: Hill and Wang.

———. 1961. The Caucasian Chalk Circle, in E. Bentley (Ed.), *Seven Plays.* New York: Grove Press.

———. 2005. *Threepenny Opera.* London: Methuen.

Buber, M. 1947. The development of the creative powers in the child, in M. Buber (Ed.), *Between Man and Man.* London: Kegan, Paul, Trench, Trubner and Company Limited.

Burniston, C. 1972. *Into the Life of Things: An Exploration of Language through Verbal Dynamics.* Southport: English Speaking Board.

Butler-Kisber, L. 2002. Artful portrayals in qualitative inquiry: The road to found poetry and beyond, *Alberta Journal of Educational Research* 48(3), 229–239.

Campbell, G., Conrad, D., Kamau, O., Smith, L., and Spence-Campbell, S. February, 2001. *Examining the Construct of Desire through Popular Theatre and Improvisational Drama*. Performance presented at the Advances in Qualitative Methods conference, Edmonton, AB.

Capote, T. 1965. *In Cold Blood: A True Account of a Multiple Murder and Its Consequences*. New York: Random House, p. 343.

Cloke, K., and Goldsmith, J. 2002. *The End of Management and the Rise of Organizational Democracy*. San Francisco: Jossey-Bass.

Coger, L. I., and White, M. R. 1971. *Readers Theatre Handbook*. Glenview: Scott, Foresman and Company, p. 308.

Cohen, M. 1995. *First Grade Takes the Test*. New York: A Picture Yearling Book.

Coloroso, B. 2002. *The Bully, the Bullied, and the Bystander*. New York: Harper Collins.

Conrad, D. 2001. Media, Advertising and Drama. Unpublished master's thesis. Edmonton, University of Alberta.

Conrad, D., Zinken, P., and Mirror Theatre. 1999. (Co-directors). *Where's the Risk in That? Living on the Edge,* Youth Conference. Drayton Valley, AB.

Cottrell, J. 1979. *Teaching with Creative Dramatics*. Skokie: National Textbook Company.

Courtney, R. 1980. *The Dramatic Curriculum*. New York: Drama Book Specialists.

Culler, J. 1982. *On Deconstruction*. Ithaca: Cornell University Press.

de Chardin, P. T. 1969. *Christianity and Evolution*. New York: Harcourt Brace Jovanovich.

Denzin, N. 1989. *Interpretive Biography*. Newbury Park, CA: Sage.

———. 2003. Performing [auto] ethnography politically, *The Review of Education, Pedagogy, and Cultural Studies* 25, 257–278.

Dodson, K. 1956. *Away All Boats*. New York: Bantam.

Donmoyer, R. 1990. Generalizability and the single-case study, in E. W. Eisner and A. Peshkin (Eds.), *Qualitative Inquiry in Education*. New York: Teachers College Press, pp. 175–200.

Donmoyer, R., and Yennie-Donmoyer, J. 1995. Data as drama: Reflections on the use of Readers Theatre as a mode of qualitative data display *Qualitative Inquiry* 1(4), 402–428.

Duch, B., Groh, S., and Allen, D. 2001. *The Power of Problem-Based Learning*. Sterling, VA: Stylus Publishing.

Dunlop, R. 1999. Boundary Bay: A Novel. Unpublished doctoral dissertation, The University of British Columbia.

———. 2002. *Boundary Bay*. Winnipeg: Staccato Chapbook.

Eco, U. 1976. *A theory of Semiotics*. Bloomington: Indiana University Press.

Edwards, B. 1979. *10*. USA: Geoffrey Productions Inc.

Eisner, E. 1997. The promise and perils of alternative forms of representation, *Educational Researcher* 26(6), 4–10.

Ellis, C. 2004. *The ethnographic I*. Walnut Creek, CA: AltaMira Press.

Falikowski, A. 1996. *Mastering Human Relations*. Upper Saddle River, NJ: Prentice Hall.

Fels, L., and Belliveau, G. 2008. *Exploring Curriculum: Performative Inquiry, Role Drama, and Learning*. Vancouver, Pacific Educational Press.

Filewod, A. 1982. Collective creation: Process, politics and poetics, *Canadian Theatre Review* 34(Spring), 46–58.

——. 1987. *Collective Encounters: Documentary Theatre in English Canada.* Toronto: University of Toronto Press.

Flinders, D., Noddings, N., and Thornton, S. 1986. The null curriculum: Its theoretical basis and practical implications, *Curriculum Inquiry* 16(1), 33–42.

Frank, K. 2000. "The management of hunger": Using fiction in writing anthropology, *Qualitative Inquiry* 6(4), 474–488.

Freire, P. 1986. *Pedagogy of the oppressed.* New York: The Continuum Publishing Corporation.

Fullan, M. 1982. *The Meaning of Educational Change.* Toronto: OISE Press.

Futterman, D. 2006. *Capote: The Shooting Script.* London: Nick Hern Books.

Gadamer, H. 1975. *Truth and Method.* New York: Crossroad.

Gallagher, K., and Riviére, D. 2007. When drama praxis rocks the boat: Struggles of subjectivity, audience, and performance, *Research in Drama Education* 12(3), 319–330.

Gearing, R. E. 2009. Bracketing, *The Sage Encyclopedia of Qualitative Research Methods.* Los Angeles: Sage, p. 1.

Geertz, C. 1973a. *The Interpretation of Cultures.* New York: Basic Books.

——. 1973b. Thick description: Toward an interpretive theory of culture, in C. Geertz (Ed.), *The Interpretation of Cultures.* New York: Basic Books.

——. 1974. From the native's point of view: On the nature of anthropological understanding, in P. Rabinow and W. Sullivan (Eds.), *Interpretive Social Sciences.* Berkeley and Los Angeles: University of California Press, pp. 221–237.

——. 1983. *Local Knowledge.* New York, Basic Books.

Giorgi, A. 1997. The theory, practice, and evaluation of the phenomenological method as a qualitative research, *Journal of Phenomenological Psychology* 28(2), 235.

Giroux, H. 1991. *Postmodernism, Feminism, and Cultural Politics: Redrawing Educational Boundaries.* Albany: State University of New York Press.

Giroux, H., and Penna, A. 1981. Social education in the classroom: The dynamics of the hidden curriculum, in H. Giroux, A. Penna, and W. Pinar (Eds.), *Curriculum and Instruction.* Berkeley: McCutchan Publishing Corporation.

Goffman, I. 1974. *Frame Analysis.* Cambridge: Harvard University Press.

Goodman, L., and Gay, J. D. 1996. *Feminist Stages: Interviews with Women in Contemporary British Theatre.* Amsterdam: Harwood Academic Publishers.

Greene, M. 1995. *Releasing the Imagination: Essays of Education, the Arts and Social Change.* San Francisco: Jossey-Bass.

Greenfield, H., and Sedaka, N. 1961. *Calendar Girl.* Toronto: EMI Music Publishing, Inc.

Hailey, A. 1971. *Wheels.* New York: Bantam.

Harman, W., and Rheingold, H. 1984. *Higher Creativity.* Los Angeles: Jeremy P. Tarcher, Inc.

Hartsock, J. C. 2000. *A History of American Literary Journalism.* Boston: University of Massachusetts.

Heathcote, D. 1971. *Three Looms Waiting* [Film]. Toronto: Omnibus: BBC Enterprises.

Heathcote, D., Johnson, L., and O'Neill, C. 1991. *Dorothy Heathcote: Collected Writings on Education and Drama.* Evanston, IL: Northwestern University Press.

Heisenberg, W. 1927. Über den anschaulichen Inhalt der quantentheoretischen Kinematik und Mechanik, *Zeitschrift für Physik* 43, 172–198.

——. 1983. On the illustrative content of quantum-theoretical kinematics and mechanics, in J. A. Wheeler and W. H. Zurek (Eds.), *Quantum Theory and Measurement.* Princeton, NJ: Princeton University Press.

Henderson, J. 1992. *Reflective Teaching: Becoming an Inquiring Educator.* Toronto: Maxwell Macmillan Canada.

Henderson, J. G., and Kesson, K. 2003. *Curriculum Wisdom: Educational Decisions in Democratic Societies.* Upper Saddle River, NJ: Pearson/Merrill/ Prentice Hall.

Herrigel, E. 1989. *Zen in the Art of Archery.* New York: Vintage Books.

Hewson, A. 2007. Emotions as data in the act of jokering forum theatre, *International Journal of Education & the Arts* 8(18), www.ijea.org/v8n18/, accessed November, 2008.

Hobbs, W. 1995. *Fight Direction for the Stage and Screen.* London: A & C Black.

Hume, D. 1987. *Essays, moral, political, and literary/David Hume.* Indianapolis: LibertyClassics.

Irwin, R. L., and de Cosson, A. 2004. *A/r/tography: Rendering Self through Arts-Based Living Inquiry.* Vancouver: Pacific Educational Press.

Jackson, T. 1993. *Learning through Theatre.* New York: Routledge.

Janesick, V. J. 2001. Intuition and creativity: A *pas de deux* for qualitative researchers, *Qualitative Inquiry* 7(5), 531–540.

——. 2004. *"Stretching" Exercises for Qualitative Researchers.* Thousand Oaks, CA: Sage.

Jersild, A. 1955. *The Search for Meaning.* New York: Teachers College Press.

Johnson, K., and Nelson, J. 2002. *I Am Sam.* New Line Cinema.

Kemmis, S., and McTaggart, R. 1988. *The Action Research Planner* (3rd ed.). Victoria: Deacon University Press.

Kieren, T. 1995. *Teaching Mathematics (in the Middle): An Enactivist View of Learning and Teaching Mathematics.* (Publication from the Center for Mathematics, Science and Technology Education, www.ioncmaste.ca/ homepage/discussion_group.html.)

Koch, T. 1995. Interpretive approaches in nursing research: The influence of Husserl and Heidegger, *Journal of Advanced Nursing* 21(5), 827–836.

Kopp, S. 1972. *If You Meet the Buddha on the Road, Kill Him.* New York: Bantam.

Koski, C. A. 1999. The non-fiction novel as psychiatric casebook: Truman Capote's *In Cold Blood, Journal of Technical Writing and Communication* 29(3), 289–303.

Kostera, M. 2006. The narrative collage as research method, *Storytelling, Self, Society* 2(2) (Spring 2006), 5–27.

Kuhn, T. 1962. *The Structures of Scientific Revolutions.* Chicago: The University of Chicago Press.

Langevin, M., Bortnick, K., Hammer, T., and Wiebe, E. 1998. Teasing/bullying experienced by children who stutter: Toward development of a questionnaire, *Contemporary Issues in Communication Science and Disorders* 25, 12–24.

Leavy, P. 2009. *Method meets art.* New York: The Guilford Press.

Lesko, N., Simmons, J., and Quarshie, A. 2008. The pedagogy of monsters: Scary disturbances in a doctoral research preparation course, *Teachers College Record* 110(8), 1541–1573.

Levinas, E. 1984. Emmanuel Levinas, in R. Kearney (Ed.), *Dialogues with Contemporary Continental Thinkers.* Manchester: Manchester University Press, pp. 47–70.

Lounsberry, B. 1990. *The Art of Fact.* New York: Greenwood Press.

Lyng, S. 1990. Edgework: A social psychological analysis of voluntary risk taking, *American Journal of Sociology* 95(4), 876–921.

Lyotard, J.-F. 1979. *The Postmodern Condition: A Report on Knowledge,* G. Bennington and B. Massumi (Trans.). Minneapolis: The University of Minnesota Press.

McGregor, R. 1990. Hunch, in J. Simpson (Ed.), *Coming of Age.* Edmonton: Fine Arts Council, pp. 1–11.

McLuhan, M. 1967. *The Medium Is the Massage.* Toronto: Random House of Canada.

McNiff, S. 2000. *Art-Based Research.* Philadelphia: Jessica Kingsley Publishers.

Merleau-Ponty, M. 1962. *Phenomenology of Perception,* C. Smith (Trans.). New York: Humanities Press.

Meyer, M. 1998. Transitional Wars: A Study of Power, Control, and Conflict in Executive Succession—Theatre as Representation. Unpublished Doctoral Dissertation, McGill University, Montreal.

Meyer, M. 2009. *Improving the Selection and Performance of School Principals: Using Theatre as a Professional Development Tool.* Lewiston: The Mellen Press.

Mienczakowski, J. 1995. The theater of ethnography: The reconstruction of ethnography into theatre with emancipatory potential, *Qualitative Inquiry* 1(3), 159–172.

Miller, D. 1966. (Director) *Summerhill.* National Film Board (Producer). Canada.

Mishlove, J. Metaphysics and modern science Part I: Consciousness and science with Willis Harman, accessed August 10, 2008, from *The Intuition Network, A Thinking Allowed Television Underwriter,* www.intuition.org/txt/harman1.htm.

Morgan, N., and Saxton, J. 2006. *Asking Better Questions.* Markham, ON: Pembroke Publishers Limited.

Myers, I. B., & McCaulley, M. 1985. *Manual: A Guide to the Development and Use of the Myers-Briggs Type Indicator.* Palo Alto, CA: Consulting Psychologists Press.

Nachmanovitch, S. 1990. *Free Play: The Power of Improvisation in Life and the Arts.* Los Angeles: Jeremy P. Tarcher, Inc.

Naisbitt, J. 1982. *Megatrends: Ten New Directions Transforming Our Lives.* New York: Warner Books.

Neelands, J. 1984. *Making Sense of Drama.* London: Heinemann Educational Books Ltd.

Neelands, J., and Goode, T. 2000. *Structuring Drama Work.* New York: Cambridge University Press.

Neilsen, L. 2002. Learning from the liminal: Fiction as knowledge, *The Alberta Journal of Educational Research* XLVIII(3), 206–214.

Norris, J. 1989a. Some Authorities as Co-Authors in a Collective Creation Production. Unpublished Doctoral Dissertation, University of Alberta.

———. 1989b. (Writer) *The Merry-Grow-Round: A Collective Creation performance.* Edmonton: Instructional Technology Center, University of Alberta.

———. 1989c. (Writer) *Examples of Some Dramatic Forms Used in Collective Creations.* Edmonton: Instructional Technology Center, University of Alberta.

———. 1989d. (Writer) *An Example of the Collective Creation Process.* Edmonton: Instructional Technology Center, University of Alberta.

———. 1989e. (Writer) *Examples of the Exploration Stage in Collective Creations.* Edmonton: Instructional Technology Center, University of Alberta.

———. 1993. Adulthood. . . lost Childhood . . . found, *Educational Action Research* 1(2), 255.

———. 1994. Advocacy: Doing what we do best, *The Drama Theatre Teacher* 6(4), 10–13.

———. 1995a. Response-able guided imagery, *Stage of the Art* 7(4), 4–9.

———. 1995b. The use of drama in teacher education: A call for embodied learning, in B. Warren (Ed.), *Creating a Theater in Your Classroom.* North York, ON: Captus University Publications, pp. 279–305.

———. 1998a. TIE/DIE: Listening to the voices of the audience, *The National Association for Drama in Education Journal* (Australia) 22(1), 61–67.

———. 1998b. Creative drama as adult's work, in B. J. Wagner (Ed.), *Building Moral Communities through Drama.* Stamford, CT: Ablex Publishing Corporation, pp. 211–230.

———. 1999. Representations of violence in schools as co-created by cast and audiences during a theatre/drama in education program, in G. Malicky, B. Shapiro, and K. Masurek (Eds.), *Building Foundations for Safe and Caring Schools: Research on Disruptive Behaviour and Violence.* Edmonton: Duval House Publishing, pp. 271–328.

———. 2000. Drama as research: Realizing the potential of drama in education as a research methodology, *Youth Theatre Journal* 14, 40–51.

———. 2008a. Duoethnography, in L. M. Given (Ed.), *The Sage Encyclopedia of Qualitative Research Methods,* Vol. 1. Los Angeles: Sage, pp. 233–236.

———. 2008b. Playbuilding, in L. M. Given (Ed.), *The Sage Encyclopedia of Qualitative Research Methods,* Vol. 2. Los Angeles: Sage, pp. 630–633.

———. 2008c. A quest for a theory and practice of authentic assessment: An arts-based approach, *LEARNing Landscapes* 1(3), 211–233.

Norris, J., and Mirror Theatre. 1996a. (Director and Coauthor) *Great Expectations II*. Keynote Paper/Performance presented at the 1996 Western Canadian Association for Student Teaching. University of Saskatchewan: Saskatoon, Saskatchewan.

——. 1996b. (Director and Coauthor) *Great Expectations III*. Plenary Paper/Performance presented at the 1996 Western Canadian Association for Student Teaching. University of Saskatchewan: Saskatoon, Saskatchewan.

——. 1997a. (Director, MC, Actor, and Coauthor) *What's the Fine Line?* Keynote performance presented at the 1997 Conference for Safe and Caring Schools. Edmonton, Alberta.

——. 1997b. *Shadows*. (Director, MC, Actor, and Coauthor) Teen Wellness Conference. Grey Nuns Hospital, Edmonton.

——. 1998a. (Director, MC, Actor, and Coauthor) *One of These Things Is Not Like the Others; One of These Things Just Doesn't Belong*. Keynote performance presented at the 1998 Western Canadian Association for Student Teaching. Victoria, British Columbia.

——. 1998b. (Director and Joker) *Under Construction*. A performance/workshops (four) presented at the Expecting Respect Peer Educator Training sessions.

——. 1998c. *Complexities and Contradictions*. Keynote performance presented at the Western Canadian Conference on Human Sexuality. Edmonton.

——. 1999a. (Director) *Respecting Diversity and Preventing Prejudice*. The Society for Safe and Caring Schools and Communities (Producer). Canada.

——. 1999b. (Director and Joker) *Crossroads*. Five performance/workshops presented at the Expecting Respect Peer Educator Training sessions.

——. 2000a. (Director) *Dealing with Bullying*. The Society for Safe and Caring Schools and Communities (Producer). Canada.

Norris, J., and Mirror Theatre. 2000b. (Director, MC, Actor, and Coauthor) *To the Movies*. Performance presented at the Safe and Caring Communities Conference. Edmonton, Alberta.

——. 2000c. (Director, MC, Actor, and Coauthor) *What's the Use?* Five performance/workshops presented at the Expecting Respect Peer Educator Training sessions.

——. 2000d. (Director, Actor) *ReSearch: RePlay*. Performance presented at the Qualitative Health Research Conference, Banff, Alberta.

——. 2001a. (Director with Mirror Theatre) *Resolving Conflict Peacefully*. The Society for Safe and Caring Schools and Communities (Producer). Canada.

——. 2001b. (Director, MC, Actor, and Coauthor) *Friends, Family, and Foreigners*. Five performance/workshops presented at the Expecting Respect Peer Educator Training sessions.

——. 2001c. (Director, MC, and Coauthor) *Last Call... Your Call*. Alberta Alcohol and Drug Abuse Commission's Launch of their YA (Youth Alternative Program) Stettler, Drumheller and Valleyview.

——. 2001d. What can we do? A performance/workshop on bullying and managing anger, *Journal of Curriculum Theorizing* (Summer 2001), 111–128.

Norris, J., and Mirror Theatre. 2002. (Director) *C5: Civility, Citizenship and Community Construction on Campus*. Performance/Workshop for University Teaching Services, University of Alberta.

——. 2003. (Director) *Examining Social Issues through Forum Theatre*. Invited presentation for the Theatre in Education Preconference of the American Alliance for Theatre and Education. New York.

——. 2004. (Director, MC, Actor, and Coauthor with Student Company) *Shadowing*. Keynote performance presented at the 2004 Western Canadian Association for Student Teaching. Edmonton: Alberta.

Norris, J., and Student Company. 1991. (Director, Actor, and Coauthor) *Snapshots of Playing Together*. Performance presented at the Western Canadian Association for Student Teaching. Regina.

——. 1992. (Director and Coauthor with Company No Spare Time) *Paradise Lost*. Paper/Performance presented at the 1992 Western Canadian Association for Student Teaching. University of Alberta: Edmonton, Alberta.

——. 1993a. (Director, Actor, and Coauthor) *Mirror/Mirror*. Performance/Workshop presented for the Faculty of Education, University of Alberta's Equality and Respect day.

——. 1993b. (Director and Coauthor) *The First Frontier*. Paper/Performance presented at the 1993 Western Canadian Association for Student Teaching. University of British Columbia: Vancouver, British Columbia.

——. 1994a. (Director, Actor, and Coauthor) *Great Expectations*. Edmonton: Instructional Technology Center, University of Alberta.

——. 1994b. (Director, Actor, and Coauthor) *Rules of the Game*. Performance/Workshop presented at International Week. University of Alberta.

——. 1995a. (Director, Actor, and Coauthor) *Great Expectations*. Performance presented at the Annual Conference of The Journal of Curriculum Theorizing. Banff Centre for Conferences, Banff, Alberta.

——. 1995b. (Director, Actor, and Coauthor) *If We Offend*. Performance/Workshop presented during Education Week. University of Alberta.

——. 1995c. (Director, Actor, and Coauthor) *'clusions*. Performance/Workshop presented at Austin O'Brien High School.

——. 1995d. (Director, Actor, and Coauthor) *What's the Fine Line?* Five Performance/Workshops presented at Steele Heights Junior High School.

——. 1996a. (Director, MC, Actor, and Coauthor) *What's the Fine Line?* Performance/Workshop presented at G. H. Primeau School. (One parent and three student shows.)

——. 2005. (Director, Coauthor with Mount Saint Vincent graduate Students) *Warts or Beauty Marks?* Keynote: Atlantic Educators Conference. Antigonish: Nova Scotia.

Norris, J., Higgins, C., and Leggo, C. 2004. *"Shh stories": The Problematics of Personal Disclosure in Qualitative Research*. Paper presented at the American Alliance for Theatre and Education: Conference. San Diego.

Norris, J., and Sawyer, R. 2004. Null and hidden curricula of sexual orientation: A dialogue on the currreres of the absent presence and the present absence, in L. Coia, M. Birch, N. J. Brooks, E. Heilman, S. Mayer, A. Mountain, and P. Pritchard (Eds.), *Democratic Responses in an Era of Standardization.* Troy, NY: Curriculum and Pedagogy, pp. 139–159.

O'Neill, C. 1995. *Drama Worlds: A Framework for Process Drama.* Portsmouth, NH: Heinemann.

Orff, C. 1977. *Music for Children,* Vol. 2. New York: Shott.

Orwell, G. 1992. *1984.* New York: Knopf.

O'Toole, J., and Stinson, M. 2009. Past, presents, and futures: Which door next? in J. O'Toole, M. Stinson, and T. Moore (Eds.), *Drama and Curriculum.* Dordrecht: Springer, pp. 193–209.

Palmer, M. 1995. *Boys Will Be Boys: Sexual Harassment in Schools.* Canadian Broadcasting Corporation (Producer). Canada: CBCLearning.

Pammenter, D. 1993. Devising for TIE, in T. Jackson (Ed.), *Learning through Theatre.* New York: Routledge, pp. 53–70.

Papin, J. 1985. The Open Hand Theatre: A Collective Creation. Unpublished Doctoral Dissertation, Syracuse University.

Phillips, D. C. 1995. The good, the bad, and the ugly: The many faces of constructivism, *Educational Researcher* 24(7), 5–12.

Piirto, J. 2002. The question of quality and qualifications: Writing inferior poems as qualitative research, *International Journal of Qualitative Studies in Education* 15(4), 431–445.

Pinar, W. 1975. Curerre: Toward reconceptualization, in W. Pinar (Ed.), *Curriculum Theorizing.* Berkeley: McCutchan Publishing Corporation, pp. 396–414.

——. 2000. *Curriculum Studies: The Reconceptualization.* Troy, NY: Educator's International Press.

Rapaso, J., and Stone, J. 1992. *One of These Things: The Sesame Street Song Book.* Milwaukee: Hal Leonard Corporation, p. 135.

Reason, P., and Hawkins, P. 1988. Storytelling as inquiry, in P. Reason (Ed.), *Human Inquiry in Action.* Newbury Park, CA: Sage, pp. 79–101.

Richardson, L. 1990. *Writing strategies: Reaching diverse audiences.* Newbury Park, CA: Sage.

Rohd, M. (1998). Theatre for community, conflict and dialogue. Portsmouth: Heinemann.

Rodgers, J. 1967. *Child of Clay* [Music]. Los Angeles: A&M Records.

Root-Bernstein, R., and Root-Bernstein, M. 1999. *Sparks of Genius.* Boston: Mariner Books.

Rosenblatt, L. 1978. *The Reader, the Text, the Poem: The Transactional Theory of the Literary Work.* Carbondale: Southern Illinois Press.

Rudlin, J., and Crick, O. 2001. *Commedia dell'Arte: A Handbook for Troupes.* New York: Routledge.

Rutledge, M. 2004. Dance as Research: The Experience of Surrender. Unpublished doctoral dissertation, University of Alberta, Edmonton.

Saldaña, J. 1998. "Maybe someday if I'm famous...": An ethnographic performance text, in J. Saxton and C. Miller (Eds.), *The Research of Practice, the Practice of Research.* Victoria: IDEA Publications, pp. 89–109.

Saldaña, J. 2001. *Finding My Place: The Brad Trilogy.* Performance at the Advances in Qualitative Methods conference. Edmonton AB, Canada.

——. 2002. Finding my place: The Brad trilogy, in H. F. Wolcott, *Sneaky Kid and Its Aftermath: Ethics and Intimacy in Fieldwork.* Walnut Creek, CA: AltaMira Press, pp. 167–210.

——. 2005. *Ethnodrama: An anthology of reality theatre.* Toronto: AltaMira Press.

Salutin, R., and Theatre Passe Muraille. 1976. *1837.* Toronto: James Lorimer and Company.

Sameshima, P. 2006. Seeing Red—A Pedagogy of Parallax: An Epistolary Bildungsroman on Artful Scholarly Inquiry. Unpublished doctoral dissertation, The University of British Columbia, Vancouver.

——. 2007. *Seeing Red—A Pedagogy of Parallax: An Epistolary Bildungsroman on Artful Scholarly Inquiry.* Amherst, NY: Cambria Press.

Schön, D. 1983. *The Reflective Practitioner.* New York: Basic Books.

Schonmann, S. 2006. *Theatre as a Medium for Children and Young People: Images and Observations.* Dordrecht: Springer.

Schunk, D. 1991. Chapter 7: Constructivism, in D. Schunk (Ed.), *Learning Theories.* Columbus: Merrill Prentice Hall, pp. 285–328.

Schwandt, T. A. 1997. *Qualitative Inquiry: A Dictionary of Terms.* Thousand Oaks, CA: Sage.

Selman, J. 1986a. *Role Play: A Practical Guide for Group Leaders.* Edmonton: Alberta Alcohol and Drug Abuse Commission.

——. 1986b. *Theatre for Education and Change.* Edmonton: Alberta Alcohol and Drug Abuse Commission.

Shakespeare, W. 1972a. *The Tempest,* in S. Barnet (Ed.), *The Complete Signet Classic Shakespeare.* New York: Harcourt Brace Jovanovich.

——. 1972b. *Twelfth Night,* in S. Barnet (Ed.), *The Complete Signet Classic Shakespeare.* New York: Harcourt Brace Jovanovich.

——. 1972c. *Hamlet.* In S. Barnet (Ed.), *The Complete Signet Classic Shakespeare.* New York: Harcourt Brace Jovanovich.

——. 1972d. *As You Like It,* in S. Barnet (Ed.), *The Complete Signet Classic Shakespeare.* New York: Harcourt Brace Jovanovich.

Shelton, N. R., and McDermott, M. 2007. A Curriculum of Beauty. Paper presented at the Curriculum and Pedagogy Conference. Balcones Springs, Texas.

Smith, A. 1996. Forum Theatre and the Role of the Joker: Social Activist, Educator Therapist, Director: The Changing Perspective of Canadian Jokers. Unpublished master's thesis, University of Alberta, Edmonton.

Smith, J., and Heshusius, L. 1986. Closing down the conversation: The end of the quantitative-qualitative debate among educational Inquirers, *Educational Researcher* 15(1), 4–12.

Smith, P., Morota, Y., Junger-Tas, J., Olweus, D., Catalano, R., and Slee, P. (Eds.). 1999. *The Nature of School Bullying: A Cross-National Perspective.* New York: Routledge.

Snowber, C. 2002. Bodydance: Enfleshing soulful inquiry through improvisation, in C. Bagley and M. B. Cancienne (Eds.), *Dancing the Data.* New York: Peter Lang Publishing.

Spolin, V. 1963. *Improvisation for the Theatre: A Handbook of Teaching and Directing Techniques.* Evanston, IL: Northwestern University Press.

Spradley, J. 1979. *The Ethnographic Interview.* New York: Holt, Rinehart, and Winston.

———. 1980. *Participant Observation.* New York, Holt, Rinehart, and Winston.

Sternberg, P. 1998. *Theatre for Conflict Resolution.* Portsmouth: Heinemann.

Strauss, A., and Corbin, J. 1990. *Basics of Qualitative Research: Techniques and Procedures for Developing Grounded Theory.* Newbury Park, CA: Sage.

Streisand, B. 1983. *Yentl.* (Director) Barwood Films & Ladbroke Investments (Producer). United States: MGM/UA Entertainment Company.

Suddeth, J. A. 1996. *Fight Directing for the Theatre.* Portsmouth. NH: Heinemann.

Swortzell, L. 1993. Trying to like TIE: An American critic hopes TIE can be saved, in T. Jackson (Ed.), *Learning through Theatre.* New York: Routledge, pp. 239–249.

Tannen, D. 1990. *You Just Don't Understand: Women and Men in Conversation.* New York: Ballantine Books.

Taylor, P. 2003. *Applied Theatre: Creating Transformative Encounters in the Community.* Portsmouth, NH: Heinemann, 2003.

Tardif, C. 2006. Motion to urge government to reconsider decision to discontinue the court challenges program, in Government of Canada, *Debates of the Senate* (Hansard) 1st Session, 39th Parliament, 143(35).

Theatre Passe Muraille. 1967. *The Farm Show.* Toronto: The Coach House Press.

Tuckman, B. 1965. Development sequence in small groups, *Psychological Bulletin* 63, 384–399.

Varela, F., Thompson, E., and Rosch, E. 1992. *The Embodied Mind: Cognitive Science and Human Experience.* Cambridge, MA: MIT Press.

Verbinski, G. 2003. (Director) *Pirates of the Caribbean: The Curse of the Black Pearl.* Walt Disney Pictures. USA.

Wagner, B. J. 1976. *Dorothy Heathcote: Drama as a Learning Medium.* Washington, D.C.: National Education Association.

Watson, L. 1994. If you have come to help me… Northland Poster Collective: http://northlandposter.com/blog/2006/12/18/lila-watson-if-you-have-come-to-help-me-you-are-wasting-your-time-but-if-you-have-come-because-your-liberation-is-bound-up-with-mine-then-let-us-work-to-gether/, accessed July 2008.

Weigler, W. 2002. *Strategies for Playbuilding.* Portsmouth, NH: Heinemann.

Werhane, P. H. 1999. *Moral Imagination and Management Decision Making.* New York: Oxford University Press.

Werner, W., and Rothe, P. 1979. *Doing School Ethnography.* Edmonton: Department of Secondary Education, University of Alberta.

Wisegeek. 2009. What are cattle calls? www.wisegeek.com/what-are-cattle-calls.htm, accessed August 2009.

Zinken, P., and Mirror Theatre. 2003. (Director) *I Bet You Can't Do That.* ASSIST Community Services Center, Edmonton.

Index

About the Author

Joe Norris, an advocate of the arts as a way of knowing, doing, and being, has spent a number of years pioneering research methodologies and instructional and assessment strategies that are based in emancipatory pedagogy and research. He strongly believes in the right and responsibility of voice and has included students' voices in many of his research projects. As cofounder and artistic director of Mirror Theatre, he, his students, and community members have cowritten over two hundred research-based scenes that examine issues of social justice and the human condition. With co-editors Laura McCammon and Carole Miller, he wrote *Learning to Teach Drama: A Case Narrative Approach*, which examines the lived-experiences of the field experience through cases written by student teachers. His latest project, "duoethnography," a research methodology, cocreated with Rick Sawyer, extends autoethnography through the juxtaposition of disparate points of view, intentionally disrupting the meta-narrative of personal texts. Joe has taught courses in integrating the arts in the curriculum, learning through drama, arts-based research, drama as a way of knowing, drama methods, Playbuilding as curriculum inquiry, curriculum theory, principles of learning, and qualitative research. After 20 years in faculties of education, Joe now makes his home in a faculty of humanities teaching drama in education and applied theatre in The Department of Dramatic Arts of the Marilyn I. Walker School of Fine and Performing Arts at Brock University, Ontario, Canada.